# Big Macs &
# Burgundy

# Big Macs & Burgundy

## WINE PAIRINGS *for the* REAL WORLD

VANESSA PRICE *with* ADAM LAUKHUF

*Photography by* MICHELLE MCSWAIN

*Illustrations by* THE ELLAPHANT IN THE ROOM

ABRAMS, NEW YORK

*for* Breanna

"Once . . . in the wilds of Afghanistan,
I lost my corkscrew, and we were forced to
live on nothing but food and water for days."
                                    —W. C. Fields

# Contents

# Hello, Stranger.
# Pull Up a Corkscrew.

**S**ancerre is a town in the Loire Valley of France that produces benchmark Sauvignon Blanc with crazy acidity, pure minerality, and cheek-puckering citrus. It goes perfectly with Cheetos.

I know this because I have paired Sauvignon Blanc with Taco Bell's entire menu, the country's most popular movie candy, almost everything in the supermarket frozen food aisle, including Hot Pockets Philly Steak & Cheese (with and without Croissant Crust), and pretty much every other mass-produced foodstuff you can think of—and returned from the field with one of the most important oenophilic discoveries of our time.

Sancerre and Cheetos go together like milk and cookies. It's a pairing so deceptively and fundamentally delicious, it has eluded almost every wine expert colleague I know—right up until the moment they polish off a bag and a bottle for themselves.

The sense science behind this unholy alliance of artificially flavored puffed corn-meal and serious wine is as elemental as acid, fat, salt, and minerals—the very same principles that explain the harmonious bond between oysters and Chablis or filet mignon and Napa Cab.

In fact, I've spent the better part of fifteen years in the wine industry as a trained sommelier thinking about exactly what makes pairings work, then testing and retesting my craziest hypotheses on unsuspecting friends and loved ones. I turned some of that hard-earned knowledge into a column for *New York* magazine's *Grub Street*, and the enthusiastic response I've received from readers like you has only confirmed what I've known for a long time: There's a whole world of entirely fun, entirely accessible, and often entirely counterintuitive wine pairings out there waiting to be discovered.

It's also been a constant reminder that there's an entire planet full of people who love wine as much as I do but have never had the opportunity to learn about it the right way—through informed experimentation. They're the same people who might drink three or four different bottles per week (or more during a pandemic), yet are so turned off by the inaccessible snobbery of winespeak that they generally avoid it altogether. Sound familiar?

If so, this book is for you. As someone who has been lucky enough to experience some of the greatest chef-sommelier tasting menus in the world, I can say with certainty that you don't need truffle-dusted sunchokes or sous-vide pheasant loins to unlock the joys of a fabulous or even just-plain-good bottle of wine. It can be done gloriously with something as basic as Funfetti cake. There are exceptional pairings to be had almost anywhere, from the local gas-station snack rack to your favorite Grubhub guilty pleasure order.

The art of pairing food with wine is not without its mysteries, but it's far from a mystical trick of culinary alchemy. At its most basic, it's the informed process of combining complementary flavors and textures, either through contrast or accentuation, to create perfect balance. And when you get it just right, your palate finds equilibrium with each swallow.

If your food has a lot of fat, it needs a sharp, acidic wine to cut through it; if it has heat and spice, a high-sugar wine will soften the intensity. Bitter foods want something deep and lush to counteract them, while certain rich and powerful dishes can call for congruent pairings, which means doubling down on all the attributes that make something delicious to begin with. The same rule of congruency applies to fresh and citrusy fare: Your ideal wine will reflect that light, bright character.

As you'll learn throughout these pages, a great food and wine pairing both heightens and, to a degree, cancels out its counterpart. It's a principle that's been put into practice for thousands of years in the Mediterranean, where wine and food have long worked in symbiosis. While wines from the land of Dionysus may seem tannic, tart, or too sweet by themselves, Greek table varieties take on an entirely different and uncommonly satisfying character when consumed with certain kinds of food. The zesty sting of Santorini yields to charred octopus, while Retsina, an exotic, resinated wine with undercurrents of pine, is tempered by spicy lamb. That's what "food-friendly" wine means. (I didn't make this term up, I promise.) And don't worry, by the time we're done, you'll understand that concept completely.

In the Burgundy region of France, they'll serve you White Burgundy with gougères, a savory puff pastry filled with a nutty cheese, typically Gruyère or Comté, which blends uncannily with the French-oak creaminess of their wine. And if you ask them how long they've been pairing those two things, they'll say "forever"—it's been going on for that many centuries.

Pairing in the modern sense—as an expensive gastronomic "experience"—has only really been a thing since the 1980s. That's when paired dishes and wines started appearing on the menus of fancy restaurants, usually in set-price, multi-course dinners with specific wines matched to individual dishes. For the most part, pairings have remained in that rarefied realm of tasting menus ever since, depriving the rest of us of one of life's purest pleasures.

As I'll explain more deeply later, Sancerre works so well with Cheetos because of its salinity, light body, and raw bite. It makes sense that the only grape that stands a chance against Chester's finger-staining orangey salt-powder is the rip-roaring acidity of white Sancerre, which has the added benefit of being highly textured—meaning that when you swish it around it coats your mouth, giving it a fighting chance against all that Cheetos buildup. Each of the fleshy areas of your mouth, from the gums to the tongue to the roof and all the way back to your throat, provide sensory feedback to your brain, which lights up with pleasure when processing this kind of robust data.

White Sancerre also has a lot of what we in the business call minerality, that category of smells and flavors that aren't fruity, spicy, or herbal, but rather flinty or chalky. Think of the subtle brine of an oyster, or of licking a rock. Sancerre's minerality keeps the explosiveness of the nacho cheese in check.

Similar principles are at work in the shockingly delicious marriage of s'mores and Recioto della Valpolicella (page 224), Sour Patch Kids and semi-dry Riesling (page 83), and, you guessed it, Big Macs and Burgundy (page 69). It is beautiful and surprising combinations like these, freed from the tyranny of three-figure ingredients and white tablecloths, that excite me most. And I'm pretty sure they'll excite you, too.

Of course, it's not just about $1 pizza and Montepulciano (which you should definitely try; see page 49), it's also about the fresh, simple, and clean foods that you eat the rest of the time, because you're a normal, healthy person. Even the blandest Netflix-night grilled chicken with steamed broccoli can be made sublime with the right glass of wine.

**There are exceptional pairings to be had almost anywhere, from the local gas-station snack rack to your favorite Grubhub guilty pleasure order.**

What follows are pairings that will make you smile and open your mind to new possibilities, with plenty of rut-breaking varieties you may have never considered. If you like Sauvignon Blanc, let's get you on the Verdicchio train. Drinking a lot of Chianti? Try tracking down a Mondeuse Noir. And you can also apply the specific pairings in this book to your broader culinary circumstances. For instance, the next time you see a Chablis on the wine list at the hottest new Japanese spot, you'll know exactly what to do with it. Because you already know that it goes perfectly with seaweed snacks, and that mineral-driven whites are good with seafood, it's probably going to be a stellar match for that sushi special roll. That's the look of your date being totally impressed.

And those are the moments I live for. When I see students or friends feeling confident enough to make the leap and apply what they've learned on their own terms, there's no better feeling—except for when I get to eat and drink their discoveries. Wine inspires me, and by the end of this book, I hope it will inspire you, too.

# But Just Who the Hell Am I, Spouting All of This Life-Changing Knowledge?

Well, you're going to get to know me and the story of how I came to wine, and how it changed my life. And hopefully, little by little, you'll start to trust me enough to lend me your summer house in France.

I'm going to tell you about the time I served Sancerre to Justin Bieber and his entourage at a club in Montauk. About how I made it in one of the most cut-throat and depraved industries in one of the most cut-throat and depraved cities in the world. About how the very same girl who once thought she was a serious wine collector because she had a kitchen shelf stocked with Arbor Mist somehow found herself sitting with the owners of Cristal Champagne giving menu notes to the world-famous chef Eric Ripert at his three-star Michelin restaurant Le Bernardin. And how it all pretty much comes down to Matt Damon.

But the first thing you need to know is just how improbable it is that I'm a sommelier at all. I was born and raised a Southern Baptist in Louisville, Kentucky, the granddaughter of evangelical ministers and the daughter of parents who didn't take a sip of alcohol in my presence until I was an adult. Drinking was once an excommunication-level taboo in my family. My mother is a successful CPA. My father is an admiral in the Navy and a corporate litigator. White-collar conservative teetotalers from the Bible Belt—that's my pedigree.

After a long and circuitous path to a bachelor's degree that involved several years as a wanna-be actress and a stint waiting tables at a local winery in Kentucky, I moved to New York City for the long haul. And I spent the next twelve years eating, sleeping, learning, dreaming, waking, teaching, writing, and definitely drinking about wine. As a wine educator, wine columnist, wine sales rep, wine importer, sommelier, and consultant for private wine collectors, I've worked with some of the most renowned winemakers, sommeliers, and restaurants in the world. I'm more passionate about wine and wine pairing than I've ever been, but I'm still just a regular girl from Louisville who feels lucky to have made it this far. And as I write these words in this unprecedented era of isolation and anxiety, when the simple comforts of food and wine have become that much more meaningful to us all, it is my great privilege to be able to share what I've learned with you.

# THE RIPE STUFF

## THE MIRACLE OF WINE, BROUGHT TO YOU BY ACID, SUGAR, AND THE SUN

# It's all about *the birds,* sugar.

**If that regrettable sentence helps you remember what comes next, then I don't apologize.** Because to understand anything about wine, you have to start with sugar and acid. And to understand just how fundamental sugar and acid are to wine, it helps to think about birds.

Let's go back to a time long before wine-making was a thing, when grapevines relied on birds (and wind and lots of other creatures, yes, but let's just stick with birds) to spread their seeds far and wide. You know how nature works: bird meets grape, bird flies away, bird poops grape seed, new vine sprouts up somewhere else and asks for a paternity test. But why does the bird eat that grape in the first place? Because the bird has a sweet tooth. And when does a grape taste sweetest? When it's ripe.

No one likes sour grapes, including birds. So if the grape doesn't have enough sugar to offer, the bird won't do its part. That's just nature. In early spring, not-yet-ripe grapes are green, and if you bite into them, they're nasty. At that point, there's nothing but acid in there. But about midway through the growing season, something happens. The sun

and the vine, with some help from the rain and the soil, begin to create excess energy in the form of sugar, and the vine starts to store those sugary spoils in its grapes. Much like neon license plates or Justin Bieber's first wisp-thin goatee, it's the grape's way of shouting, "Hey birds, my seed is ready for you now—come and get it!"

The magic moment, called véraison, is when grapes start to change color and ripen. Their taste begins to transform from sour and bitter to sweet, and their smell from herbaceous to fruity. But something even more important is happening inside the grape. As the sugar levels rise, all that acid from the beginning of the growing season starts to dissipate. The plant science is complicated, but the best way to think about it is that there's only so much room inside each grape, so the sugar and acid are locked in a constant battle for space. Like the two sides of a Yin and Yang, they're opposing forces set against each other at an inverse ratio: the higher the acid, the lower the sugar, and the lower the sugar, the higher the acid. When you pick a grape too early, the acid tells you as much with a firm smack to the taste buds. And when you pick a grape too late, you've got an overripe little boo-boo bloated with sugar. Birds don't like those, either.

That ratio of sugar to acid is the key to understanding wine. Picking a grape at just the right time, when the balance is perfect for whatever style of wine you're making, is what separates great vintners from average ones.

# How Grapes Become Wine

WAIT, IS THAT A SCIENTIFIC FORMULA? You thought I said this book was going to be fun! I know, I know. Just bear with me, I promise this will help.

This is the simple equation that explains how we turn grapes into wine:

$$Sugar + Yeast$$

$$=$$

$$Alcohol + CO_2$$

After grapes get picked, they're brought to a winery and crushed to break open their skins and release their juice. Yeast is then added, which eats the sugar in the grape juice and converts it to alcohol. The more sugar in the grape, the more alcohol there can be in the wine.

A winemaker could stop the fermentation before all the sugar is converted to alcohol, as they do for sweeter dessert or fortified wines, but these are the exceptions, not the rule. $CO_2$ is also created, but as a by-product

that the wineries let dissipate out of the wine until it is completely still, even in the case of Champagne. (Fun dinner-party fact: Even your favorite Merlot was once sparkling and your Champagne was once flat.)

Most wine made with high-sugar grapes isn't sweet. When that sugar is transformed into alcohol, it adds to a wine's body, and the more booze in a wine, the more body it typically has. What exactly is body? It's how heavy a wine feels in your mouth. The more mouth-feel and texture, the fuller the body. If the wine is light and zips right back without a lot of fuss or feeling, it has a lighter body. The lighter the body, the lower the alcohol, which means the less sugar—and more acid—in the grapes.

I'll repeat that one more time: Wines that have less alcohol tend to have less body and more acidity. That's because they come from grapes with less sugar, and sugar and acid mostly work at inverse ratios in both grapes and wine. The more acidity in the grape, the crisper the wine. The more sugar in the grape, the more alcohol—and body—in the wine and (usually) the less acidity. The more alcohol in the wine, the richer it will be. Now go back and read all of that again until it makes sense. And then read it again until it sticks. Once it does, it will seem obvious.

|  Start of Growing Season | Middle of Growing Season | Harvest |
| --- | --- | --- |

*Sugar* ↓ *Acid*

The ratio of sugar to acid in any given grape differs widely depending on the type and where and how it's grown, but generally speaking, the longer it's on the vine, the more a grape gains sugar and loses acid. The moment those levels become ideal for a particular grape or wine means it's time to harvest.

# The Four Elements of Wine

THERE ARE FOUR BASIC ELEMENTS that matter most when we talk about wine, and they're essential to decoding what your mouth registers when you drink it, in terms of both taste and feel. Discussing these four things alone—sugar, acid, alcohol, and tannin—is a much more valuable way to describe your experience with a wine than flowery language like, "Aromas of dried rose petals, rich dark currants, nectarine marmalade, and dried tobacco with a smashed metallic finish." Of course, I love to parse the nuances of wine with colorful brushstrokes, but you can't paint the ceiling of the Sistine Chapel without the four walls that hold the thing up.

**ALCOHOL** in a wine is tied to how much sugar was in the grapes used to make it. Alcohol content can help us judge how light or heavy the body of a wine is. The more alcohol in a wine, the more viscous, or heavy, it becomes. Because higher alcohol wines are heavier, they have more body. Lower alcohol wines, in turn, have less body.

**TANNIN** is a word thrown around a lot, even if what it actually means often seems as clear as the hieroglyphics in Nefertiti's tomb. It's a type of polyphenol found in many plant species but in the case of wine comes from grape skins, stems, and seeds, or is imparted through time spent in newer oak barrels. As with alcohol, tannins assist in boosting the body of a wine. Grape tannins add one layer of body; putting a wine in oak adds another. Because

tannin is extracted from the grape skins at the same time color is, the two are usually correlated. So, typically the deeper a wine's color, the more tannin it has. (As with everything in wine, there are exceptions.)

**ACID** is what makes a wine fresh and gives it vibrancy. Industry people say it gives wine a structural backbone, which means it makes the wine sturdy and stable enough to be able to age long term. You often hear words like "crisp" or "bright" to describe wines with more acidity. You will read this word a lot moving forward: I warn you now—there's just no way around it.

**SUGAR** is what makes a wine sweet. When a wine is sweet, the sugar was either added in the winery or is the natural residual sugar purposefully left over after fermentation.

# HOW YOUR MOUTH PERCEIVES . . .

### ACID

You'll pick up a tingling sensation near your jaw and experience prolonged salivation after you swallow. If I tell you to think about biting into a super-sour lemon wedge, do you feel how, with just your imagination, your mouth starts to pucker? That's because when you put a high amount of acidity in your mouth, your body reacts to tame it, rushing in more saliva to dilute the acid and restore equilibrium—even if you're only just anticipating it. Have you ever heard someone say the word "finish" when it comes to wine? They're referring to how long the flavor persists in your mouth after you've swallowed. Typically, the longer the finish, the higher the acidity, and the shorter the finish, the lower the acidity. (Again, there are exceptions to this rule.)

Acid is what drives a lot of good food and wine pairings, because it takes rich food and cuts right through it, acting as a palate cleanser. It can also round out the sensations in your mouth, enhancing the flavors of the food. Unlike your dinner party guests, it makes everything more tasty and then cleans up afterwards.

### TANNIN

It's pretty close to that feeling you get when the dentist removes the cotton balls. Tannin produces a momentary drying sensation in your mouth, which you can perceive with your tongue, gums, and even lips, almost like a vacuum whoosh. Tannins are compounds that appear naturally in grapes, driven by a need to find protein and bond with it. You have trace amounts of protein in your saliva. So whenever you drink a tannic wine, the tannin will bond with the protein in your saliva. And when you swallow, those bonded compounds get washed right down the hatch, leaving your mouth feeling sucked dry. But if you pair that same tannic wine with food that is high in protein—anything from quinoa to a rack of lamb—the excess protein you've consumed will saturate the tannins from the wine, leaving only the delicious lingering of all the yummy things you just ate and drank. Because it is also astringent, tannin causes all of the bitter taste receptors in your mouth to fire, which sounds unpleasant but is actually the same satisfying sensation behind dark chocolate, coffee, savory herbs, and the seeds that season your everything bagel.

## SUGAR

While you can perceive sugar anywhere in your mouth, most people get a slightly tingly sensation at the tip of their tongue when there's sugar present in a wine. Sometimes the tingle hits when you drink; sometimes it pops up after you swallow. Sugar in a wine can cause you to feel oiliness in the middle of your tongue (called the mid-palate). Sugar can also make the wine feel more full bodied because it is more viscous. (See the section titled "Alcohol" below for more on that.) Warning: Don't let a wine that just smells sweet trick you into thinking you are tasting sugar. The presence of sugar is what makes a wine sweet. That sounds obvious, but barely a day goes by that I don't hear someone say a wine is "sweet" when it is actually dry. When grapes come from warmer climates, the wines they produce can smell very fruity or ripe, which can make us automatically think sugar. But those wines can still be dry—as in they don't contain sugar because all of it has been converted to alcohol.

## ALCOHOL

The liquids that comprise wine are alcohol and water. Because alcohol (ethanol) has a higher viscosity than water, we can use alcohol to measure body in our mouths. "Viscosity" is a science-y term wine pros use that refers to how easily a liquid flows; honey, for example, has a much higher viscosity than milk. The heavier the wine feels on your tongue and the slower it moves from the front to the back of your palate, the fuller bodied the wine is—and the more alcohol it contains. If wine has higher alcohol you can also register the sensation of heat in the back of your mouth and throat (think about the burn when you take a tequila shot). The range of low to high alcohol is relative: 12 percent is low for your average table wine and 15 percent is high. Each percentage point of alcohol was created by converting around 17 grams per liter of sugar, and so for your body, processing each additional point is no small feat. Guaranteed I can go toe to toe with someone twice my size if I'm drinking 12 percent Muscadet and they're drinking 15 percent Napa Cab. Just watch who taps out first. (Bonus: I won't have purple teeth.)

## Climate Climate Climate

WHEN I SAID WINE WAS ALL ABOUT the birds, I really meant a bird in sunglasses. Grapes are sugar and acid, and their sugar-to-acid ratio is directly dictated by the climate in which they grow and the ripeness at which they're picked. How much sugar is in a grape when it is picked affects both the body and the flavor of the wine it will make.

When that grape is turned into wine, the more sugar it has means the more alcohol is produced, which means more body. (Has the broken record worked on you yet?) In addition to being able to produce more alcohol, the riper the grape, the fruitier the wine will taste. Grapes that are less ripe, on the other hand, will produce wines that have more mineral, herbal, and earthy characteristics. So different climates make the same type of grape taste different.

In both the Northern and Southern Hemispheres, the vast majority of quality wine is grown between the 30th and 50th parallels. And while the same grape may be grown anywhere within these latitudes, the style of wine it will ultimately create varies drastically. For example, a Chardonnay grape grown in Chablis, the coolest and northern-most wine district of Burgundy, sitting just below the 48th parallel, will have high acid and minerality for days, while a Chardonnay grown in Napa at the 38th parallel, which has more sun and an average temperature that's five degrees warmer, will have far more sugar, making for a fruitier version with more alcohol and body and less crispness than its Chablis counterpart. To be clear, a grape that has reached its perfect level of ripeness in a particular climate can only ever be that ripe, no more and no less. So grapes from warmer climates are always "riper" when picked at full

maturity than those from cooler climates, even though they're both picked at the ideal ripeness for their growing conditions. (That is, you can't just leave a Chardonnay grape on the vine in Chablis for an extra three weeks to get it to taste like Napa Chard.)

Since white grapes ripen faster than black grapes (black grapes are what the wine world calls grapes that make red wine), white grapes do well in cooler climates with less sun. The opposite is true for black grapes, which do better in warmer climates because they ripen more slowly—they need more warmth and sunshine to get the job done. You can easily taste the difference climate makes. This is why most regions focus more heavily on one color of wine, even if they grow both grape colors. Alsace, Germany, and Austria have cool climates, so they grow mostly white grapes. In warmer climates like the Rhône Valley, Napa Valley, and Barossa Valley, they grow a lot more black grapes.

# The Two Worlds of Wine

NO MATTER THE AMOUNT OF ACID or sugar or alcohol or tannins, all wines fall into two overarching categories: Old World and New World.

**Old World** wines come from anywhere that wine and winemaking originated, primarily Western and Eastern Europe—Spain, England, Italy, France, Hungary, Romania—as well as what some call the "Old-Old World" centered around the Fertile Crescent. The area is considered the birthplace of wine, which includes places like modern-day Georgia, Turkey, Israel, Cyprus, and Lebanon, as well as parts of North Africa like Egypt, Morocco, and Tunisia.

**New World** wines come from anywhere the vine species (*Vitis vinifera*) used to make the wine—along with the techniques necessary to do it—were brought by the Old World colonizers who settled into these lands during or after the Age of Exploration (fifteenth to seventeenth centuries), which include North America, South America, South Africa, Australia, New Zealand, India, China, and Japan.

There are two main reasons these categories are important to understand:

## STYLE

These are broad silos, but white wines from the Old World tend to be mineral driven (think chalkiness and salinity) and Old World reds tend to be earth driven. In the New World, both reds and whites are driven by pure and unadulterated fruit. That doesn't mean Old World wines don't have fruit or New World wines can't be earthy. The term "driven" means it's the first thing you smell, and it's what informs you of the wine's style.

| Geographic Label | Grape Label | Fantasy Label |

SAUVIGNON BLANC IN THREE DIFFERENT OUTFITS

## THE WAY A WINE IS LABELED

In the Old World, there are places that have been making wine for an uninterrupted millennia. I once had a Sancerre in my import portfolio that has been planted continually since 1040. With that much time and experience, you start to figure out the best combination of factors that lead to great wine—what soils go with what grapes go with what climates. And as those higher-quality practices started to be identified and adopted, so did the need to legally define them. That gave rise to what are now iron-clad laws.

The type of grapes that can be grown in an identified geographical area, called an appellation, are strictly regulated in the Old World, so putting the name of the grape on the label becomes redundant. Sancerre, for example, is not a grape, it's a place, so if it's a white grown in Sancerre, the only grape it can be is Sauvignon Blanc. But they don't write Sauvignon Blanc on the label—knowing it's from Sancerre tells you all you need to know. Same with Chianti, which is a place

known for wine that comes primarily from the Sangiovese grape. Ditto Rioja, Barolo, and down the line. There are a few exceptions, most notably in German wine production, but in general this rule will serve you well.

In the New World, on the other hand, winemakers can grow whatever they want. They just need to stay within the legally defined geographical area if they want to use a specific location on their bottles. This is why we label by the area as well as the grape in the New World. There are no legal requirements that can give us an indication of what grapes are in the bottle—just what the winemaker has chosen to put on the label.

Some winemakers choose to go with what's called a Fantasy Label. In the Old World, this is done when the grapes used in the wine fall outside the bounds of what is typically grown in the region in question (so they can't use the name of the geographical area). In the New World, a winery can choose to label by name instead of by grape or area as they see fit, since there are no laws to say they must do otherwise.

# PUTTING IT *Together*

## READY TO SEE HOW WINE WISE YOU ARE?

Let's say I am a grape called Sylvaner from Germany. Hopefully you've never heard of that grape before. Given all that you've learned, try to make some informed inferences:

**Is it from a cool or warm climate?**

**Is it a white or a black grape?**

**Will the grape have more or less sugar?**

**Will the grape have more or less acid?**

**Will the wine have more or less alcohol?**

**Will the wine have more or less acid?**

**Will the wine have a shorter or longer finish?**

**Will the wine be light, medium, or full-bodied?**

**Will the wine be fruit, earth, or mineral driven?**

If you concluded Sylvaner is a white wine from a cool climate with lower alcohol, higher acidity, lighter body, mineral-driven characteristics, and a longer finish, you nailed it.

Now let's say I'm a Petit Verdot from Southern California. Ask yourself the same set of questions. If you concluded that Petit Verdot is a red wine from a warm climate, with higher alcohol, lower acidity, bigger body, fruit-driven characteristics, and a shorter finish, you're killing it.

Now take a moment to think about that. Brain tingling yet? You have accurately described wines you most likely have never tried—or even heard of. Since this method is a way of generalizing wine, it isn't a perfect metric, but it's a great way to start anticipating the style of unfamiliar wines you come across on a menu or shelf.

# The Twelve Styles of Wine

PRETTY MUCH ANY WINE you can think of will generally fit into one of these categories, and you're probably already familiar with most of them. Some may even fit into more than one. Simply knowing a wine's style alone can be a great hint as to the type of foods it might go well with.

### LIGHT-BODIED WHITE

Light-bodied whites are usually lower in alcohol and often described as refreshing and easy to drink. Pinot Grigio is a classic example. Muscadet from the Loire Valley in France is a lesser-known star in the category.  Unoaked, they typically come from cooler climates and have smells that are citrusy or minerally, making them some of the most popular wines in the world for everyday consumption. Sometimes dismissed as the "beer of wine," there's actually much more diversity to the style beyond the handful of grapes that tend to dominate shelves.

### AROMATIC WHITE

Yes, they can smell strongly of perfume or fancy soap, but these oft-misunderstood wines can be some of the most exotic and enticing you'll ever taste. Made from grapes such as Gewürztraminer (Alsace in France) or Torrontés (Chile), they are usually medium bodied and range from dry to a category called "semi-dry" or "off-dry," meaning there's a perceptible amount of sugar but not enough to make it fully sweet. These are some of the oldest grapes still grown and cultivated in the world today, with some dating back to ancient Egypt.

### FULL-BODIED WHITE

Perennially popular oaked Chardonnay is the doyenne of the category. Full-bodied whites get their girth from higher alcohol as well as techniques employed in the winery. To follow our earlier example, Chardonnay that hasn't been oaked, like in Chablis, will be a light to medium-bodied wine at most. It's the addition of the oak, as well as the alcohol, that helps fill it out. California Chardonnay is the best example of this, but there are other wines like Grenache Blanc, which is a white mutation of the red version, that are just as big and powerful.

### PALE PINK (ROSÉ)

The classic French style originated in Provence but has become a global obsession—and is now made around the world. In a shade of delicate pink, rosés are citrusy. In the Old World, they often display similar aromatics to a jar of herbes de Provence—rosemary, thyme, and lavender. In the New World, they express more fruity notes like strawberry, raspberry, and sherbet. They're made the same way as reds, except with less time spent in contact with the grape skins. Their body is light to medium, and they're almost always dry.

### RICH PINK (ROSATO/ROSADO)

The hot pink styles at the more vibrant end of the rosé spectrum have a body that is medium to full, and they're explosive in their expression of juicy fruitiness. They can be slightly more tannic because of the longer extraction of color from the grape skins to the grape juice. Spelled with a "d" in Spain and a "t" in Italy, this style is also made the world over and runs the range from dry to sweet. Pale pink rosés tend to hog all the attention in summer months, but don't discount the neon-hued iterations. They can be marvels of smell, texture and flavor.

### SKIN CONTACT

Commonly known by the limiting label of "orange wine," they can actually range in color from light honeyed gold up to vibrant persimmon orange. In the simplest sense, they are white wines made like reds: Instead of removing the skins from the juice, as with most whites, the skins are left in during the fermentation process, as they are for reds. This enhances body and tannic presence without using oak, which diminishes the expression of a wine's acidity. Since the fermentation can last from a few hours to a few months, the variations in color can be extreme.

### LIGHT-BODIED RED

Because color is extracted at the same time tannin is, lighter-bodied reds tend to be paler in color and have less tannin. Sometimes the color can be translucent, which means if you hold your wineglass up, you'll be able to see through it. The most popular light-bodied red wine grape is Pinot Noir, but there are many more just as worthy, such as Gamay (Beaujolais). Because high-tannin wines can dull the mouth's ability to grasp the textural sensation of acid, lower-tannin reds tend to have more perceivable zip.

### MEDIUM-BODIED RED

Medium-bodied reds have more heft than light-bodied reds and less chew than full bodied. They can be fruity or earthy and sometimes partially oaked (meaning a portion goes in the barrel and the rest is stored in concrete or stainless steel). In addition to a step-up in body, they typically maintain a zestiness that makes them an easy go-to for food pairing. Merlot is the standard bearer of the category; if that is a grape you like, find others like Barbera (Piedmont in Italy) and Touriga Franca (all over Portugal) and prepare to be delighted.

### FULL-BODIED RED

Big, full, dense, rich, strong, and powerful are the words most associated with this category, which finds one of its most thunderous expressions in Cabernet Sauvignon. These wines have deep, opaque color, formidable flavors, and supercharged tannins that can be unctuously velvetine or chewy and bitter. Equally sumptuous alternatives in this bold arena can be found in Sagrantino (Umbria in Italy) and Tannat (Uruguay). These wines require dishes that are as powerful and rich as they are.

## FORTIFIED

The only category more powerful than full-bodied red, fortifieds range from white to red, and dry to Slurpee sweet. What makes them so robust is the extra alcohol added—a type of flavor-neutral spirit similar to brandy—which amplifies the body, strength, and flavor of the finished wine. Port, sherry, and Madeira are the most common examples. Another bonus for these styles: the added layer of alcohol acts as an antioxidant, so you can open a bottle and it will keep much longer (weeks to months, depending on the style) than a typical table wine.

## SPARKLING

All things bubbly are all things holy in my book. They can run the spectrum from $7 André Spumante all the way up to prestige cuvée Champagnes that go for hundreds. What they all share in common is an effervescence from $CO_2$ trapped in the wine. How big the bubbles are, how aggressive the fizziness feels in your mouth, and how refined the wine is overall will vary based on the quality. The better ones will also have a steely backbone of acidity that works like a shiv on food as it moves through your mouth. Some can be sweet, but the majority are dry.

## SWEET

Just because it's sweet doesn't mean it's cheap. Some of the most coveted wines in the world have more sugar than Hershey's syrup. The difference between entry-level and higher-quality sweet wines is in the amount of acidity present to distinguish them from a bottle of chocolate sauce. Because this style has so much sugar, the wines feel thicker and richer. Sauternes is the most famous of them, but it has rivals for prestige in sweet wines like Tokaj from Hungary and Passitos from Italy. They range from red to white and come still, sparkling, or fortified.

# Now You're Ready for the Concept of Terroir.

*Terroir* **(tare-wahr) is a French word that is so ubiquitous and seemingly untranslatable that it has been adopted by the rest of the world's languages.** It's the idea that a wine can only taste how it tastes because of the place it came from.

Think of terroir as a way of explaining why the same grape can taste so different when it comes from two different places. The ultimate expression of an identical grape is determined by the land on which it's grown. More specifically, the soil, the elevation, the aspect, the region's weather in a particular year (a.k.a. the vintage), the general climate of the area, surrounding environmental elements like nearby beaches or rosemary fields, and even the hours of sunshine in a day, all get wrapped up into one total expression in a glass. Like humans, two grapes might have nearly identical DNA, but exactly where and how they were raised has a profound effect on their unique identities as individuals, and no two people or wines are exactly alike.

Generally speaking, the finer the wine, the more defined the terroir expression will be, and often this implies small-batch production. Bulk-produced wines can lose their terroir expression because too many grapes are being mixed from too many places to be able to retain any real character. In the coming chapters, I'll expand upon the abiding joys and mysteries of terroir, which is the very language—and essence—of wine.

# WHAT GROWS TOGETHER
# GOES TOGETHER

When regional cuisine and local viticulture develop simultaneously over time, they become organic mirrors of one another and the land from which they come. This applies to places in the world that have long histories of specialty cuisines and winegrowing. Txakoli and sardines or Albariño and barnacles are both timeless regional Spanish matches. Ever wonder why Pisanello tomato red sauce pasta and Chianti are always so perfect together? They're grown in the same place.

# WELCOME TO FLAVORTOWN

## GREAT TASTING IS THE KEY TO GREAT PAIRING

# *The Science of* Eating & Drinking

## Smell's Tasty

YOU KNOW THOSE INSUFFERABLE people who stick their noses deep down into a wineglass before they drink, causing everyone else's eyes to roll back in their sockets? I hereby give you full permission to become one of those people. In fact, I insist upon it.

You have to jam your nose into the glass. There's just no way around it. I assure you it's not actually weird; it's perfectly normal. And if you do it often enough, you'll understand why. It will eventually become second nature. Don't fight it.

Smell is one of the first senses we develop before we're even born, and it's the earliest fully formed sense that babies use. There are more genes in the family of olfactory DNA than any other genetic code humans possess.

Imagine for a moment that someone blindfolded you and pinched your nose shut, then gave you a piece of chocolate to taste. (OK, just go ahead and try it.) There's a very good chance you won't be able to guess what you're eating. Without your sense of smell, chocolate might taste sweet or bitter, with a consistency that melts in your mouth, but you might not be able to distinguish it from unsalted butter or soft ricotta cheese or canned fruit of similar texture.

We've got nothing on dogs, who have more than forty times the scent receptor cells we do, but the average human can still detect more than a trillion unique and discernible odors. Those odors are comprised of different smell combinations of airborne molecules called odorants. When we whiff a glass of wine, clusters of odorants pass through the air and into our nostrils to the back of the nose, where they run into a little piece of tissue called the olfactory epithelium. It has special neurons for sensing smell, almost like taste buds for your nose, which pass the information on through the olfactory tract, like a smell highway to your brain. But unlike sight and sound, which travel directly to a central relay station for processing before being dispersed, smell data gets blasted to multiple areas of the brain at once. That's why certain smells can illicit visceral reactions, like fear, nostalgia, or melancholy triggered by something as simple as glue, depending on your individual experience at Camp Kikapasaukee.

Our mouths also have a secret air passage in the back that leads up to the same smell computer. As you chew your food, air pushes up through your nasal passage, carrying the aromas with it. You may think you taste that pumpkin spice, but you're really smelling it.

## Taste's Smelly

NOW STICK OUT YOUR TONGUE and look in the mirror. You'll notice lots of small bumps called papillae. These papillae contain our taste buds; each bud has microscopic hairs called microvilli that send their own messages to our sensory processor about how something tastes. The average person has between five thousand and ten thousand buds, but most scientists agree that our tongues can only perceive about twenty different "tastants," and we use just a handful of those to actually "taste" food.

Our tongues can only handle roughly five primary tastes (and I'll circle back to them in a minute; see pages 36–37), but they're biggies: sweet, salty, sour, bitter, and savory. Because we have substantially fewer taste receptors than scent receptors, smell is constantly informing the brain about what we're actually tasting—and it has about a trillion ways to help. Our noses are basically valedictorians of nuance that our loud, remedial tongues have been cheating off of for millennia.

*Smell + Taste =*
*Flavor*

# Flavor Savor

TASTE AND SMELL ARE separate senses with their own electronic circuits communicating on distinct channels with the mothership, yet they are inextricably linked. This is why you can easily imagine how something might taste simply by smelling it (you won't always be right), and why you can barely taste anything when you're stuffed up with a cold. The word "taste" comes up all the time when we talk about food and wine, but it turns out we don't actually taste much at all. Most of what we think we taste—like strawberry or cinnamon or chocolate—is really the end product of this crazy computation our brain performs simultaneously with the raw data from our tongue, mouth, and nose. Ultimately, taste and smell converge in the frontal lobe of our cortex, and this convergence is what we call flavor.

Flavor is the all-encompassing impression you get about a food or wine after you've processed its taste, smell, temperature, and mouthfeel in symbiosis, and we humans have the ability to discern about one hundred thousand different flavors.

# Uncorking Taste

PUTTING ASIDE FOR THE moment everything I've been preaching about the crucial importance of smell, when it comes to wine and food, those five fundamental tastes that your dumb-jock taste buds are able to recognize on their own are the cornerstones of wine pairing. For our purposes, I'm somewhat scandalously adding spicy and fatty to the list of primary tastes, though any good scientist will tell you they're not technically tastes. (The cellular receptors for spice and fat, like the ones that sense alkaline, metallics, starch, calcium, and water, sit right up next to our taste buds on our tongues, but operate by their own set of rules.)

## SALTY

Salt is the ultimate flavor enhancer; it's how we bring out the tastes and aromas of almost all of our ingredients. Salty foods soften wine and can make them seem fruitier or sweeter than they are, so your wine should have enough power to stand up to the salt. That oomph could come in the form of high acidity, as with Champagne or Riesling, or in the kind of rich, concentrated flavor that comes with Cabernet.

## SWEET

When we eat sugar, even the natural kinds we get from fruits and honey, our brains are triggered to release endorphins. And due to some kind of twisted evolutionary fail-safe, sweeter foods make wine taste drier and more bitter. So while it may seem counterintuitive, with sweeter foods you actually want a wine with just as much, if not more, sugar—or your wine will end up tasting sour or fruitless. But equally crucial is that the wine also has enough acid so your mouth doesn't feel like a Skittles dispenser.

## BITTER

The aversion we often have to bitterness is rooted in evolution. It can be a sign that something is inedible or even toxic. We actually have the most varied receptors for it—twenty-five of them, compared to three for sweet—able to detect different kinds of bitter proteins that produce a sharp, pungent taste. But we also know that plenty of bitter things, like coffee, chocolate, and kale, are delicious. Bitter foods are the toughest to pair with wine because, when met with their equal counterpart, they tend to exacerbate the other's bitterness. Bitter foods also mask acidity and tannin, while bringing a wine's sweetness to the forefront. With bitter foods, avoid bitter (or tannic) wines, and try something with a lot of acidity. Sauvignon Blanc is a great rescue option for a bitter green salad.

## SAVORY

Also known as umami, this distinct profile was confirmed by Japanese scientists in the early twentieth century and has only recently become widely accepted as a primary taste. It comes from amino acids in protein-rich foods like meat and cheese, which often develop a lot of glutamate through the aging, drying, and curing processes. Sometimes mistaken for mere saltiness, it's defined by a uniquely savory depth that's pretty unmistakable but less easy to describe. There's a comforting aspect to umami sensations, which are most often associated with deliciousness. And like potato chips with MSG, once you pop you can't stop. (To be clear, your wine doesn't have MSG.) These foods make wines seem stronger and more bitter than they are, so go with varieties that are lower in tannin and higher in acidity, like Aligoté or Beaujolais. Dry fortified wines such as Fino sherry can also do the trick.

## SOUR

Not to be confused with bitter, sour is a taste that comes from acidic solutions like lemon juice, sour cream, and pickles. Acidic foods make wines seem sweeter and softer, so you need just as much or more acid in your wine to achieve balance. That's why so many Asian dishes based on a sweet-and-sour profile are a natural coupling with Riesling. You need enough acidity to fight sour food's tendency to soften and diminish the flavor of any given wine.

## FATTY

Fat just might be the sixth elemental taste, though it remains unofficial and hotly debated in scientific circles. Still, there can be no denying the thick, creamy, pleasurable texture we perceive in soft cheese, buttered popcorn, or crisp, oily fried anything. Fatty foods dull acidity (sour) and tannin (bitter), so you need double the amount of one or both of these in your wine to ensure your whole experience doesn't devolve into a flabby or flavorless mess. The more power the better. That's why rib eyes and Napa Cabernet have long been partners in the hallowed halls of Gastronomy.

## SPICY

Some scientists believe it's a biological accident that we can even register spice, a mistake in our genetic code that allowed a mutation in perception to form. We don't actually "taste" spice at all. We sense the temperature of heat. Sensory cells in our mouths pick up on capsaicin, the neuropeptide-releasing agent in spicy foods. That's why your mouth burns and you may even sweat when you eat them. Your body is reading that spice as a temperature, and, in theory at least, you could eat enough ghost peppers to pass out or even kill yourself. Spicy foods make wine seem dry and bitter, so a good way to combat that is with a little sugar in your wine to soften the effects. Lower alcohol wines are also a better bet, so the alcohol doesn't exacerbate the heat of the food and overload your senses.

# The Science of
# Pairing Food & Wine

## The Two Kinds of Wine Pairings

PEOPLE ALWAYS TELL ME how intimidated they get trying to pair food and wine because it seems like there are so many variables to consider. This is true, but it's actually a good thing, not a bad thing. It means there isn't just one right answer. There are usually a lot of right answers. And even if the pairing you choose is "wrong" but you like it anyway, you're still right.

If you think of wine as an ingredient, determining its ability to pair with specific foods starts to feel much more natural. It would be weird to add parsley to chocolate cake, right? Trust those same instincts when you pair wine with food. Just like the ingredients on your recipe list, wines have tastes like acidity, sweetness, and bitterness, and flavors like rose, peach, chocolate, and green bell pepper that make each of them unique. The trick is learning which wines make sense as ingredients for a particular recipe.

While there may seem like a lot of different ways to go about pairing wine, at its most basic, there are really only two distinct paths you can take. You just need to decide whether to pursue a congruent (parallel) or contrasting (headlong) match between your food and wine.

**CONGRUENT** pairings involve foods and wines that share similar characteristics, meaning they run right alongside each other, enhancing their shared flavors. The sensory elements of both are amplified and balanced by their similarity.

**CONTRASTING** pairings are achieved with sensory elements that oppose each other in a way that creates balance and tension, resulting in combinations of flavors that feel intense and complex to the palate but still very pleasing.

Fried chicken, for example, is savory and fatty. Champagne, with all its acidity and effervescence, is a natural contrasting pairing, because it cuts through that greasy fat like a buzzsaw and washes your palate for the next mouthful. To create a congruent pairing with fried chicken, you could crack a wine like Meursault (oaked Chardonnay from Burgundy in France) because it will be just as savory, and the saltiness and creaminess of the wine will melt right into the salt and fat of the bird, producing a blissful blend of parallel sumptuousness. Both work beautifully for very different reasons.

# Getting Started: Pairing 101

LIKE A BLIND DATE ON the Lifetime channel, it's all about domination and intensity. Keep these basics in mind and you'll always find a great match.

## START WITH THE FOOD

Foods have more components to worry about than wines do, with a mix of ingredients that have their own individual identities and often change depending on how you combine and cook them. Wine is less complex—you just pop the cork and pour it, and it's rarely altered before you drink it. This makes it easier to pair wine with food than the other way around. There are always more wines to choose from that will match a given dish, which is why most people pick their food first and their wine second. Hard-core wine lovers (myself included) may start with the wine, and there is absolutely nothing wrong with that, but it will potentially limit your food options.

## THINK ABOUT THE DOMINANT COMPONENTS OF THAT FOOD

Because there are often many elements to a dish, pick the most obvious headlines to focus on. For example, tater tots are potatoes dominated by fat and salt. And if you eat them with ketchup, you've also got acidity in the form of tanginess and a mild sweetness on your list of primary components. To create a contrasting pairing, you need a fruity wine with high acid, low alcohol, no tannin, and prob-

ably some bubbly fizz, like a Cava or a Prosecco. The more ingredients in the food, the more complex the pairing becomes. I always go back to the most obvious dominant flavor and then adjust course based on any additional flavors and textures. I know I'm generally going to want a medium-bodied red for a basic ground-beef burger without any bells and whistles. If the patty comes with cheese and ketchup, a plump Australian Shiraz will do very nicely. But with added bitterness from raw onions and sourness from pickles, I might turn up the intensity with a northern Rhône Syrah, which is very similar in style to the Shiraz, but with more bold tannin and acidity to meet the added bitter-sour ingredients.

It's in these nuances, which you will start to learn in time, that the art of pairing comes alive. The next question to ask is a matter of degrees.

## HOW HEAVY OR INTENSE IS THE FOOD?

Beef Bourguignon is a deeply rich dish, and though it consists primarily of carrots, onions, mushrooms, and beef, those ingredients on their own could just as easily be a salad. It's when you brown the meat and vegetables in bacon fat and simmer them all together in a slow cooker for eight hours with garlic, wine, and chicken stock that it becomes a thick and succulent comfort-stew (and about as far from a salad as it gets). The bigger, richer, and more intensely flavored the food, the bigger, richer, and more intensely flavored your wine will need to be. Any light wine you might pair with a steak salad will likely be overwhelmed by Beef Bourguignon. So while it's important to identify the individual ingredients and dominant flavor components of a particular food, there's always a bigger picture to consider when pairing. Is the dish rich and creamy, or light and citrusy? Is it spicy and intense, or soft and sweet? Asking these simple questions will already start to push you toward the right style of wine.

## KEEP IN MIND THE SAUCE, SEASONINGS, AND HOW THE DISH IS PREPARED

Sometimes it isn't the protein that determines the intensity of a dish but what comes on top of it. A white fish drizzled with fresh lemon juice would do well with a light, crisp, citrusy wine because it's an airier, zestier dish. But if you put a heavy sauce on that same white fish, you'd want to move to a richer, creamier white wine. The cooking method, seasoning, and sauce impact the flavor, texture, and intensity of any given set of ingredients—and the wine you choose to pair with it.

## TRUST YOUR PALATE

Some people love spice. Some can barely tolerate it. And a wine that seems outrageously sharp to some might only be mildly tart to others. Your own perceptions are what matter most. The more you experiment, the more you will be able to calibrate pairings that work with your own preferences.

# Three Steps to Tasting Like a Pro

No one just wakes up one day and proclaims their wine has a perfumed bouquet with notes of rustic bramble fruit and a long pronounced finish. It takes years of technical wine tasting and comparative analysis to get to the point where every sip of wine becomes an intellectual assessment. Wine's ultimate purpose is to give pleasure, and that's where most people leave it, but there is a way to approach wine that will greatly enhance your ability to discern its nuances.

## 1. LOOK

First look at the wine. Color can tell you a lot. If it's a white and the color is clear to light yellow, it is probably a light-bodied, crisp wine like Pinot Grigio or Sauvignon Blanc—the kind that is refreshing on a hot summer day. If the color is deeper yellow to golden, the wine is probably fuller bodied and may have been aged in oak, like Chardonnay. That means the wine will be smoother and richer. If it is a red wine and the color is translucent, there is probably less tannin, making it a lighter-bodied red wine like Beaujolais or Pinot Noir that can be described as fresh. If the color is more opaque, the wine will be bigger bodied with more tannin, either from the grape or oak aging or both. Just remember that color is an indicator, not a fail-safe.

## 2. SMELL

If you're wafting your nose several inches above the glass assuming that should be sufficient to smell a wine, you're missing the point, which is happening inside the glass. You want the hilt of your nose right at the top of the inside of the glass, which creates the greatest distance between nostril and wine, allowing for the most smells to be conjured in the air pocket between. The closer you get to the wine, the more you'll only be smelling alcohol, which dulls your ability to smell anything else.

If you're having trouble smelling anything, tilt the glass toward one side and roll the wine around to coat the inside walls. This increases your wine-to-air ratio, so more aromatic particles will be released for your nose to pick up. You can also swirl a wine to increase the perceptible aromatics, but don't overdo it: you can just as easily over-swirl them all away. (For more on how to swirl, see page 98.)

## 3. TASTE

If you just knock it straight back, you're not going to get a very good sense of the wine. All the different fleshy bits of your palate provide you with various sensory information. So make sure the wine coats your whole mouth before you swallow. That doesn't mean swish it like mouthwash. Just naturally move it around—you'll also prolong the flavor of the sip.

After you swallow, keep your mouth shut and think. Where did you feel the wine? What did you taste? What textures did you experience? How long did the flavor continue to persist? The answers will help you to understand the wine and also inform you about what you do and don't like about it. When you add in the variable of food, try to process what you're eating and drinking as two halves of a whole. Each bite should be followed immediately by a sip so the food and wine can interact with each other and heighten your experience of both, while also setting up your palate for the next forkful. I drink wine at a much faster clip when I'm eating than when I'm not.

# *Recommended*
# WINES & PRODUCERS

With each pairing, I've included information about the grape and the place the wine comes from, and I hope you'll use this as a starting point to explore the many different types of bottlings those two specific data points can produce. You'll also find the names of a few specific wines and producers below each entry to help you on your way. Still, what you can find in a store in Texas or Ohio is almost never exactly the same as what you can find in New York or Michigan, so I've attempted to keep my picks as broad and inclusive as possible. Getting too specific tends to send people down a rabbit hole when a particular bottle isn't readily available, and often unnecessarily leaves many other excellent options out. That being said, you can now find just about anything on the internet if you're willing to put in a little work.

You'll see the following symbols throughout the book wherever producer names and wines are mentioned, which will come in handy the next time you suss out a bottle of something new. Note that wineries included in the farming and winemaking categories are practicing these methods, but not necessarily officially certified.

$   A Good Value-Priced Wine (under $25)

$$   A Wine to Share with Friends ($25-$75)

$$$   A Wine Worth Splurging On ($75+)

  Practicing Sustainable Farming

  Practicing Organic or Biodynamic Farming

  Vegan-Friendly Wine

  Natural Wine

  Well-Known Wine or Winery of the Region

  Status Symbol Collector Wine

BIG MACS & BURGUNDY

# THERE ARE NO WRONG PAIRINGS!

I am giving you the tools of the trade, but feel free to chuck them out the window. Chef Eric Ripert of Le Bernardin has a saying: "Bordeaux avec tout," or "Bordeaux with everything." And he really means it, all the way down to Red Bordeaux and oysters—a pairing that would make most people wince. If one of the most famous and respected chefs in the world sees no reason to apologize for his unconventional wine and food pairings, neither should you.

# CHAPTER 1

# Subsistence Pairings

*For the* SHOESTRING SOMM, SCRAPPY
DOESN'T HAVE *to* MEAN CRAPPY

**A**ll we heard was "You don't know who I am, do you?" Who actually says that? It turns out Matt Damon actually says that, at least in 2003, outside a club in Miami, where I was with a high school friend who'd moved there after graduation. The bouncer genuinely had no clue who Matt Damon was, but he did know me and my friend after our three-week tear through the night spots of South Beach. "He's with us," we assured the man with the velvet rope, to which Matt Damon chuckled, "You girls are funny. Thanks for the in."

The series of events that followed are fuzzy, but I can tell you that by the end of the week I had a gig as an extra on a terrible movie called *Stuck on You,* a three A.M. answering machine message that included the words, "Hi! You girls might not remember me, my name is Matt," and an early morning that ended with a paparazzi shot of me and my girlfriend in a national tabloid, skulking out of Matt Damon's all-night session "frolicking with various blondes and brunettes at a Miami mansion."

What *Star* magazine described as "a regular sin bin" was actually entirely innocent, with the possible exception of some pot we smoked out of an apple Jason Bourne'd into a bowl by Matt himself.

The one thing I couldn't forget was the hours-long conversation we had about acting, which had been a pipe dream of mine since my theatrical triumph as The Little Match Girl in high school. He told us that when he dropped out of Harvard to finish *Good Will Hunting*, everyone told him he was crazy.

When I got back to Kentucky, I couldn't get them apples out of my head. One of the conservatories in New York he had told me about happened to be holding an open call in Nashville that week. I drove down to audition without telling anyone, and a month later was accepted with a partial scholarship. My parents were shocked. Their daughter was about to drop her life and move to New York City to become a struggling actress, and they had Matt Damon to thank for it.

The first thing I learned when I moved to New York was that *Sex and the City* is a vicious lie perpetrated by monsters on nice young women from out of town. As a teenager, I'd always dreamed about what it would be like to have my own apartment in the city, and the sadists at HBO fluffed those country-girl fantasies like Rainbow Brite at BronyCon. My reality was a rent budget equivalent to roughly one half of one pair of Carrie Bradshaw stilettos, which I soon discovered meant you could forget about Manhattan entirely—and say hello to the Cosmo desert that was the outer boroughs.

My acting-school classmate Sarah, who was and always will be "Roomie" to me, was in a similar financial predicament, but we were both scrappers. We found an apartment in the basement of a single-family row house in the farthest industrial reaches of Long Island City, Queens, an area that's on the verge of coolness today, but was decidedly not back then. We carted everything we owned there in multiple subway loads from the temporary digs I'd found in Hell's Armpit, an area between Port Authority and the Lincoln Tunnel best known for its diverse bounty of car horns and methadone. In Queens, we slept like Mole People in bunk beds in a single, subterranean room with cheap black-and-white linoleum tiles. The Greek family upstairs resented our very existence—a financial necessity to make their mortgage—and they liked to poke their noses in just to make sure they still despised us. And by that I mean unlocking the door and coming in anytime they liked.

Those first few months, Sarah and I were the kind of broke where half your lunch is dinner and also tomorrow's breakfast. Thankfully, our friend Steve worked the closing shift at Starbucks in Lincoln Center, and he'd let us dumpster dive through the leftovers he was about to throw out for the day (just like Charlotte and Miranda!). As it happens, gently aged Starbucks pastries are actually pretty good when they're free, even if you have to commute by public transit for an hour at midnight to get them.

Of course, traveling by subway late at night also got me nearly mugged, which is another thing Candace Bushnell mostly leaves out. In a safety class at my acting school, I had been taught that you drop your house keys between your fingers in a clenched fist if you ever feel like someone is about to attack you, which seemed kind of *SVU*-ish to me at the time. But it turned out to be really relevant information when a man started following me much too closely as I was exiting our station. Instinct and my twenty minutes of training kicked in, and I locked my keys into position as he grabbed me and pushed me against a wall. I swung my arm wildly and caught his lip. He screamed and I screamed, and then I ran very fast. I called Sarah mid-stride on my state-of-the-art flip phone and she held the door open until I made it home. We drank a lot of bad wine that night.

Still, as broke and Manolo-less as I was that first year, it wasn't all creepy landlords, foiled muggings, and dumpster croissants. I got my first New York City restaurant job as a hostess at the hottest brunch spot on the Upper West Side, where a Samantha-worthy cast of who's-whos would gather every Sunday to see and be seen.

My third week on the job, Steve Martin walked in, blissfully unaware that he was about to be the second real-life celebrity this doe-eyed Kentucky fawn had ever met in person. He just walked right up to the host stand and announced himself like a perfectly normal person.

"Hi, I'm Steve Martin, we're a party of four, I think you should have my reservation?"

There I was, a fellow actor, practically best friends with Matt Damon, and all I could do was stare blankly and think, *That's Steve Martin.*

"Um, I'm Steve Martin, I think you should have a reservation under my name?" he kindly attempted again. And still I stared.

"I'm pretty sure I have a reservation," he tried a third time. "I'm pretty hungry and I know we would all love to eat."

"You're Steve Martin," I finally said. He waited politely for more, but nothing came.

"Sure am!" he said. "Do you have a table for four?"

At some point I walked him to one, because I remember being too embarrassed to even glance at that side of the room for the rest of the night, and then reliving it over wine and leftover Chinese when I got home. Back then, I was partial to $8 General Tso's, because it was cheap and plentiful enough to make two very good $4 meals. And it still does. I'll always love a good down-and-dirty night of cheap comfort food and bodega grocery staples, but now I can do it like a grown adult on an upstairs couch with throw pillows instead of a rickety basement futon.

## 99-Cent Pizza
## & MONTEPULCIANO D'ABRUZZO

I no longer spend 80 percent of my income on rent, but I'll still grab a dollar slice on my way home to eat with some Netflix and a Montepulciano from Abruzzo. Cheap slices always have plenty of red-sauce tomato acid, and you want a wine with a good amount of acid, too, so it won't taste flat or strangely sweet in comparison to the pizza. The fatty mozzarella is even more reason to pick a crisp, sharp wine. Montepulciano, which is a grape grown all over Italy, is naturally high in acidity and a dear friend to the budget slice. The vivid, plummy, medium-bodied red is notable for its aromatic herbs—oregano and pepper in particular—which seamlessly fill out the flavor deficits, namely blandness, that come with pizza that costs as much as Breath Savers. Its spritely tannins also ensure that any oiliness from those low-quality ingredients doesn't linger in your mouth. These wines are best enjoyed with a slight chill, so drop them in the fridge first.

The most famous wine made from this grape is also the herbiest, Montepulciano d'Abruzzo, named for the region it comes from east of Rome. And d'Abruzzo's winemakers craft some of the most beautiful wines in the world. The great news for the 99-cent pizza demographic is that they aren't oppressively expensive. In fact, many of them are downright budget friendly.

*$ Valle Reale Montepulciano d'Abruzzo* ☀ ⸎

*$$ CantinArte "Ode" Montepulciano d'Abruzzo* ☀

*$$$ Emidio Pepe Montepulciano d'Abruzzo* ✷ ⸎ ☀ ❁

## Lucky Charms
## & WACHAU RIESLING SMARAGD

I wish I had kept track of how many bowls of Lucky Charms I ate in my first years in New York. The sheer amount of milk alone must be staggering. To this day, the marshmallows still make me happy, and I always leave my favorite rainbows for last. Had I only known then to introduce Austrian Smaragd Riesling to my Charms, I could have been so much happier. Wachau is an appellation in Austria that has its own insular system for defining the ripeness levels at which growers can pick, which in turn determines different label and style designations. Smaragd is the top level of three categories, and the wines are as dry as a Maggie Smith retort, with at least 12.5 percent alcohol. Yet, despite having no actual sweetness, they do have a voluptuous body so full of ripe stone fruits and citrus they could make a Leprechaun blush. They're a pot of extra-dry Austrian gold for milky, sugary bowls of frosted oats and marshmallow clovers.

I love these wines because you can drink them young and saucy or old and refined, and as long as you've got yer Lucky Charms, they're magically delicious.

*$ Domäne Wachau "Weissenkirchen" Riesling Smaragd* ⸎

*$$ Alzinger "Ried Loibenberg" Riesling Smaragd* ⸎ ✷

## TexMex Quesadilla
## & RED RIOJA

I was raised on what was commonly called Mexican food. Anything with salsa, meat, cheese, and sour cream got lumped into this category, which was really just the Americanization of a proud and multifarious culinary tradition that has thankfully long since gotten the respect it deserves. (As an adult, I also figured out that real Parmesan doesn't come from plastic shakers.) Still, the gringo-fied version of Mexican cuisine known as TexMex will always have its place in my heart, and it seems strangely fitting that this food born of the Americas matches up so well with its European colonizer.

Spanish Rioja was the first region in Spain to create modern "fine wine" aged in oak barrels and export it commercially abroad. The tradition of making wine here stretches back in written record to the 800s. Yes, three digits, not four. Globally, Rioja is Spain's most prominent region, and it deserves its place at the world's big-kid wine table. I've tasted Riojas that are more than a century old and still full of life, vibrancy, and tension. They might not have the fruitiness you associate with young wine, but where the fruit has dissipated, crazy tones of earth, leather, spice, and all-around funk have dutifully taken their place.

Rioja's four-tier system of quality management is easy to decipher and a reliable indication of what you'll get at each age level. Ranging from youngest to oldest, the grades are Rioja, Crianza, Reserva, and Gran Reserva, and each tier requires more time in barrel and bottle before being released to the market. All the elevated aging is meant to beef up the wine for a potentially very long life after it's sold, and the more time and energy the winery puts in, the more the Rioja will cost. At the top-quality level, bottlings can start around $75, which might seem like a splurge until you realize this is a wine that can easily outlive you—and gets better each year.

The thing about a TexMex quesadilla is that its laundry list of ingredients—cheddar, ground meat, onion, jalapeño, spicy beans, more cheddar, salsa, and sour cream—goes with every level of Rioja, which is comprised primarily of Tempranillo and Garnacha grapes. Each tier has the spicy exuberance and bitter tannin the quesadilla needs to achieve equilibrium in your palate—it's just a matter of how mature you'd like that expression to be. If you're headed to a dinner party, take a Reserva. If you're celebrating, go with a Gran Reserva, which you can open younger if you want fruit (though it will probably need a good decant). Pop it older (twenty-plus years) if you want to know how delicious barnyard cow can be.

$ *Bodegas y Viñedos Artadi Viñas De Gain Tinto* ☀ ✳ ⟡

$$ *La Rioja Alta "Viña Arana" Gran Reserva* ✳

$$$ *Marqués de Murrieta "Castillo Ygay" Gran Reserva Especial* ⦚ ✳ ⚱

## Meatloaf TV Dinner
## & DRY CREEK ZINFANDEL

While both of my grandmothers would tell me it's sacrilege to eat frozen meatloaf, sometimes you just need a good TV dinner, and at the very least, the meatloaf version feels the tiniest bit enough like home to distract you from the fact that you're eating a TV dinner. What you do get is a warm and gooey hit of salinity that only processed gravy can deliver. And before you say gross, let me double down on that and tell you about California Zinfandels from Dry Creek Valley in northern Sonoma, California. They are dominated by saddle-leather aromas that remind you of sweat in the yummiest possible way. Their tannic structure is abundant but fleshy, and married together with the beefy loaf and salty gravy of a TV dinner, these two iffy-sounding things become a minor revelation.

What's nice about Zinfandel is that no matter where it comes from, it's going to be really big and really juicy and really alcoholic (as high as 17 percent abv, or alcohol by volume, without any additional alcohol fortification). The grape likes hot and dry places, and when

# WOULD YOU LIKE SOME WOOD WITH THAT?

**W**hen you hear someone say a wine has been "oaked," it means the wine has spent at least part of its time in the winery in a wood barrel. When bourbon first comes off the still, it's clear and sharp, just like vodka. Aging bourbon in oak barrels allows it to oxidize and soften, developing richer flavors over time. Same idea for wine. Putting a wine in oak can soften it, add body in the form of tannin to it, and give it a deep range of flavors like vanilla, butterscotch, dill, and coconut, depending on the type of oak and the amount of time the wine stays in contact with it. It does this by exposing a wine to small amounts of oxygen (barrels are liquid-tight but not air-tight), which makes it smoother and more concentrated in flavor. What flavors are imparted and how intense they are is a function of many factors, from the size and age of the barrel to how much the wood is toasted and what country or even specific forest it comes from. One thing oaking a wine will always add is expense. A single 225-liter oak barrel, which holds about three hundred bottles, can cost several thousand dollars.

SUBSISTENCE PAIRINGS

it gets those conditions, it rewards you with a borderline gluttonous abundance of overly ripe blackberry and strawberry, stone fruit puree, licorice, and sweet tobacco. Dry Creek Valley is arguably the best place to grow Zin in the continental forty-eight. But the gravy on top is that the Zins from this particular area also tend to offer a slight tomato note, meaning they basically add their own ketchup to the meatloaf, which makes it even better when you break out the actual Heinz.

$$ *Ridge Vineyards "East Bench" Zinfandel* ☀️✳️
$$ *Dashe Cellars Zinfandel Reserve* ☀️

# Mozzarella Sticks
## & AUSTRIAN ZWEIGELT

Thank the food gods for fried tubes of questionably real mozzarella. Whether or not to add the marinara is a very personal decision, and I respect your choices, but I'm going to assume you're a dipper. The most important thing to keep in mind with mozzarella sticks is that their shells are usually packed with ground Parmesan, herbs, and black pepper. That distinct Italian flavor profile, combined with the greasy crunch, creamy center, and sharp red-sauce finish, has an ideal bedfellow in Zweigelt from Austria.

A bright, violet-hued cross between Blaufränkisch and St. Laurent grapes, it's the most widely planted red grape in the country, and it embodies all the characteristics you need for fried cheese. Don't let the crazy name scare you. It's pronounced the way you think—zwhygelt—which is only moderately easier on the tongue than Rotburger, its original name before 1975, when they rather inexplicably decided to rename the grape for the Nazi who invented it in the 1920s, Fritz Zweigelt.

A red with soft tannins and a medium body, Zweigelt is packed with red cherries, cinnamon, and violets, with a juicy freshness and a firm thrust of acid that's as saucy as it is demure. That unusual tension is one of the wine's greatest attributes. Zweigelts are similar to spicy Beaujolais or richer Pinot Noirs, but also aren't entirely like either one. They're in their own category, much like our fried wonder wands. The Italian herbs in their breadcrumb-coated crust highlight the black licorice and ground pepper notes in the wine. And in turn, the Zweigelt's red fruit and sweet baking spices sing a vibrant falsetto with the marinara's tangy soprano, which straddles that hair's breadth between savory and sweet that keeps us dunking.

While you can find Zweigelts all across Austria, look for bottles from the regions of Burgenland, Kamptal, and Kremstal, which will be listed on the label along with the grape.

$ *Weingut Kollwentz "Eichkogel" Zweigelt, Burgenland* 🎵🎶🌿✳️

$$ *Weingut Leo Hillinger "Hill 1" Burgenland* ☀️

$$ *Weingut Judith Beck "Bambule!" Zweigelt, Burgenland* ☀️🌿🎵🎶

## Mac & Cheese
## & VIOGNIER VIN DE PAYS

I don't know you, but I know you love mac and cheese. Everyone does. It's one of the first foods we all eat and learn how to make. Whether or not you've graduated from blue boxes and powder to more refined versions, it's a comfort food equal to any occasion. And while it might be tempting to grab something high in acid—or even sparkling—to spar with its richness, the dish is actually perfect for a congruent pairing. So, we go big on all the attributes that make mac and cheese great to begin with—namely salty, creamy cheese. Contrast is great, but it's often achieved with acid, and in the case of mac and cheese, which is such a monolith of same-same flavor, too much contrast and acid can be a record scratch that subtracts from the experience. A creamy, low-acid wine like Viognier from the southern coast of France, on the other hand, magnifies it.

A soft, opulent wine for a soft, opulent dish, Viognier is unique in the spectrum of white grapes. When you first smell it, you're hit with floral notes like rose petal and honeysuckle, plus bright citrus fruits like bergamot, orange, and tangerine. But don't let the sweet aromatics fool you—these wines are dry. When you taste Viognier, it starts subtly but grows broader as it moves through your mouth, developing a texture that feels almost oily. That's exactly what we want for creamy sauce. And when you swallow, Viognier's light bitterness cuts in the same direction as the sharpness of the cheese. The best bottles come from an area of the Rhône called Condrieu, an appellation that's beloved among serious wine drinkers (and priced accordingly). Vin de Pays is a French classification for larger areas producing good quality wines above the entry "vin de table," and they offer some of the best values on Viognier in France. Next time you're craving mac, track one of them down and pour yourself a glass of creamy comfort to go with your bowl of the same.

*$ Triennes Sainte Fleur Viognier* ❀

*$$ Patrick & Christophe Bonnefond "Sensation du Nord" Vin de Pays Viognier* ❦ ❧

*$$$ Domaine Georges Vernay Condrieu* ❀ ✳

## Grilled Cheese
## & CAHORS

Whether you're nine or ninety-nine, the soft, creamy, salty, buttery-crisp, steaming-hot joy of grilled cheese is universal. And the bread-and-cheese sleeve of crunchy ooze is simple enough even for those who can't boil an egg to execute. A cheese sandwich of such immense staying power wants a red wine with generous reserves of supple tannin, fruity pop, and firm body to slice and dice the greasy starch and fatty dairy.

That red wine is Malbec—not from Argentina but from southwestern France. It's a fifth or sixth fiddler in premiere appellations like Bordeaux, but in Cahors (Cow oar), French Malbec has made a name for itself as the biggest fish. Here the wines are surprisingly distinct from the Southern Hemisphere versions you might know. Where the Argentine edition has a velvety texture that might whimper at the onslaught of melted lipids, Cahors has a bitter chew that eats through them like a wood chipper. These rustic wines have more tart in the form of dark fruits like plum and blackberry, and their tannins are as taut as Simon Cowell's brow. It's a savory little package with the grilled cheese that makes me buckle at the knees.

*$ Clos la Coutale Cahors* ❀

*$$ Fabien Jouves Mas del Périé "La Roque" Cahors* ❀ ❦ ❧

*$$$ Château du Cèdre "Le Cèdre" Cahors* ❀ ✳

# SWEET NOTHINGS

At times, wine people have a hard time communicating with normal people because they're using the same words with different meanings. Wines that are ripe and fruity are often misconstrued as being "sweet." But they can only be sweet if they have sugar levels high enough to outweigh the ratio of acidity by more than two grams, the threshold of sweetness we can physically perceive. Otherwise, those rich flavors and extra fruity smells indicate the wine was made from grapes that were picked very ripe. It could still be bone dry because it doesn't have sugar.

The word "dry" itself is another big one that gets lost in translation. Dry means not sweet—that there isn't enough perceptible residual sugar in the wine. (But just to confuse things further, "off-dry" actually means that the wine is a little sweet!) If you taste a wine and it dries your mouth out texturally, that means the wine has tannin, which is causing a bitter astringency in your mouth. It has no bearing on whether the wine is dry or sweet. Use the word "tannic" instead.

# Packaged Ramen
## & ALSACE PINOT GRIS

These are boom times for noodle lovers, thanks in part to the explosion of ramen-mania that has gripped America for the last decade. But even if the quality of preparations and ingredients has improved immensely since the days when "ramen" meant packets of instant noodles destined for the microwave, the basic structure of the dish has not. There's concentrated broth, an array of toppings, the tare (soy, miso, salty umami), and the springy, alkaline noodles. Within that framework, there are nearly limitless combinations of ingredients, but no matter what type of ramen you choose, you're going to want to drink Alsace Pinot Gris with it.

All ramen is dominated by rich, savory flavors. This kind of unbridled umami calls for a wine with both a touch of residual sweetness and a truckload of acidity to level the flavor. Alsatian Pinot Gris is often off-dry, which translates to "a little sweet," with a light sugar element that will temper the broth's saltiness by softening its intensity. Because you also need a wine with enough body and texture to avoid falling flat against the broth, Pinot Gris, with its glorious ability to sing a high, bright note while remaining grounded in richness and weight, is the ultimate ramen lover. (If that name sounds similar to "Pinot Grigio," that's because it's the same grape varietal; Pinot Gris is the French name, and Alsace, which has a cool climate but also gets a lot of sunshine, is the perfect place to grow it. For more on this see page 159.)

With its easy texture, high acidity, and soft sweetness, it's positioned to get the most out of the many toppings you see in high-end ramen. It can manage all the fatty, savory, and bitter you want to throw at it, particularly all at once.

*$ Trimbach Réserve Pinot Gris* 🎏☀

*$$ Domaine Schlumberger "Spiegel" Grand Cru Pinot Gris* 🌼☀

*$$$ Domaine Zind-Humbrecht "Rangen de Thann Clos Saint Urbain" Grand Cru Pinot Gris* 🌼☀

# Marie Callender's Pot Pie
## & BADEN SPÄTBURGUNDER

Frozen pot pies are one of those delicious things I wish I could eat more often without knowing that half of one serving pretty much blows out every daily recommended calorie, starch, carb, sugar, and salt guideline I have to work with.

But when I do indulge, the guilt is easier to swallow knowing I'll be doing it with Spätburgunder (Shpate-bur-gun-dher), Germany's much more fun name for Pinot Noir. Baden is the most southerly wine region in Germany, but it's still quite far north for winegrowing as a whole, at 48°N, just one degree south of Champagne, making it a lean, mean, Pinot machine. And while climate change is now making it possible for reds to fully ripen in all thirteen of Germany's wine regions, I still prefer a good Baden version. The wines have a classic cool-cherry vibe with an allspice fleck and earthy base that give them more substance than you might expect from their thinner color. The pie's creamy, molten innards need acid, and German Spätburgunder has enough of it to clean the clock of the heaviest protein-and-veggie mash. The wine's earthiness also makes a pretty backdrop for everyone's favorite part, the buttery crust, helping its flavor to linger.

*$ Weingut Ziereisen "Tschuppen" Spätburgunder* 🍃🍂☀

*$$ Enderle & Moll "Buntsandstein" Spätburgunder* 🌼🍃🍂

# General Tso's
## & BEAUJOLAIS

When the General calls, most would tell you to make an easy beeline for some Riesling, which is a perfectly reasonable pairing for sweet and spicy food. But there are more interesting ways to go, particularly if you're partial to red. Beaujolais, which comes from a subregion in the southernmost stretch of Burgundy, is chief among them.

While most Burgundy is based on Pinot Noir and Chardonnay grapes, Beaujolais is made from Gamay, a grape whose name got dragged through the mud when the region's Nouveau style of wine became over-commercialized in the eighties. But all that's changed due to a massive shift in the mindset and philosophy of the area's winemakers.

In fact, Beaujolais—an area once known for producing wine in such bulk that the Japanese created outdoor pools where you could bathe in it—is now leading the conversation about natural wine, thanks to a group of forward-thinking viticulture revolutionaries known as "the Gang of Four," Marcel Lapierre, Jean Foillard, Jean-Paul Thévenet, and Guy Breton. Back in the eighties, they gave up all synthetic herbicides and pesticides and started working with old vines that yield less fruit but higher quality. They also harvested later to ensure more structured wines, rigorously sorted the fruit to purge subpar grapes, reducing their production again, and stopped adding sugar and outrageous amounts of sulfur. In other words, they signed up to make less wine that was also harder and costlier to produce at a time when few cared about any of the things they were taking a stand against. Today, most of these practices are considered beneficial to the vineyard and the wine and have been widely adopted.

The more natural approach to winemaking often practiced in Beaujolais is a throwback to the way wine was made in the area before modern technology, using a technique called carbonic maceration. By packing grape clusters on top of each other in a vessel without oxygen, fermentation happens naturally. The high concentration of $CO_2$ starts the fermentation inside the berry, so there is little tannin compared to typical red winemaking. Grapes in the bottom of the vessel are crushed due to the weight of the clusters above them, providing enough color and tannin to make the wine red.

This technique produces a style that's light in body, much like Pinot Noir, with a lot more fruitiness. In the case of tangy General Tso's, that juicy mouthfeel moves in tandem with the heat of the spice, and the light and fresh fruit flavors bond with the sweetness. The deep-fried chicken is underpinned by Beaujolais' acidity. And because Gamay from the region also tends to have a hint of earthiness, those occasional cuts of dark meat will get their due, too.

*$ Clos de la Roilette Fleurie* ⁝⁝ ⸙⁕

*$$ Domaine Marcel Lapierre Morgon* ☀⸎ ⸙⁕

*$$$ Jean Foillard "Cuvée 3.14" Morgon* ☀⸎ ⸙⁕

# Bagel Bites
## & PAARL PINOTAGE

South African Pinotage is a grape that was made by crossing Pinot Noir and Cinsault in the early 1900s in the hopes it would have the sensual appeal of Pinot Noir without its growing challenges, and be as easy to cultivate as Cinsault. Unfortunately, they ended up with a grape known for primary characteristics like tar, burnt-tire rubber, and nail polish remover. But what a difference a century makes. These days, there are majestic versions of Paarl Pinotage that are rewriting the grape's outdated résumé—just in time to redeem a miniature novelty pizza that's always had a reputation problem of its own.

Paarl is a respected wine-producing region that's typically outshined by its older South African neighbor, Stellenbosch, which also makes some great Pinotage. But just a little to the north, Paarl makes a version that's packed with red, purple, and black fruits, rooibos tea leaves, licorice of both colors, sweet tobacco, and bacon. They can be beguilingly complex—in ways a Bagel Bite rather proudly isn't. And while they don't have much in the way of acidity, they do have a soft tannic structure that offers a hint of sweetness. All those factors come together in just the right measure for that semi-sweet, semi-artificial, enzyme-enhanced tomato-and-cheese-ish bite of unfrozen genius that's about to burn the roof of your mouth.

*$ Nederburg "The Winemasters" Pinotage* ✳

*$$ Lievland Bushvine Pinotage* ✳

# PB & J
## & LAMBRUSCO AMABILE

Whether you go for the super-smooth, no-stir peanut butter or the organic, pricey Justin's kind, the salty-sweet staple of PB&J tastes better with Lambrusco, the wine to peanut butter's jelly. Produced in Emilia-Romagna and Lombardy, Lambrusco belongs to the rare category of lightly sparkling wines from northern Italy called red frizzante, which is largely misunderstood. Some of the early Lambrusco wines that were available in the United States were considered sweet or cheap or both, but that's no longer the case today. The best versions of Lambrusco are made dry (secco), or let their light sweetness shine through gently (amabile). Six primary red grapes are used to make the wine, all of which have Lambrusco in their names, and what they share in common are bright berry notes, toe-curling acidity, and a pleasant, mildly bitter pinch. Crucially, good Lambrusco delivers ripe, brambly flavors that link up with the grapey sweetness of the jelly (amabile in particular), while that hint of bitter folds into the nutty sweetness of the peanut butter. And the light, bubbly edge cleanses the sticky roof of your mouth like a squeegee.

*$ Cleto Chiarli "Vecchia Modena" Lambrusco di Sorbara*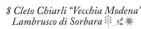

*$$ Cantina della Volta "Rimosso" Metodo Ancestrale Lambrusco di Sorbara*

# CHAPTER 2

# Southern Comforts

BLUEGRASS BASICS *for* COASTAL ELITES

**W**ay back before I was a wine expert, I waited tables at a winery in Louisville—yes, they make wine in Kentucky, sort

of—which is where I first caught the vine bug. I was a year out of acting school, living paycheck to paycheck in New York and sinking deeper into debt, when my father called me with an offer I couldn't refuse. If I'd come back to Kentucky to get my bachelor's degree, he'd happily pay.

My father is in the Navy and a corporate lawyer—the acting thing tested the limits of his comprehension. He had indulged my thespian dreams, but he also adamantly believed I needed a college education. Playing pretend with other unemployed adults was great, but now it was time to grow up. And as hard as it was for me to admit, I knew he was mostly right.

I loved acting, but I also loved eating and indoor plumbing. And I was watching my high school friends wrap up their final years of college, ready to head out into the world

with pieces of paper that said they were hirable for non-table waiting jobs.

Back home, I wasn't interested in partying or the full college experience. I wanted in and out, so I could get back to New York and acting. That diploma was the obstacle standing in my way, so I fast-tracked my curriculum and took on colossal course loads. I managed to graduate in two years, and no, my major wasn't Communications—I got a far more useful Philosophy degree.

I knew after tasting independence in the city I couldn't go back to living at home, so I got a job as a waitress at a restaurant and winery in downtown Louisville to pay rent. To my surprise, it quickly went from an obligation to the best part of my week.

For the first time, I became interested in wine as a subject: how to taste it, how to make it, how to talk about it. I know now that most

SOUTHERN COMFORTS

59

of what we were making was your average local fruit swill, but even with our basic setup, there was a very real culture around the wine. The way people behaved around it and spoke about it was provocative to the point of seeming almost mystical to me. After I found a decent comfort level with the wines we made, my Virginia Slims–smoking boss, Dave, said I was welcome to come in on Sundays to help with grunt work in the winery for extra cash.

The work wasn't glamorous—it was cleaning floors, hauling cases, and counting inventory—but everything about being there energized me, down to the unique smell. In a winery, the air is cool and humid, with a subtle yeast scent that permeates everything and is weirdly pleasant. When you spend time in one, watching the wine rest quietly and patiently in its barrels as it ages, and you see the care and pride the winemaking team puts into each bottle, it's, well, intoxicating.

Before I knew it, I was hooked, even though I didn't really understand anything about wine. I fell in love with the science of fermentation, the centuries of history behind the craft, and even the challenge of trying to describe the nuances of a wine to customers. I liked how it made me feel, which I think to my younger self was worldly and sophisticated. It tapped into something beyond my immediate existence as a half-actress student waitress with no clue what she was going to do with her life.

I went from knowing nothing to studying just enough not to mispronounce Merlot as Mer-LOT. And I even started "collecting" for the first time, which meant stockpiling a mixture of fruit-flavored Chardonnay and high-fructose corn syrup known as Arbor Mist. (It came in pretty colors!) I displayed the whole range of flavors on a rack I bought at Target, but rarely drank them—I

> **No matter how far you take me out of the South, I'll always be a southern girl, and the love I feel for Kentucky stays with me like a tune. It helps that I've always been able to bring its food culture along with me.**

preferred to ogle my bottles as decor the way I assumed fancy people did. (I wasn't totally wrong about that.)

Just after graduating, when I was getting everything in order to return to New York, my father and I went out for a run, which was his not-so-secret Dad method of talking to his kids about what was going on in our lives. By this time, he had finally come around to the idea that I had my heart set on the bright lights of Broadway or Hollywood.

"So you're moving back to New York to become a famous actress, eh?" he asked, with what I think was sincerity.

Without missing a beat, I answered, "Nope, I'm going back to be a sommelier."

He stopped dead in his tracks. "A sum-all-what?"

No matter how far you take me out of the South, I'll always be a southern girl, and the love I feel for Kentucky stays with me like a tune. It helps that I've always been able to bring its food culture along with me. (The accent follows without permission.) From Hot Browns and beer cheese to dirt cake and brisket, wherever I am, I keep going back to these Kentucky classics, now paired for her pleasure—and citified tastes. It only takes a bite to bring the song rushing back.

# Kentucky Fried Chicken
## & BRUT CHAMPAGNE

There is no bad time to drink Champagne. This is a universal truth that needs no undoing. The only question becomes: What do you want to eat with it? For this Bluegrass girl, the answer is always a bucket full of fried chicken. In fact, there may be no better accidental relationship on earth than the one that exists between fried chicken and Champagne, the ultimate Voltron of grease, protein, bubbles, and acid.

When Champagnes are made, they go through a process called autolysis, during which the wine spends time *sur lie*. This is a French phrase that is a much more beautiful way of saying the wine was aged on the dead yeast that's left over after fermentation ends. The liquid in each bottle eventually takes on the flavors of that yeast— it's the toasted brioche that comes through when you smell and taste good Champagne.

Those bread flavors also align with the golden goodness of fried chicken, and I'm honor bound to stand behind the Colonel's Original Recipe here. The secret spice blend is packed with savory, umami-driven pleasures, which along with the chicken grease call out for Champagne's natural acidity. The bubbles bring home the crunch of the skin and the coating.

As for the Champagne, look for Brut Multi-Vintage (Brut meaning dry, and Multi-Vintage, or MV meaning a blend of grapes from different years, also known as Non-Vintage, or NV). This is the style every Champagne house hangs its hat on, and because it makes up a majority of those houses' production, it's easy to find. They're designed to taste the same year after year, so you can always expect a consistent bottle. Each house has a distinct profile that they work to replicate every time by blending multiple vintages together. Some people think this is just an entry point for Champagne, and while it is usually the least expensive in a house's lineup, it's also arguably the most difficult to make in both artistic and scientific terms.

Almost all Champagnes are Brut-level dry, so it won't be hard to find; you just want to make sure the wine is on the drier side because a Champagne that's sweeter than Brut would clash with the savory chicken. And unlike Vintage Champagnes, which require time to develop the kind of complexity you want from this particular pairing, Multi-Vintage Champagne is ready to drink when it comes to the market. The autolytic character of the Champagne engulfs those eleven herbs and spices in toasty rapture.

$ *Nicolas Feuillatte Réserve Brut MV (375 ml)* 🌿
$$ *Louis Roederer "Brut Premier" MV* ❀ ✳ 🌿
$$$ *Egly-Ouriet Brut Grand Cru MV* ❀ ✳ 🥄

# SPARKLING WINEMAKING METHODS

I hate to be the bearer of bad news, but your André California Champagne is neither Champagne, nor produced in the same method as Champagne.

Sparkling wine is a broad category, made across the globe through a number of different techniques. Some producers make it the same way it's made in Champagne, France, which is known as the Traditional Method, or Méthode Traditionnelle. It requires two fermentations, the second of which happens in the same bottle you drink the wine from, and anywhere from fifteen months to more than a decade to produce a bottle this way, making it the most involved and costly of all the myriad methods to make bubbles. Still, even when a sparkling wine is produced the same way it is in Champagne, it can't be called Champagne—only the stuff that comes from that famous region earns that honor.

There are other ways to make sparkling wine, like the Charmat Method (also called the Tank Method), which in Italy is used to produce Prosecco. It also requires two separate fermentations, but it's batch-fermented in tanks before being bottled, allowing for larger bulk production that doesn't need the long aging times. And similarly, only Prosecco comes from Prosecco.

The oldest way of producing sparkling wine, the Ancestral Method, is making a centuries-later comeback. Ever had a *pét-nat*? That's short for *pétillant naturel*, which translates to "natural sparkling" wine. Producers take an unfinished or mid-fermentation wine and bottle it, letting the first fermentation finish in the bottle you drink it from. It can be a game of Russian roulette from a consistency standpoint, but it's a wild ride that a lot of newcomers to the style are happily taking.

Sparkling wines can also be made through a lo-fi process called Injection Carbonation, which most critics find wanting. It works in exactly the same way your Coca-Cola gets its fizz.

# The Hot Brown
## & PATAGONIA PINOT NOIR

We borrowed it from Austin and Portland, but the local business slogan in my hometown is "Keep Louisville Weird." And I love that my people lean in, at least when it comes to their arteries. The Hot Brown was invented at an iconic spot in downtown Louisville called the Brown Hotel as a late-night snack for revelers who attended its huge dance parties in the 1920s. And though you might visit Derby City for the big race or the bourbon, I have to insist that you make a stop at this local landmark to try its namesake dish. It's an open-faced sandwich on Texas toast with turkey and bacon smothered in Mornay sauce, which is basically an ungodly amount of butter, heavy cream, and Gruyère cheese with a pinch of nutmeg and paprika. It all gets broiled until the bread crisps and the sauce, well, browns. And it's just as gloriously weird as it sounds.

The wine to drink with it, Patagonia Pinot Noir, was not made by the same company that supplies hedge funders with their favorite vests. The natural wonderland of Patagonia in Argentina is the southernmost wine-producing region in the Americas, and its arid valleys make some of the best Pinot Noir in the world. Its extreme winters and cool summer nights make for a prolonged growing season that's particularly well suited for Pinot. Bright and high toned enough for that thick Hot Brown sauce, it's also notable for its earthy undercurrents, which the

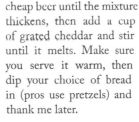

turkey and bacon lap right up. A dish so rich needs all the tannin and acid you can muster— and Patagonian Pinot delivers those by several lengths. If a visit to the Brown isn't in your immediate future, think about similar iterations of grilled bread, cheese, protein, and rich sauces. A decadent croque monsieur can do a tasty tango of its own with this lithe Argentine.

*$ Bodega Noemia de Patagonia "A Lisa"* ☼
*$$ Bodega Chacra Pinot Noir* ☼ ✳

# Beer Cheese
## & BRAZILIAN BUBBLES

You may have never heard of beer cheese or sparkling wine from Brazil. That's because you haven't been living your best life, and you need to make some changes. Beer cheese is a specialty of my home state, and I had always assumed that everyone loved this trailer-park-to-table spread as much as Kentuckians do, until I discovered that the rest of the world is still living in the dark ages. It's a simple recipe: over medium heat, whisk two tablespoons of butter and flour with a pinch of salt, pepper, and garlic powder, stir in a cup of cheap beer until the mixture thickens, then add a cup of grated cheddar and stir until it melts. Make sure you serve it warm, then dip your choice of bread in (pros use pretzels) and thank me later.

As for Brazil, bubbles are so popular there that LVMH set up an outpost of Domaine Chandon in the country just to keep up with local consumption. Rio Grande do Sul, the southernmost state of Brazil known as the "Tuscany of the Southern Hemisphere," produces 90 percent of the country's wine and its best bubbles. They're newer to U.S. shelves, but if you're adventurous enough to try something called beer cheese from a state best known for horses and brown liquor, you can handle "Espumante Brut."

These wines are Carnivale in liquid form. Made from everything from Chardonnay to Riesling Italico (different from German Riesling but still packing plenty of spritely textures and high-toned aromatics), they flaunt more colorful fruit than Carmen Miranda, with Traditional Method bubbles that samba in tiny sparkly costumes. The effervescence helps clear your palate's dance card for more beer cheese, and the softer Brazilian acid profile lets the spotlight shine on the bristling cheddar.

*$ Família Geisse "Cave Geisse" Brut*

## BBQ Brisket & Ribs
### & CÔTE-RÔTIE

BBQ is in my blood, and I genuinely believe that the act of pit-smoking giant slabs of meat is one of the world's great culinary art forms. I also know that there are many bottles that can amplify the smoky, fatty sublimity of perfect brisket or a rack of tender ribs. But one above all, Côte-Rôtie from the Rhône Valley of France, can help BBQ achieve transcendence.

The Rhône Valley is a diverse, dynamic region that stretches approximately 120 miles north to south and can be cut in half both geographically and stylistically. The southern part makes wines that are based on the grape Grenache and can have a lot of other red and white grapes blended in. But in the north, it's all about the magnificent red grape we call Syrah.

Within the northern Rhône, there are five smaller appellations—each with its own distinct characteristics and idiosyncrasies—that use Syrah as their base. What makes Côte-Rôtie such a unicorn among them is actually explained in its name. In English, it translates to "the roasted slope," because the steep inclines where the vines grow face south toward the Rhône River and get a lot of sunshine. That allows the grapes to ripen to their full and most powerfully tannic potential, and the resulting expression yields a robust set of aromas and flavors like olives, white pepper, bacon fat, and black fruits of all kinds, along with a distinct smokiness that's a dead ringer for charcoal. No matter what type of barbecue you love, these wines will get the very most out of every juicy, smoky hunk. The appellation is small and prestigious, so the wines start on the pricey side and only go up from there. But Côte-Rôtie is so consistently good, you get what you pay for every time.

*$$ Domaine Lionel Faury Côte-Rôtie* ⚬ ⚬
*$$$ Domaine Jamet Côte-Rôtie* ⚬ ⚬ ✳ ⚬

# Dirt Cake
## & BANYULS

Most likely a descendant of the Mississippi mud pie, the dirt cake is a classic from the 1970s that the South has never quite quit. It's about as easy as baking gets, in that you don't have to bake anything, and it's equally as odd, in that it's supposed to look like dirt. The "cake" is typically served in a real flower pot and consists mostly of pudding and crushed Oreos, with gummy worms on top to complete the effect. And obviously it's delicious.

Such a strange confection calls for a peculiar wine, and Banyuls happens to be the right kind of down and dirty. The fortified wine from southern France is based mainly on red Grenache grapes and made through a method known as *Banyuls traditionnel*. About halfway through fermentation, when the wine is still sweet, they add a neutral grape spirit that stops the fermentation process and preserves all the sweetness. For the style I recommend, they employ a mad-hatter strategy of transferring the

wine between oak barrels of various ages and sizes to simmer. In some cases, they put the wine in giant glass bottles called demijohns and let them bake directly in the sun (the grand cru bottlings go for two and a half years or more). Yes, unlike dirt cake, they actually bake the wine.

All this work produces a wine with an aroma profile called rancio, which sounds a lot like "rancid" because that's exactly what it is. (I told you this was an odd couple.) Fortunately, that doesn't mean it smells like someone hid cafeteria meat in the locker room—it means that it was intentionally exposed to oxygen, in this case to create a wine that tastes like a bowl of candied fruit and nuts, with a little bit of chocolate and herbaceous mint on the bottom.

The Banyuls' rancio notes act like a garden rake on the cookie-and-pudding dirt, bringing all the rich flavor to the surface and exposing the juicy gummy worms as the real star. The alcohol level (around 16 percent) isn't as high as other fortified wines, making the profile soft enough so that the pudding doesn't get trampled. For Oreos on their own, see my pairing with cream sherry (page 84), which allows for more of the salty and bitter components of the cookie to come through without all the distractions of fruity gummies and creamy pudding.

*$ Maison M. Chapoutier Banyuls Rimage* ✳ ✳ ⚬
*$$ L'Étoile Banyuls Grand Cru Cuvée Reservée* ✳
*$$ Domaine du Traginer Banyuls Ambré MV* ⚬ ✳ ✳

CHAPTER 3

# Extra Value Meals

MCDONALD'S: *on* PROPERLY LOVIN' IT

**I**spent the better part of seventh grade eating defrosted McDonald's Happy Meals. I do not recommend this for the optimal enjoyment of

Happy Meals. But it was a sacrifice I was more than willing to make for the object of my obsession in 1997. Like so many other kids—and an even weirder amount of adults at the time—I was fully in thrall to the sack of plastic pellets and synthetic plush known as Beanie Babies.

More specifically, I was hell bent on acquiring the complete collection of Mini Beanie Babies that came with McDonald's Happy Meals that year, a seemingly modest ambition that was, in fact, more like an epic grail quest, if Indiana Jones was played by Snooki (and the grail was a Red Bull–branded Mazda). Getting the full set was a volume game that involved my mother driving my brother Forrest and me to what may have been every McDonald's in the state of Kentucky. And as my parents discovered, we would not stop until we achieved satisfaction.

Naturally, both siblings had to have their own sets. Sharing was not an option. And as our father failed to fully appreciate, despite the many times we explained it to him in detail, they all needed to be in mint condition in their original plastic packaging, so they could be sold for unfathomable, life-changing fortunes at a later date. By my projections, the potential value of these Mini Beanie Babies on the collectibles resale market was plainly obvious. It was actually *insane not to buy all of them.*

Of course, McDonald's being the geniuses they are, you couldn't just roll through any old drive-thru and request a Happy Meal with the Mini Beanie Baby you required. You had to cross your fingers, open the box, and take what you got—gratefully, I might add—because you were lucky if that particular location even had any of those chubby little uncut diamonds left.

For months, my mom would pick us up after school and we'd light out for various McDonald's far and wide, in suburbs we'd never heard of, hunting down the elusive Minis that would complete our sets. We'd hear rumors about a rare cache of Pinchers the Lobster that had landed downtown on Third Street. Or that an Inch the Inchworm, the nearly impossible-to-find Sasquatch of Mini Beanie Babies, had been sighted at a location in East Louisville.

Each and every time, my mother would load us into Big Bertha, our purple Ford mini-van, and perform what I only realized later were selfless acts of love. And she wasn't just going through the motions—her commitment to our mission was full and unwavering. You should have seen her at the drive-thru them, and we were *absofrickenlutely* not the kind of family that wasted food. So all those extra hamburgers and fries went straight into the freezer. We were defrosting and eating them for months. (About a minute in the microwave does the trick.)

Thanks to the heroic actions of my mother, we did eventually get all of our complete sets. And I couldn't tell you where they are today. My father says he thinks he found a garbage bag full of them when he was cleaning out the basement once, and may or may not have tossed them, completely unaware of their immense value.

Despite the squandered millions, I wouldn't trade that trash bag full of memories for anything. (And as it happens, "No amount of money in the world" is pretty much exactly

## It's a primal kind of craving. The Hamburglar gets his mitts on you young, and even now, try as I might, I find it impossible to shake him.

intercom, displaying an aptitude for maternal skullduggery that was a joy to behold, as she tried to finagle confidential information out of often amused and endlessly patient drive-thru employees about which Beanies may or may not be on premises—and what exactly could be done to perhaps get one of those specific Beanies to fall into her bag?

We had quotas for each day, right up until the moment my father realized that something insane and sinister had overtaken his family and tried to put limits on our right to pursue happiness. This, of course, amounted to treason and did not last, because no man could stand between us and what was obviously the very future of our family's fortunes.

It turns out he was actually more concerned about the stockpile of ice-cold Happy Meals that was taking over our house. We were buying them faster than we could eat what they're worth now.) Besides, they don't have a section on eBay for moms willing to go to extremes just to make their crazy children happy. Who can put a value on that?

For most Americans, there's at least one item on the OG McDonald's menu that brings them back to a simpler time, a bite that's inextricably linked to their childhood or to a pure moment of satisfaction—a very specific flavor combination that sets off, however briefly, the sensation of olfactory nostalgia. And as hard as it is to ever get that feeling back as an adult, that doesn't stop us from chasing the golden dragon. It's a primal kind of craving. The Hamburglar gets his mitts on you young, and even now, try as I might, I find it impossible to shake him. The good news is that you can turn that weakness into a strength, or at least a pretty good excuse, by dressing it up as a sophisticated wine-tasting experiment.

# Big Mac
## & RED BURGUNDY

When it comes to its list of ingredients, the most iconic burger of all time has the Pledge of Allegiance beat for sheer staying power in our collective memory. Those two all-beef patties, special sauce, lettuce, cheese, pickles, and onions on a sesame-seed bun have had us in their clutches for more than fifty years—and to this day still sell at a clip of 550 million a year in the United States alone. We're powerless to resist those beefy twins drizzled in tangy sauce, swaddled by a crucial center bun that remains one of the great innovations in burger history, originally added because the double-stack was too messy without it.

There have been plenty of attempts over the years to deconstruct the special sauce. While McDonald's guards the recipe like the Maharaja's necklace, there's general agreement that it consists of varying proportions of mayo, sweet pickle relish, yellow mustard, white wine vinegar, paprika, garlic, and onion. Altogether, it's creamy and just a little bit mouth puckering with a hint of sweet. Add that to the beef fat and the mild nuttiness of the sesame-seed bun, and the Big Mac's power ballad of flavor calls for a soloist with higher acidity and a touch of tannin.

The lusty Frenchman that fits the bill is Bourgogne Rouge, or red Burgundy, probably my favorite wine on planet Earth. While Burgundy is the name of the region southeast of Paris where the grapes are grown, the actual grapes that make red Burgundy are Pinot Noir. (There's also white Burgundy, made mainly from Chardonnay grapes grown in the same place.) Because of its nearly perfect ratio of soil, sun, and slopes, the Burgundy region has proven over centuries of winemaking that the vines grown in its earthly bosom provide the most complex expressions of Pinot Noir. This is the storied land where some of the most expensive wines in the world were born: One

bottle of 1945 Romanée Conti recently sold at auction for $558,000. But you don't have to mortgage your house to get in on most of the exceptional wines on offer here.

In Burgundy there are no duds—there are quality designations across the price spectrum—but the entry point for most people will be the wines known as regional Burgundies (for more on these quality levels, see page 70). Light, fresh, and delicious regionals can be had for less than $25 a bottle.

One of the hallmarks of red Burgundy is its earthy, mushroomy flavor, which is slightly subtler in regional bottlings, where the wine's fruitier elements tend to take the main stage. Red Burgundies hit you first with a very distinct salvo of red cherry, followed by red hibiscus and raspberry. That very specific tang hitches a loud and proud ride on the Big Mac's special sauce, while the Burgundy's low hum of mushroom forms a backbeat with the sesame seed bun. Its gentle tannic kick clears away the fat of the beef and cheese, and the pickles enhance the Burgundy's fruity autotune.

*$ Domaine Thévenet et Fils Bourgogne Rouge "Bussières Les Clos"*

*$$ Domaine Méo-Camuzet Bourgogne Rouge*

*$$$ Maison Leroy Bourgogne Rouge*

# CHUG, MARRY, SPILL
## *The Burgundy Power Rankings*

Within the Burgundy universe there are four levels of quality. What makes one better than another is determined by rarity, how long it can age, and the land from which it comes. Some places simply grow superior grapes because of a long list of factors determined by their terroir, like soil, drainage conditions, and aspect. While the reputation of the winery—called a domaine if they grow their own grapes and a négociant or maison if they buy them from others—can also make a big qualitative difference, it isn't accounted for in the ranking levels. In this case the sole basis of the ranking is the land. In order of quality from lowest to highest, they are:

REGIONAL Bourgogne (Bore-gun-yah)—The entry tier makes up a little more than half of the total production in Burgundy and blankets the whole region. Chardonnay and Pinot Noir grapes grown anywhere in Burgundy can carry this quality level, and the label will bear the name Bourgogne.

VILLAGE (Vee-lahj)—Smaller circles within the bigger circle of the Burgundy region, these more specific appellations cover the area around the village that gives the wine its name, like Puligny-Montrachet and Chambolle-Musigny. There are forty-four different villages from north to south.

PREMIER CRU (Pree-meer Crew)—Sometimes written as "1er Cru," which is pronounced the same as when it's spelled out (not "one air crew"), these wines come from even more specific plots (smaller circles inside the two previous circles), known as climats, that are located within the villages themselves. They're labeled with the name of the village followed by the name of the Premier Cru climat, such as Puligny-Montrachet Premier Cru Champ Gain or Chambolle-Musigny 1er Cru Les Sentiers. These climats have proven they can produce higher quality wines than the rest of the village.

GRAND CRU (Grahnd Crew)—Just like it sounds, they're the grandest wines made in Burgundy. They account for just 1 percent of the total production and are as rare as they are expensive. There are thirty-three Grand Crus, and at this level the label simply indicates the name of the climat the wine comes from. For example, "Montrachet" is a Grand Cru in Puligny-Montrachet. "Musigny" is a Grand Cru in Chambolle-Musigny. If that sounds a little confusing, it's because vintners got tricky a long time ago and started adding the name of their most famous climats to their village names to elevate the status of their village wines. So you can blame the French for these perfectly accurate logic expressions: Montrachet Grand Cru > Puligny-Montrachet 1er Cru Champ Gain > Puligny-Montrachet Village > Bourgogne Blanc. Or, Musigny Grand Cru > Chambolle-Musigny Premier Cru Les Sentiers > Chambolle-Musigny Villages > Bourgone Rouge.

# Filet-O-Fish
## & AUSTRIAN BLAUFRÄNKISCH

McDonald's first blessed its menu with the Filet-O-Fish back in the 1960s as an option for Catholics on Good Friday. And though its appeal may remain niche, fans of its seaward charms are devoted. There's something about that first bite, when the squishy steamed bun gives way to the crisp Alaskan pollock and a warm ooze of creamy tartar sneaks through. It's a simple pleasure known only to those unfairly maligned mavericks who choose the Filet-O-Fish. And it is for these intrepid souls that I proffer a red wine—not a white—to pair with their O-favorite. The assumption that white is only for fish and red is only for meat is outdated cockypot, and it's time for that rule to be broken.

For fried fish, you'll want a lighter red, chilled in the fridge as if it were white. And for the Filet-O-Fish in particular, a tarty little number from Austria called Blaufränkisch cannot be bested. Blaufränkisch is an older grape, but it's become so popular in recent years that some are now calling it the Pinot Noir of the East. One of the many things that make wine so confusing is that sometimes the same grape has a different name depending on where it's planted. That's the case with the Blaufränkisch grape, which is grown in countries across Eastern Europe. Called Blaufränkisch in Austria, the very same grape is known as Blauer Limberger in Germany, Frankovka in the Czech Republic and Serbia, Frankovka modrá in Slovakia, Kékfrankos in Hungary, and Franconia in Italy. The grape itself produces a wide range of wine styles, but for our purposes it's the lighter and fresher medium-bodied iterations that work best, where the tannins aren't so intense as to overpower our crispy fish, yet sturdy enough to echo the rich tartar sauce. And one of the hallmarks of Blaufränkisch is the spiciness it exhibits in spades, which is just the kind of kick that lands so beautifully in a pillowy steamed bun. The tastiest appellations seem to come from the places with the craziest names, like Mittelburgenland, which makes a hot pepper spicy style with a fruit density that ranges from red licorice to fruit roll-up.

*$ Markus Altenburger "vom Kalk" Blaufränkisch, Burgenland* ☼☽🍃

*$$ Weingut Moric Blaufränkisch Reserve, Burgenland* ☼☀

*$$$ Christian Tschida "Felsen I" Blaufränkisch, Burgenland* ☼☽🍃

# Quarter Pounder
## & RED SUPER TUSCAN

The primary difference between a Quarter Pounder and a Big Mac? Ketchup and mustard instead of special sauce, one additional slice of American cheese, more meat, and no middle bun. That bun-to-meat ratio turns out to be a key factor when it comes to picking the right wine for this McDonald's mainstay. With more cheese and meat, you need a bigger wine, but you don't want to sacrifice that great synergy of acidity and fat you get with the Big Mac and Burgundy pairing. What you need is more cowbell, in the form of tannin, and for this we head to Italy, specifically coastal Tuscany, the land of the oft-misunderstood Super Tuscan.

Confoundingly enough, the term "Super Tuscan" is a made-up coinage with no technical or legal definition. All it means is that the wine comes from one or more grapes—like Cabernet Sauvignon, Merlot, or Syrah—that are physically grown in Tuscany but not originally native to Italy. (Or in some cases when native grapes like Sangiovese or Montepulciano are used outside of the specific parameters of a producer's appellation.)

Super Tuscan styles can vary, but what they all share is a unique broadside of freshness and power, and a juiciness that snaps to attention with ketchup, mustard, and pickles. The wine's guaranteed acidic streak supersizes that pucker, and the beefy tannins from all the thick-skinned grapes work overtime on the quarter-pound patty and extra cheese.

*$ Tenuta Prima Pietra "Dainero" Toscana*

*$$ Uccelliera "Rapace" Toscana*

*$$$ Tenuta San Guido "Sassicaia," Bolgheri Sassicaia*

# Hot Caramel Sundae
## & 20-YEAR TAWNY

Even among the relatively few people who are familiar with it, Port is often dismissed as too sweet or cheap to be good. But as one of the three oldest appellations in the world, these dessert wines deserve so much more respect. Fortified wines are spiked with distilled grape spirits, usually a type of brandy, and the added booze strengthens their ability to fight spoilage for decades—and sometimes even centuries. So they're fortified on multiple levels.

Traditionally, Port was shipped out of the port town Oporto on the northwest coast of Portugal. But the grapes are actually grown, harvested, and fermented in Portugal's Douro Valley, which is farther inland. With a few exceptions, all the wines are then sent to Oporto for aging and eventual export to the world. (For many centuries, the bulk of it went to England, where Port remains popular to this day.)

Ports are mostly lumped into ruby or tawny varieties, based on their color and aging processes. Ruby Ports are blood red and fresh and fruity, with just a touch of bitter. Tawnies are browner because they're exposed to oxygen as they age, and the older they get, the better they get, developing more deeply in complexity, richness, and unctuousness. The darker the color, the more profoundly luscious they are. The designations of quality ascend by age from entry to reserve, followed by ten, twenty, thirty, and, if you're really lucky, forty-year tawny. Entry tawnies come to the market young and simple (but still plenty tasty), and they're what most people are exposed to. As you move up the age ladder, the characteristics go from dried fruits and almonds to baked fruit and balsamic aromas, and by the time you get to the rarefied thirty- and forty-year tawnies, the scarcity is as pronounced as the price.

It's a very normal thing to walk into a winery in Oporto and see barrels dating back centuries. Because tawny Ports don't come from a single vintage—they're always a blend of several—the age designation is an average of what's in the bottle. That means at the twenty-year mark, which is where we're hanging, there might be wines that are anywhere from five to fifty years old. Something happens at that twenty-year level that makes Port the ideal first mate for McDonald's Hot Caramel Sundae. They both share that creamy-soft, toasted butter-and-sugar luxuriousness, and the twenty-year's layered dried fruit and sweet baking spices melt so seamlessly into the hot caramel, you'll have trouble discerning which is which. I suggest you only try this pairing if you're ready to embark on a lifelong obsession with Port.

*$$ Ramos Pinto "Quinta do Bom Retiro" 20 Year Tawny Port*

*$$$ Quinta do Noval 20 Year Tawny Port*

# THE MARCHESE'S FORBIDDEN FRUITS

Sassicaia, the original Super Tuscan, is now widely considered to be one of Italy's greatest wines, but it started out not too long ago as a very controversial experiment. Its origins date back to the 1940s, when a man with a very complicated name, Marchese Mario Incisa della Rochetta, recognized that the Bolgherian climate and soils of northern coastal Tuscany shared more in common with the French region of Bordeaux than it did inland Tuscany. At the time, the grapes used to make Bordeaux, including Cabernet Sauvignon and Merlot, were illegal to plant in Italy, which for hundreds of years had been the exclusive domain of indigenous grapes like Sangiovese and Montepulciano.

But because estates on the northern coast of Tuscany had always struggled to produce wines remotely as good as their more famous competition in inland Tuscany, Marchese decided to take a chance and go rogue. In the beginning that meant planting outlawed French grapes that would make more sense for the soil and climate of Bolgheri—and producing just enough for the family to drink. If they weren't released commercially, there was no scandal. It wasn't until 1971, when his sons convinced him to release the 1968 vintage, that the rest of the world got to experience what had until then been the stuff of rumor.

Italians are insanely serious about their wine, but they're not crazy—the Carabinieri didn't raid the vineyard or march the brash Marchese off in handcuffs. But because the grapes he was using were banned, the wines he produced from them couldn't carry any designations of quality on their labels, which in Italy is akin to the mark of the beast: His bottles were officially deemed Vino da Tavola, or lowly table wine.

Most Vino da Tavola is simple country wine not meant for aging, let alone broad commercial distribution. And yet the wine he eventually made from those scofflaw vines, Sassicaia, was soon commanding global attention and serious prices.

Eventually, enough rebel wineries followed the Marchese's lead that the Italian government was forced to create the Indicazione Geografica Tipica designation, or IGT, a tier that allows winemakers to be more creative with their grapes. Most Super Tuscans are now lumped into this broad category, which still doesn't allow for any meaningful distinctions in quality. In 1994, Sassicaia was granted its own status as an appellation (called Bolgheri Sassicaia DOC), but it is the only wine—and only Super Tuscan—from a single estate in Italy to enjoy this privilege.

# *McNuggets*
# & THE WINES OF 'MERICA

Plump and irresistible as the little morsels are, most reasonable people would agree that the primary function of the McNugget is to serve as a crispy conduit for the dipping sauce of one's choice. Like Mary-Kate and Ashley, one is basically pointless without the other. And a person's choice of sauce is a one-ounce window into his or her soul, a culinary Rorschach that contains multitudes. We won't cast judgment upon such deeply personal preferences here, except to say that anyone who prefers the newfangled Honey Mustard to the classic Hot Mustard is most likely profoundly disturbed. Because McNuggets are as all-American as the Arches they serve, it seems only fitting that we complete their patriotic destiny with strictly American wines. The good news is that for every little pot of dipping gold in the sauce rainbow, there's a colorful domestic wine just as unique.

## Tangy BBQ
### & KENTUCKY CHAMBOURCIN

At heart a tomato paste with layers of sweet hickory smoke and savory spices, Tangy BBQ makes a fine companion for Chambourcin, a tarty hybrid wine grown throughout the eastern United States that's known for its peppery, gravelly, and chocolatey finish. (I once helped make these wines in my dear old home state of Kentucky.) Chambourcin's high acid and low tannin provide their own big, bright, red, and fruity sass to sync up with all that BBQ vinegar.

*$ Prodigy Vineyards & Winery*

## Hot Mustard
### & SOUTHERN OREGON BACO NOIR

The mad king of fast-food sauces is a blazing triumph of flavor engineering, in a shade of Chernobyl-orange so unnatural it practically dares you not to eat it. If there was ever a sauce designed to be more craveable, it doesn't exist outside of secret government facilities. Equally as strange and delightful is Baco Noir, a North-American red-grape hybrid wine that ranges in style from light and translucent to inky-rich and dark, known for its signature smokiness, sharp acidity, and particularly distinct "foxy" aroma. But it's the lighter ones coming out of southern Oregon, exploding with blackberry and black cherry, that match up so flawlessly with Hot Mustard's unhinged intensity. The region's Baco Noirs are charged with a current of clover, tobacco, and herbs, which come together with all the black fruit to provide the beauty to McDonald's beast. Think Pinot with a little funk in the trunk.

*$$ Girardet Vineyards Baco Noir S. Oregon*

## Honey Mustard
### & TEXAS MOURVÈDRE

If you're one of those people who prefer the sweetly mild Dijon of McDonald's Honey Mustard to the loud razzle-dazzle of its hot cousin, go with a Texas-size red. The added layer of richness in Mourvèdre and its bitter tannic influences make for an uncanny amalgamation of forces. Mourvèdre is a classic *Vitis vinifera* vine from warm European areas like Provence in France. But the fruity versions coming out of Texas are only getting tastier, lending themselves well to the sugary zing of McHoney Mustard.

*$$ William Chris Vineyards Mourvèdre, Texas High Plains*

## Spicy Buffalo
### & VERMONT LA CRESCENT

Cayenne peppery, buttery La Crescent is a white hybrid grape grown across the eastern United States that's showing particularly good promise in Vermont. A kissing cousin to Riesling, these wines have a similarly sizzling citrus, which helps combat overtly spicy or creamy sauces. The Buffalo vinegar will submit easily to the off-dry sweetness of most wines made here.

*$$ La Garagista "Vinu Jancu" La Crescent*

## Habanero Ranch
### & VIRGINIA VIOGNIER

Rich buttermilk inflamed with habanero peppers, it's probably the spiciest of McDonald's sauces. And when you have that much heat, you want a wine without too much acidity, because acid only exacerbates the aggressive spice. But since there are so many layers of flavor to Habanero Ranch, from hot pepper to herbs and cream, the wine still needs to have strong aromatic pungency to match the dipper's fire. Viognier, the iconic white grape coming out of Virginia, has lower acidity, which softens the wine, with a perfumed bouquet and creamy body that yields pleasant results against this saucy hybrid.

*$ Horton Vineyards Viognier*

## Creamy Ranch
### & MICHIGAN MARQUETTE

The onion and garlic of this mild American standard sneak up on you like a cowboy to a steer. So does the acid-forward hybrid grown across Michigan called Marquette. The wine's sour cherries and black peppercorn, along with its grapefruity astringency, lines the creamy edges of McDonald's ranch. And as a red with relatively little tannin, it won't buck against the lightness of the sauce.

*$ Mackinaw Trail Winery Estate Marquette*

## Sweet and Sour
### & IDAHO RIESLING

McDonald's stone-fruit flavored conundrum is simultaneously sweet and sort of sour, but not exactly either, and layered with savory spices and ever-so-slight lingering heat that form a question mark on your tongue. The base consists of apricot and peach puree, which happen to be the very fruits your palate perceives in a mouthful of acid-rich, imperceptibly sweet Idaho Riesling. Grown at high elevation—around 1,800 feet (500 m) at the foothills of the Rocky Mountains—these wines have been benefiting from climate change, as devastating frost and severe winters have become less of a threat.

*$ Ste. Chapelle "Chateau Series" Riesling*

## Honey
### & HAWAII PINEAPPLE WINE

I like honey in my tea almost as much as I like it on my nuggets, which is a lot. To counter something so sweet, I make a rare but divine exception for pineapple wines. They're made in the same way grape wine is: Fruit is crushed and fermented, then bottled to drink. But in Hawaii, they make a pineapple style that's unique in its ability to sustain preposterously high amounts of acid and sugar at the same time. Usually off-dry with a lot of astringency, the finest versions are sparkling, with strong citrusy notes that keep it all from toppling over. They can say aloha to my honey and nuggets anytime.

*$ Tedeschi Vineyards "Hula o Maui" Sparkling Pineapple*

# HYBRIDS VERSUS CROSSES

When the flower of one grape species is fertilized with the pollen of a different grape species, you get a hybrid grape. American vine species like *Vitis labrusca* and *riparia* were first crossed with the European species *Vitis vinifera* in an attempt to breed resistance to diseases like powdery mildew and phylloxera. The early results were lackluster, and many gave up on the practice, but hybrids are making a comeback thanks to some younger, energized winemakers in the United States who have picked up the torch. Today, hybrids like Seyval Blanc, Chambourcin, Baco Noir, and Vidal Blanc are being grown across the country, and they're better than they've ever been.

Crosses are similar to hybrids, but while hybrids are created by combining two different species, crosses are the result of either intentional or natural inter-pollenization between grape varieties of the same species, and they account for most of the grapes you drink. Cabernet Sauvignon, for example, is the happy result of a natural crossing between Cabernet Franc and Sauvignon Blanc, and Pinotage, a newer red in South Africa, is an intentional cross between Pinot Noir and Cinsault.

# CHAPTER 4

# Roadside Attractions

SNACK-RACK SISTER ACTS,
AVAILABLE *at a* GAS STATION NEAR YOU

**M**y only sister, Breanna, is nine years younger than I am, which means we never really got to argue about boys or clothes. By the time she got interesting, I was already out of the house. Growing up, our personalities seemed entirely different. She graduated from high school at sixteen, I'm pretty sure just to show me up. But as adults, those perceived differences started to fade away.

A few years ago, she called me on a frozen day in January to announce she was moving back home to Kentucky. She had been living in Santa Barbara with her long-time boyfriend, and after a lot of years and a lot of cities together, their relationship was *mort*. In typical Breezie fashion (that's her nickname), she already had a plan and didn't want to wait. She would be driving solo across the country in the dead of winter and was going to take the long route. So I volunteered to go with her.

The weather conditions were looking so dismal that I had friends promise to pour one out over my grave if we didn't make it home. I said that was fine, as long as it was good wine.

A couple of days with my sister follows a pretty standard sibling trajectory. First we catch up, happy to see one another. Then we start with the jabs. Pretty soon everyone's annoyed. And by day four or five, it's all-out war. Our road trip had been going great until we got to South Dakota. That's when the snow started coming down so hard we could barely see a foot in front of us. When we weren't hydroplaning, we were inching forward at five miles per hour.

One of the things that makes the Black Forest that borders the Dakotas so awesome is the long stretch of road that hugs the sides of the mountains with sheer cliff drops and no guard rails. And, as you can imagine, the road is that much more thrilling when you can't control your car. So after a few brushes with death, we decided it was time to give up and hunker down. And of course, nothing cuts through tension like time, close quarters, and silence.

It was me, my sister, and her American Eskimo dog, Luna, in a gleaming white SUV on the side of the road to nowhere. And because we were in the middle of a white-out snowstorm, we blended right in, with the occasional eighteen-wheeler and giant salt truck plowing through unable to see us. The car was packed to the roof with all of my sister's worldly possessions, including a lamp shade that had been poking the back of my head for eleven states. I brought up the ex, which was my first bad idea. Then I brought up future plans, which was an even worse idea. And by the time we got to the parental divorce, we were locked in a gale-force snowstorm screaming at each other from a distance of one foot. It went back and forth from, "I can't ever say anything right!" to "You're always so dramatic!" until the tears came, followed by the Pounding of the Dashboard. At some point, poor Luna buried her head under the lamp shade.

Eventually, and for an incredibly awkward amount of time, it was eerily quiet as my sister and I both stared out the windows. We couldn't see a thing, and couldn't escape the other if we'd wanted to (we both wanted to).

**Wiping away tears, I started to dig around for some of the packaged cheese and gas-station snacks from our rations and pulled a bottle of red wine from under the seat.**

Wiping away tears, I started to dig around for some of the packaged cheese and gas-station snacks from our rations and pulled a bottle of red wine from under the seat.

Breezie looked at me and without saying a word dug around in her bag until she found a corkscrew. If we were going to wait it out, we were going to wait it out properly. We poured that delicious Brunello (from an estate called Castiglion del Bosco) into our coffee cups and ate garbage cheese with Funyuns. Before long, Luna came out of hiding. And pretty soon we were laughing like a couple of crazy chicks from Kentucky stuck in a South Dakota blizzard with Funyun breath. We got out of the car and ran around in the snow, without another human in any direction as far as we could see; and when the cold finally got to us, we hunkered down in the car to sleep. When we woke a few hours later, the storm had passed, and the roads were starting to clear.

"You ready?" she asked. "Yep." I answered.

*Since the writing of this story, my beautiful baby sister was taken from this world too soon. While I still grieve, I am grateful for the twenty-six years that I got to be her big sister, especially with memories like these.*

# Cardi B Cheddar Bar-b-que Chips
## & CENTRAL COAST PINOT NOIR

As a rabid member of the Bardi Gang, I have to admit I was pretty excited when she came out with her own line of Rap Snacks. She's got four flavors, including Cardi B Habanero Hot Cheese Popcorn, but my favorite is the Cheddar Bar-b-que chips.

BBQ chips get their flavor from an entourage of granulated ingredients like hickory smoke powder, barley malt powder, garlic powder, tomato powder, honey powder, and onion powder, just to name a few. There's also yeast extract, which always lends an insatiable zing. It's part of the reason you always want more, and is the very essence of umami. Beyond the cheddar cheesiness, Cardi's version has a vigorous little booty pop of spice at the end.

The same umami principle makes it impossible to have just one sip of Pinot Noir from the Central Coast of California, a large American Viticulture Area with several notable sub AVAs like Arroyo Grande Valley, San Benito, Santa Maria Valley, and Sta. Rita Hills. (AVAs function similarly to European appellations but are far less regulated than French AOCs and Italian DOCs, which stand for Appellation d'Origine Contrôlée and Denominazione d'Origine Controllata, respectively—for more, see page 229.) Being on the coast has its advantages, because the vines benefit from the wet, cold air that gets pulled in from the ocean and forms clouds that cover the crop in the early part of the day, keeping the grapes from becoming overripe. This is why they're always so fresh and so clean.

My girl Cardi is East Coast for life, but Pinot Noir is one grape we have to concede to the WC. They just do the thing. And they do it right. All that savoriness in the chip is everything the cool-red cherry, earthy, spicy Pinot could hope for.

*$ Laetitia Estate Pinot Noir, Arroyo Grande Valley*

*$$ Sandhi Sta. Rita Hills*

*$$$ Sea Smoke "Southing" Pinot Noir Sta. Rita Hills (Monopole)*

# Cheez-Its
## & WHITE PRIORAT

There's a reason Cheez-Its manage to stand out among America's many cheese-flavored snacks. They're as salty and crisp as you'd want a cracker to be, with a unique what-the-hell-is-that tang. What's more, they actually kind of taste like cheese, which makes them a natural candidate for wine. And white Priorat loves it some cheese.

Wine from Priorat, Spain, is relatively easy to find, but most of what you see are red versions. White production in the region is just as old, but as reds got more popular, many of the white vines were uprooted to make way for more red-producing grapes. Whites now make up only about 10 percent of the region's total output, which is surprising given how special they can be. The main grape used in white Priorat is Garnacha Blanca, the white version of the more famous black grape Garnacha, and the wines can range from light- to full-bodied, depending on whether the style is intended to be enjoyed young or aged. The best versions can live for a decade plus, and the more aged the better for Cheez-Its.

That aging is usually done in oak and, depending on how much time the wine spends in it, the levels of salty, oily, and mineral-driven characteristics can range widely. These are the same notes you'll get in Cheez-Its, with the wine's singed-fruit character exalting the cracker's mystery zip. The overall effect is umami Xanadu.

*$ Conreria d'Scala Dei "Black Slate La Morera"*

*$$ Vall Llach "Aigua de Llum"*

*$$$ Terroir al Limit Pedra de Guix*

# Twinkies
## & SAUTERNES

Among wine lovers, certain food pairings are more or less unimpeachable—combinations that improve what you're eating in a way that's so special, people wonder if they'll ever be able to enjoy one without the other again. These are pairings like steak with a big Napa Cab, oysters and Chablis, or rich foie gras with the sweet wine that's produced in Sauternes, France. The latter is a small appellation in Bordeaux legendary for making wine capable of aging for centuries, and is thus among the most coveted in the world. But there's one thing the French don't know that can improve Sauternes wine even further: chasing it with a Twinkie.

In Sauternes, where they use Sémillon, Sauvignon Blanc, and Muscadelle grapes, the best wines are made following a process that seems counterintuitive to people new to winemaking. Most vintners want clean, healthy grapes at harvest time—the less rot and disease the better—so they can make great wines from the best possible fruit. But in Sauternes, they pray for rot, specifically a fungus called *Botrytis cinerea*, lovingly referred to as "noble rot." This very special condition acts to dehydrate the grapes and, in the process, concentrate their sugar and acidity. The final wines aren't just sweet; they have levels of complexity and savoriness that lift them up with the angels and prevent them from tasting like grape sherbert.

There are other regions that use the same method of producing dessert wines, but none have quite captured the élan of Sauternes. And yet even in France, the winemaking can be hit or miss, as the conditions needed to spur the rot at harvest are fickle. The combination of complex process and inconsistent supply also produces a substantial price tag.

So why pair this very desirable, expensive wine with Twinkies? Because the day you do will be the happiest of your week, and you're all about self-care. Twinkies may not be foie gras, but Sauternes' toasted baking spices, honeyed apricot notes, dense citrus, and layered minerality are a tractor beam for the bright yellow snack cake's signature creamy center and fake-but-familiar flavors of vanilla and butter. The sponge is industrially engineered to achieve a perfect balance between moistness and lightness; the wine achieves its own implausible dichotomy of textures and flavors—deep richness and searing acidity—the natural way.

Pro tip: If you find yourself dining in midtown Manhattan, The Grill stocks three centuries of these fabled wines. BYOT (bring your own Twinkie).

$ *Château Clos Haut-Peyraguey (375 ml)* 🎋

$$ *Château Rieussec Sauternes Premier Cru Classé* ✳

$$$ *Château d'Yquem Sauternes Premier Cru Supérieur* ☀ ♀ ✳

# Cheetos
## & SANCERRE BLANC

Cheetos are a shade of blinding orange that's never occurred in nature. And if the flavor resembles real cheese in any way, that is surely a coincidence. Even the long-time slogan, "Dangerously Cheesy," sounds more like a threat than a boast. And yet, we are powerless to resist them. They are somehow both crunchy and fluffy, and they leave our fingers coated in fluorescent oil dust because we ate the whole bag. And

even when that leaves us feeling guilty, we know we'll do it again. And at some point in your Cheetos-eating life, you will wonder, shouldn't I be drinking wine with this?

Of course you should, and after some strenuous research I can tell you that the wine must be Sancerre. You'll find red and rosé wines from this appellation in Northern France, but the white is what you want here. What salt is to food, acidity is to wine. Without them, both can be dull and flat. Cheetos may be the saltiest food known to man, so it makes sense that the only wine that stands a chance against the cheesy saltpocalypse is the acid queen, white Sancerre, made from Sauvignon Blanc. While it may seem odd to pair wine produced a few hours south of Paris with a cheese snack invented in Dallas, the acidity of white Sancerre engenders a natural symbiosis with the corn, cheese, and salt of Cheetos.

White Sancerre also tends to be highly textured, which means that when you swish it around as you drink, it will allow your mouth a chance to reclaim its ground against the tyranny of orange goo. And White Sancerre's geological ferocity drops a limestone bolder through Frito-Lay's artificial flavor fortifications.

The town of Sancerre is located in the Loire Valley, which snakes along from just outside of Paris all the way west to the Atlantic. The valley makes world-class whites of all different expressions, but the hallmark of nearly all of them is their flintiness. So you've got chalky rocks striking each other and a lot of citrus front and center. And that's buffered by herbaceous notes of grass, thyme, and chamomile. Together with Sancerre's D battery of acidity, that pretty much puts Chester out of a job as the perfect sidekick.

$ Foucher-Lebrun "Le Mont" Sancerre

$$ Pascal Cotat "La Grande Côte" Sancerre

$$ François Cotat "Cuvée Paul" Sancerre

# Sour Patch Kids
## & SEMI-DRY FINGER LAKES RIESLING

Trust me when I say there's a right way and a wrong way to do this. As you know by now, "like with like" is one of my favorite rules, and there's only one wine with the sweet and sour constitution to play in this particular candy patch: semi-dry Riesling from the Finger Lakes region of New York.

Semi-dry, also called off-dry, is a unique category of Riesling that winos cherish for its ability to pair with a broad range of foods. It has just enough residual sugar left over after fermentation to buffer the wine's tartness, so you get flavors of rich orchard fruit, like peach and apricot, without masking the lemon-lime citrus that keeps it crisp and refreshing. Sour Patch Kids are semi-dry Riesling with the volume cranked up at the stereo store. They open with an even louder rush of sharp and sour acid that's mellowed by a far sweeter finish, and together with the Riesling they take your taste receptors to the speaker room for some hair-raising sonic vibrations. It's as good as wine-candy collaborations get.

Because the local climate in the Finger Lakes closely mirrors the climate in Mosel, Germany, which sets the standard for the world's greatest Rieslings, you get the foundation of classical with all the rock and roll of New World fruit.

*$ Hermann J. Wiemer Vineyard Riesling Semi-Dry*

# Oreos
## & CREAM SHERRY

Let's get this out of the way: I know you think the only thing to pair with an Oreo cookie (or six) is a glass of milk, probably via the twist-and-dunk method. I once thought that, too, until I tried Oreos with a glass of sherry. Consider me a convert.

I know, sherry? If the Oreo marketing team has done a terrific job keeping their sandwich cookie relevant over the decades, the people who make this fortified wine from southwestern Spain . . . not so much. And it gets worse, because the style that works best with Oreos is cream sherry, which might as well be called grandma's cough medicine.

But hear me out. Sherry—especially dry sherry, which has names like fino and amontillado—is already making a comeback. Cream sherry has had a harder road, but it's on its way. For the record, it contains no actual cream—it's simply a mix of dry and sweet sherries—and it got its name mostly because it's a little thicker than traditional sherry. The cream version is a shade of dark mahogany, with a flavor that tastes sweet but not stickily so. The aromas and flavors also hit all sorts of dessert notes like walnuts, caramel, toffee, dried figs, and dates. They're sorcery with that super-sweet filling and chocolatey Oreo cookie. The important thing is to make sure you look for top producers who blend quality sherries, as opposed to bulk producers who use flavor additives. It's the difference between a wine that's heavy, sweet, and unbalanced and a wine that starts lusciously and ends on the savory, drier side. And, yes, you can even dunk the cookie in the wine. In fact, I recommend it.

*$ Harveys Bristol Cream Sherry*

*$$ Emilio Lustau "Solera Reserva" Rare Cream Superior*

*$$$ González Byass Matusalem "Vinum Optimum Rare Signatum 30 Años"*

# White-Cheddar Popcorn
## & WHITE BURGUNDY

You'd be an idiot if you didn't like white-cheddar popcorn. That's why they call it Smartfood. It is a crucial and irresistible member of America's snack canon. (OK, maybe not as important as Doritos, but it beats the hell out of Corn Nuts.) White Burgundy honors that service.

Burgundy is the most recognizable wine region on the planet for Pinot Noir and Chardonnay, and it's considered the benchmark against which all other areas producing these grapes are measured. Unfortunately, the wines of Burgundy are held in such high esteem that their pricing has reached stratospheric levels, even at the entry point for the top producers.

Burgundy produces wines at hierarchical quality tiers known, from top to bottom, as grand cru, premier cru, village, and Bourgogne (for more on this, see page 70). The latter is a regional tier, where you get simple wines meant for opening when you buy them. Bourgogne Blanc is the entry white, and they're often fermented in stainless steel or old oak barrels, so they have a salty-apple raciness with a touch of butteriness, and never feel too heavy on your palate.

When you drink them with Smartfood, you've found your tiny little corner of nirvana. The airiness of the popcorn and the light body of the wines are a natural fit, and there's usually an underlying aroma similar to cheese rinds to these wines that sounds odd but is—I promise—very appealing, especially with white cheddar. In fact, America's best-selling popcorn is almost like a For Dummies version of gougères, the legendary puff pastry made with Gruyère or Comté cheese that's typically served with Bourgogne Blanc as an appetizer in Burgundy. And taking a cue from a pairing that's lasted hundreds of years makes it even smarter food.

*$ Joseph Drouhin Bourgogne Blanc*
*$$ Domaine Pierre Morey Bourgogne Blanc*
*$$$ Domaine Leflaive Bourgogne Blanc*

# COLD COMFORT

Some foods are notoriously difficult to pair with wine, but no one's losing sleep over asparagus and Brussels sprouts. Ice cream, on the other hand, is one of those "do not pair with wine" rules that's worth rewriting.

The chief complaint about ice cream is that it's cold, and cold numbs the mouth. While a wine's flavors come through after you've swallowed and your mouth warms up, you tend to miss out on some of the finer points of a wine when you chase it with ice cream too fast. And the butterfat coats your taste buds so well that wines are often diminished at best and nearly imperceptible at worst. There's also the problem of extremes. Acid clashes with dairy—for the same reason it doesn't sound appealing to squeeze a lemon on a creamy treat. And there's so much sugar in ice cream that it shuts down any flavors and textures that get in its way.

But I have a simple way to deal with this. Wait exactly eight seconds after swallowing your ice cream, which will give your palate just enough time to acclimate so you can actually register what's happening with the wine and all the residual flavor of the ice cream. Just make sure your wine is bold enough to play David to these frosty Goliaths, who in this case go by the names Ben and Jerry.

# Cherry Garcia
## & AMARONE DELLA VALPOLICELLA

If Cherry Garcia's vanilla-based ballad of sweet-and-sour stone fruit and fudge flakes is the music, Amarone della Valpolicellas are the lyrics. Made from grapes called Corvina Veronese with some backup from Rondinella and Molinara, they come from the fabled land northeast of Lake Garda in the Veneto region of northern Italy known as Valpolicella. The "valley of many cellars" is one of Italy's largest DOCs for quality wines.

Unlike the majority of other dry red wines, the grapes used for Amarone della Valpolicella are left on the vine a little longer to make sure they're extra ripe, which is a practice more often associated with dessert wines. When they're picked, they're laid out on straw mats to dry for the winter in a process called *appassimento*, in which they lose about 40 percent of their liquid volume, essentially turning them into raisins. The sugars and flavors become super concentrated, so it's one singularly decadent raisin. But all the sweetness is fermented right out, leaving these wines dry and bitter, despite how thick and rich they feel in your mouth. Producers only use their choicest fruit for these wines, and the rest become a "normale" red wine simply called Valpolicella, so be alert at the store for the distinction. Amarone (which means "the Great Bitter") has higher alcohol and bigger body, and needs at least a decade or two to come around.

Once the raisins are ready, they're gently pressed to extract pure nectar that's then fermented for as long as two months, and the unusually lengthy process yields a particularly dense wine, which is then aged in wood ranging from neutral chestnut and cherry to new oak.

There are two general style distinctions that won't be on the label—traditional and modern—so knowing your producers can be helpful. Traditional producers like Bertani, Bussola, and Quintarelli are known for strong acid and threads of red cherry and peppercorn, with a foundation of pure kinetic energy—and can take about twenty years to come out of their shells. Modern producers like Allegrini, Dal Forno, and Masi peak earlier, and the newer oak they're aged in imparts streaks of vanilla and cocoa.

Whether you go modern or traditional, be ready for a scarlet fire of cherry flavors to go with the real kind in your Garcia, followed by a ripple of plummy chocolate that's a natural extension of the fudge flakes. And the downy tannins, bitter snap, and high alcohol make this dry, red friend of the dairy devil something to be grateful for.

Tip: For a more affordable "Baby Amarone," look for Valpolicella Ripasso, which is a regular Valpolicella that's spent time with the skins left over from the previous Amarone.

$$ *Masi "Costasera" Amarone della Valpolicella Classico* ☙✳

# Strawberry Cheesecake
## & NAPA MERLOT

Strawberry cheesecake with a thick graham cracker swirl—the most delectable of sweet bramble fruits tied together with crunch. As an ice cream, it's a great pairing on its own, but you never really hear anyone talking about it. In the pantheon of Ben & Jerry's bestsellers, it's the red-headed stepflavor. And sadly enough, Merlot receives the same kind of second-class treatment in Napa Valley, where Cabernet Sauvignon dominates. Once beloved, the grape fell victim to its own popularity—and overproduction—in the nineties. And by 2004, thanks in part to the movie *Sideways*, Merlot had a bad rap everywhere (see page 191). But some contemporary producers are beginning to restore the grape's former glory. By foregoing some of the winemaking trends that favored Big Red soda-pop fruit, the new guard is tempering that spiked-plum mainline to the vein with more sophistication and depth. What makes these Napa Merlots so unique are their refined aromas and gentle nobility. The handful of producers who take the grape seriously also plant it on the best terroir, giving it everything it needs to reach its full potential. And the monovarietal bottlings they make are far superior in style and quality to mediocre Merlots—and sometimes even better than the Cabernet Sauvignons that compete for the same prized dirt. Done right, Napa Merlots offer a profound expression of bright red plum, followed by bay leaf, vanilla, dark red cherry, and a hint of bittersweet chocolate. Flavorwise, they're the soft, cuddly sister Ben & Jerry's strawberry stepchild never knew it had.

$$ *Colète Merlot Napa Valley* ☀ ✳

# The Tonight Dough
## & MONTILLA-MORILES PEDRO XIMÉNEZ OLOROSO

For a shared birthday one year, some wine friends and I had an extravagant dinner at Casa Lever in midtown, where the sommelier was a friend of ours. During dessert, everyone at the table suddenly went quiet and seemed to be looking over my shoulder. I felt a tap and turned to find Jimmy Fallon about a foot from my head. Mick Jagger was right behind him.

"Hey! I heard it's your birthday! So happy birthday!" Fallon beamed. "Have a great night!" Jagger followed with "Happindjafhhskdjhfs," which we interpreted to be similar sentiments. The pair had apparently noticed our very loud group as we were eating (and drinking) everything, and asked about us. Just one of those New York moments that make all the pizza rats worth it.

Which brings me to the Tonight Dough, the caramel and chocolate ice cream named for a very sweet and classy host. Jimmy's mix comes with chocolate cookie swirls, chocolate-chip cookie dough, and peanut butter cookie dough, and if you were to take all those flavors and translate them into a wine, it would lead you straight to Montilla-Moriles Pedro Ximénez. A fortified from southern Spain made in a similar style to sherry, it smells like toffee, peanuts, and burnt salty caramel, not to mention layers of peanut brittle, chocolate, coffee, and sweet baking spices.

Pedro Ximénez is the actual name of the grape as well as the wine, and industry insiders often just call it PX. It's a white grape that is used to make styles of wine that range from dry to sweet—some of the sweetest in the world—but for Jimmy it's the dry Oloroso that kills. Because the fruit is so ripe when it's picked, and the sugar is fermented out, the wines have massive body, high alcohol, and abounding aroma and flavors. You end up with a white that's naturally dry but gives you the impression of sweetness because it's just so round and strong.

$ *Bodegas Pérez "Gran Barquero Oloroso" Montilla-Moriles* ✳ 🍦

# Half Baked
## & RIVESALTES

Ben & Jerry's most popular flavor of all time is half chocolate, half vanilla, and loaded with chunks of cookie dough and fudge brownies. Much like the wine to pair it with, it's a smooth medley of elements that wouldn't typically exist in the same package. Vin Doux Naturel has a long history in France that dates back to 1285, when the king's doctor invented a winemaking method called mutage. (He also claimed the world would end in 1378 and was imprisoned for heresy.) The process involves adding a flavorless alcohol to a wine while it's still fermenting, which stops the yeast from eating the sugar, leaving you with a wine that's, well, naturally sweet, or *doux naturel*.

Located in Roussillion, Rivesaltes is the largest appellation for Vins Doux Naturels and is made mostly of Grenache. It comes in several styles that are all equally soul comforting, but I specifically recommend the *tuilé*, or oxidized red, for Half Baked. With a minimum of 15 percent alcohol and 45 grams per liter of natural sugar, it's like a boozy blackberry and raisin soda with bright-toned plum flavors, cocoa bits, hazelnuts, and a pungent candied flower depth. The label for tuilé may also include Hors d'Age, which means it has been aged for at least five years before being released to the market, further magnifying all the baked fruit and nut flavors. It also softens the tannins to velvet-blanket levels. The vines that produce tuilé are uncommonly old—between fifty to eighty years—and just like us, as they get more refined with age, their output diminishes. So while the grapes they produce are fascinatingly complex, an entire vine may only barely fill a single bottle. (The average vine can fill about five to ten.)

For a wine so rare and rich, it has a relatively low profile in the United States, though that might change when people figure out that it's Half Baked's other half. Toss that choco-vanilla kitchen sink at its stewed prunes, warm baking spices, raisins, berries, and cocoa, and you'll start to feel the other kind of baked.

*$$ Domaine Cazes Rivesaltes* ✳☀

# Americone Dream
## & MOSCATEL DE SETÚBAL

While there are no words for how much I still miss *The Colbert Report*, it always makes me happy to see my other favorite late-night host on *The Late Show*—just not quite as happy as when I'm downing a Moscatel de Setúbal with Stephen Colbert's Americone Dream.

A bit like tawny Port with its rich, candied layering, Moscatel de Setúbal is a fortified white made in southern Portugal from a grape called Muscat of Alexandria, one of the oldest genetically unmodified vines still in existence. Born an Egyptian, it's a white grape that loves a scathingly hot climate. And because no one has ever heard of it, you can get exceptional bottles of high quality and decent age for under $25.

Moscatel de Setúbals have the baking spice for Colbert's vanilla base and the honey tones for his fudge-covered waffle cone, with plenty of roasted nuttiness to go with the caramel swirl, but their fruit compote of figs, dates, and apricots are what really bring the Dream to life.

*$ Jose Maria da Fonseca "Alambre 20 Anos" Moscatel de Setúbal* ✳☀ⵌ

# CHAPTER 5

# Fast-Food Fixes

HAIR *of the* HOT DOG

T hings have changed a lot in New York in the past ten years, and the social scene has spread much further afield into areas of Brooklyn like Bushwick, Crown Heights, Bed Stuy, Greenpoint, and Gowanus, where recent college grads and creatives can actually afford to live—for now.

But for anyone of a certain generation who moved to Manhattan in their twenties and stayed through their thirties, going out in the city follows a pretty standard trajectory, which at least in theory still applies today.

You start out in your twenties with virtually no standards, and you find yourself on any given night at the most tragic of bars in, say, Murray Hill, that your friends happen to be meeting at. You don't know it at the time, but you're better than that.

You start gravitating downtown, to the equally collegey dive bars in the East Village or the Lower East Side, which are a little bit less Chad-heavy. At some point, the club scene starts to seem more interesting, because they have bouncers and door policies, so you're not always contending with a LAX-bro-to-female ratio of get me the hell out of here.

You figure out that the clubs with better crowds and tougher ropes are more appealing than the ones for jabronis, mostly because you want to be exactly where they don't want to let someone as uncool as you in. Just like the popular table in high school, except the pretty girls are actual models, wearing the stuff Forever 21 is going to knock off for the high school girls next year.

And when you get into the hot club, because now you know the guy at the door, you're hardwired to wish you were in the VIP area. And the people in the VIP area wish they were in the real VIP area downstairs. But the people in that VIP area are actually about to leave, because this place is so over—like it used to be cool but the crowd got so lame?

At some point you find yourself dating a club promoter who everyone seems to like because he's always got the free bottle service and you once saw him high-five Lil Wayne. And of course there are red flags but dancing is so much fun and—wait, that's Justin Timberlake—pour me another free vodka cranberry! Then come the exclusive private parties held every single night across the city, most of which you're not invited to, but a few of which you are. And from there it's a blur of plus ones and getting on the lists, and four A.M. nights where you wind up at after-parties in lofts you have no idea how people can afford. And at some point you realize there are thousands of Peter Pan rich kids in the city who don't ever have to grow up (or get up for work), and they all know each other and go out every night. And before you know it you start bumping into them at fashion, charity, and art-world events held in decommissioned insane asylums and pencil-sharpener factories you can only get to by barge, with secret performances by Jay-Z and spoken-word poetry by Dasha Zhukova, where everyone gets sapphire-encrusted Supreme iPad skateboards in their gift bags. And you keep chasing the good parties and the fun, and it all spirals from there . . .

**My years of research have confirmed that sometimes the only cure for a hangover is more wine and some all-American grease.**

Until you eventually lose all interest.

Congratulations. It crept up on you slowly, but you're over it, and now you almost exclusively go to the same handful of four or five restaurants and bars within a five-block radius of your apartment or office, and your social life is far less stressful, annoying, and complicated. You aged out, and it takes some people a lot longer to get there than others, if they ever do—but it's almost definitely going to happen to you. So for those of you fresh to the city, even if you live in outer Brooklyn, where the entry-level neighborhood social scene tends to be a lot less overrun, here are a few nightlife lessons to save you some trouble. (I'm pretty sure they apply to any city.) And I know you won't listen to any of them—I wouldn't have either—but you can check back here after you've learned them the hard way.

• Avoid bars that start with "O'." Actually, to be safe, just avoid all Irish apostrophes. And let's throw in anything owned by former professional baseball players.

• "Speakeasies" where you enter through a false door in a telephone booth or a fake storefront are almost never cool almost all of the time.

- Parties that are never as good as you think they're going to be, in no particular order:

  - Ones that involve purchasing tickets that are "going to sell out soon!" or are related to Halloween, "Swedish Midsummer," or the "Summer Solstice."

  - Ones with one-hour open bars from ten to eleven and no RSVP required, sponsored by a vodka you've never heard of.

  - Ones hosted by cell phone manufacturers, gaming consoles, kombucha brands, or tech thingies that sound made up, with invites that flaunt long lists of co-hosts, energy drinks, or DJs that also sound made up.

  - Ones held in department stores from six to seven p.m.

  - Ones where you get there and there's a line halfway down the block for the "general RSVP list" but the PR girl with the iPad seems to have a whole different list for people she's letting in right away, and you're not on that list.

  - Ones where there's a sign outside that says, "filming in progress, by entering these premises, your face and likeness may be used for promotional purposes..."

No matter what social life cycle you find yourself in, you will at some point overindulge and not get enough sleep. But when you drink for a living like I do, hangovers can become a regular part of your workweek. My years of research have confirmed that sometimes the only cure for a hangover is more wine and some all-American grease.

# Popeye's Spicy Chicken Sandwich
## & CHENIN BLANC PÉT-NAT

It seems like ancient history now, but the unprecedented frenzy that surrounded the launch of this sandwich was borderline deranged. Before Popeyes eventually ran out of chicken because of all the media hype, even the *New Yorker* got in on the love fest, with a headline declaring "The Popeyes Chicken Sandwich Is Here to Save America." I braved long lines on two separate occasions to get my hands on one, and I wasn't disappointed. The chicken is moist and tender and it intersects with the salty crunch of skin that's so perfectly crisped, you have to scoop up all the extra bits with your fingers. The mild heat comes after, followed by a touch of sweet from the brioche bun and some sour from the pickle.

To make the most of it, you're going to require a *pét-nat*, a category of sparkling wine that's made a major comeback of late. It's short for *pétillant naturel*, but the name is always truncated for the sake of both brevity and affection. One of the oldest known methods of winemaking, it's considered by many to be a more natural process than the ones used to make other sparkling wines (see page 62 for more on sparkling winemaking methods).

*Pét-nats* are made in a way that's so ancient, the French call it *Méthode Ancestrale*. And it probably won't surprise you that they also tend to be made by producers who believe in minimal interference in both the vineyard and the winery. In contrast to Champagne, the fermentation is allowed to start before the juice is moved to individual bottles midfermentation, so there's no need to add anything more to inoculate the transition from grape juice to wine. The resulting wines can vary widely, but there is usually some cloudiness, and there are fewer bubbles than there

are in Champagnes. *Pét-nats* also tend to have a tartness and are usually dry, though sweet options do exist.

For Popeye's spicy fried chicken sandwich, you want a *pét-nat* from the Loire Valley, which has been a leading region in the movement to bring these types of wines back into the mainstream. Specifically, look for those based on the Chenin Blanc grape, which is naturally high in acidity and thus key for pairing with fried foods. The wines have a yeastiness that matches the chicken's crisp, and Chenin Blanc–based *pét-nats* are usually a little citrusy, which is great for the spicy Cajun sauce.

You often hear these wines described as having a certain funk to them, which, while true, isn't super helpful. What it usually means is that the wine has a strong odor of sciencey things like volatile acidity or *Brettanomyces* (wine folk call them "VA" and "Brett" for short), which are naturally occurring and more common in low-intervention wines. On the pleasant side, they provide intrigue in the form of barnyard pungency and high-toned fruitiness. On the other end of the spectrum, they can wander off into a vinegary, nail polish remover kind of place that some find overwhelming. But when those horns hit just right, it's like Funkadelic playing just for you.

*$$ La Grapperie "La Bueilloise" Pét-Nat* ☀🍃

*$$ Les Capriades Pet' Sec Methode Ancestrale* ☀🍃

FAST-FOOD FIXES

# FORGET ABOUT THE LEGS!

Everyone is obsessed with legs. They're great on people, but if they're the kind running in streaks down the inside of your glass, they have little relevance outside of blind tastings. Theoretically, legs can be an indication of how high the alcohol or sugar content is in a wine because elevated levels of either make a wine more viscous, causing it to move more slowly and abundantly down the glass. But it's an antiquated practice at best and nonsensical at worst. It is nearly impossible to accurately read wine legs, and I've personally never seen anyone do it to a technical degree they couldn't just get from tasting the wine. In the real world, simply reading a wine label will much more accurately inform you of its alcohol content, and a Google search can answer any questions you might have about sugar content that aren't already solved for you on the back label.

## Katz's Deli Pastrami Sandwich
## & CHILEAN CARMÉNÈRE

There is perhaps no New York sandwich more iconic than pastrami from Katz's. The meat itself takes weeks to make. The curing, spicing, and smoking develop deep layers of flavor that most people are going to tell you can only go with Dr. Brown's Cel-Ray soda, the all-time classic pastrami pairing. And you won't hear me cast doubt upon that culinary doctrine. But I will say that Chilean Carménère makes a very convincing case for itself as an alternate headliner.

Carménère is one of the forgotten grapes of Bordeaux, and while it still grows there in small quantities, where it's used for blending, it's turned itself into a star attraction in Chile. It wasn't exactly an overnight success—the grape migrated from France to South America more than a century ago—or even an intentional one. It wasn't until DNA testing was done in the mid-1990s that Chilean wine growers realized that about half of what they thought was Merlot planted in their vineyards for the past hundred years was actually Carménère. Fortunately, the case of mistaken identity wound up leading to a distinctly savory red that's a mitzvah for pastrami on rye. Framed by rich fruit

and bold spikes of peppercorn, herbs, eucalyptus, and green bell pepper, the wine is instantly at ease with Katz's classic pastrami spice blend.

$ *Casa Lapostolle Cuvee Alexandre Apalta Vineyard Carménère, Apalta* ☀

$$ *Viu Manent "El Incidente" Carménère, Colchagua Valley* ❄☀

$$$ *Errazuriz "Kai" Carménère, Aconcagua Valley* ☀

## Doritos Cheesy Gordita Crunch
## & DEUTSCHER SEKT

Germans like to have a lot of Sekt. Like more than any other country. And get your head out of the gutter, that's German for "sparkling." Of the roughly two billion bottles of sparkling wine produced annually around the world, a quarter of it is consumed in Germany alone, and they produce 80 percent of what they drink domestically, so we don't see it in the U.S. as prolifically as Champagne or Prosecco.

When you see bottles of German fizz, look for labels that say "*Deutscher Sekt bestimmter Anbaugebiete*" or "*Winzersekt*." The first means a quality sparkling wine of distinction made in one of thirteen designated wine regions, so it didn't just come from anywhere, which is the case with wines just labeled "Sekt," the lowest quality level. Winzersekt is the top quality designation, and when you see it on a label it means the wine was made from only one kind of grape and was estate grown. The wines are mostly made of Riesling, but they can come from Chardonnay, Pinot Gris, Pinot Blanc, and Pinot Noir, if it's a pink bubble. The levels of dryness are similar to Champagne, so Brut still means dry, which is most of what you'll find and should try.

These unique sparkling wines are both sprightly and sophisticated, as if someone taught a Tasmanian devil to eat with a knife and fork. And whether you go fiery, nacho cheese, or cool ranch for your crunchy Dorito shell, their interplay between youthful fruitiness and invigorating acid wraps any meat-and-cheese Taco Bell gordita in an extra-firm hug.

$ *Sektkellerei Ohlig Sekt "50 Degrees N" Brut Weiss, Rheingau* ☷

$$ *Weingut Robert Weil Riesling Sekt Brut, Rheingau* ☷✳

$$$ *Peter Lauer Reserve Riesling Sekt Vintage Brut, Mosel* ☼✳

# Hot Dogs
## & ITALIAN ROSATO

Everyone has their own firmly held convictions on the best way to dress a hot dog. (I like spicy mustard, a drop of ketchup, and lots of sauerkraut.) It can be tough to find a wine that can abide everyone's personal condiment politics, but there's a crowd-pleasing candidate in the oft-overlooked category of Italian Rosato.

Rosato is the Italian equivalent of rosé, but it isn't the style of rosé that's typically flowing in the Hamptons all summer. These wines, especially the versions made in southern Italy, have an Amalfi Coast chic all their own, with a boisterous flair that brims with strawberry, watermelon, and prickly pear. Their color ranges from pomegranate-pink to deep-red ruby, and how intense they are depends on where they're grown and the amount of skin contact during the winemaking. The rambunc-

tious grapes often used to make these wines, like Aglianico and Cerasuolo, produce a style best described as summer in a glass. Turquoise coasts and sunny days are evident in every sip, along with a shimmer of sea spray to go with the densely packed fruit. For those in my condiment camp, the wine's tang mollifies the sauerkraut, and its salinity gives ketchup an extra pout. These Mediterranean wines are high in tannin and acidity, which help mitigate the fattiness of the frank and provide a thorough palate clean-up.

$ *Feudi di San Gregorio Ros'Aura, Campania* ✳

$$ *De Fermo "Le Cince" Cerasuolo d'Abruzzo* ☼☙

# Arby's Roast Beef
## & LOIRE VALLEY CABERNET FRANC

When someone asks me what my favorite red grape is, Cabernet Franc is always on the short list. No, not "Cab." The original gangster Cabernet. No matter where in the world it comes from, I always find it to be the most interesting. Young, old, fancy, simple, tank-fermented, oak-aged—it doesn't matter. Bourgueil (Bore-guy) and Saumur-Champigny (So-meer Shamp-in-nee) are two of the original appellations representing this legendary grape in the Loire Valley of France. (Cabernet Sauvignon is actually the offspring of Cabernet Franc and Sauvignon Blanc.) If you don't know good Cabernet Franc, then perk up your ears. They have all the red fruit like strawberries, currants, and raspberries that you love about Cabernet Sauvignon but with an added dimension of lead pencil, green pepper, and dried tobacco. These are the kinds of wines

# HONING YOUR SWIRL GAME

The point of swirling or charging air into a wine is to coax the aromatic compounds out. It's called "opening up" a wine. But it's a slippery slope. There's a right amount of air to reveal a wine's full characteristics and a wrong amount of too much air that can completely oxidize and crush a wine. This is why I always recommend smelling your wine before you swirl or decant to see how expressive it is. If aromas are blasting out of the glass full-throttle, don't prematurely swirl them all away. But if you don't smell much, swirl at will or try coating the inside of the glass.

Keep your mouth open slightly when you smell. There's a reason the ear, nose, and throat doctor is the same person—they are all connected inside your head. So if you leave room for that passage of air in your mouth, the aromatics your nose picks up will be enhanced in your palate before you even take a swig.

There's no need to take a massive whiff, vengefully inhaling everything in the glass. You'll actually blow out your receptors' ability to pick up much of anything. Take slow, gentle sips of air, paying attention to what you smell as you breathe out and in.

that are so fascinating and addictive that you smell them and immediately need to smell them three more times. If you want to be a real pro, call it Breton, which is what the locals do.

Whether they're on the simple and easy side or the complex and dense side, they all share a spiciness and medium body that fit like puzzle pieces with Arby's medium-rare roast beef and sesame-seed bun. But the crucial element comes when you mix the sweet and zippy Arby's sauce with their satanically good horsey sauce—both are required for the full experience, along with a half-pound of napkins. Tang and spice is what Cab Franc was born for, and it has a little something for everything you hurl at it.

*$ Gauthier Père et Fils, Domaine du Bel Air Bourgueil "Jour de Soif"*

*$$ Catherine et Pierre Breton "Les Perrières" Bourgueil*

*$$$ Clos Rougeard "Les Clos" Saumur-Champigny*

# Shack Burger
## & AUSTRALIAN SHIRAZ

You know Shake Shack. You can't get enough Shake Shack. There are many reasons—they use meat that's free of added hormones and antibiotics, their crinkle fries are flawless—but it mostly comes down to this: The Shack Burger, with its griddled patties, Shack Sauce, and potato roll, is one of the best hamburgers there is. In many ways, it ushered in an era of newfound respect for the lowly fast-food burger. Australian Shiraz is in similar need of some image rehab, as the mass-produced, nondescript versions that have been peddled in its good name have cheapened its rep. But once you try the good stuff, you'll know why there are so many imitators.

Shiraz is the Australian equivalent of French Syrah—it's the same grape, pronounced (and spelled) differently. The warmer climate down under makes a wine that's dazzling and peppery with big, dense tannins that shout g'day to the Shack's charred beef. And the sweet Martin's roll loves this Australian's ripe fruit and subtle earthy notes.

Traditional styles found in areas of South Australia like Barossa Valley and McLaren Vale are big in body, alcohol, and spirit with a fruit and tannin impact that's quintessential high-quality New World juice. Slightly more mid-bodied and elegant styles come out of the cooler climates to the south, like Yarra Valley and Geelong (where they sometimes choose to label it as Syrah because the style is more reminiscent of the Rhône Valley's version). Other regions like Coonawarra and Eden Valley offer some delectable styles in between. So next time the Shack attacks, skip the cheap Aussie Shiraz you think you know and seek out the high-quality producers that do the grape real justice.

*$ Torbreck "Woodcutter's" Shiraz, Barossa Valley*

*$$ Clarendon Hills "Hickinbotham" Syrah, McLaren Vale*

*$$$ Penfolds St. Henri Shiraz, South Australia*

# CHAPTER 6

# Wine with Breakfast

*The* BEST PART *of* WAKING UP
*is* FERMENTATION *in* YOUR CUP

**T**he email subject read "PRINT THIS." As instructed, I opened the attachment and printed it. My new boss seemed very busy, so I walked into his office and placed the papers on his desk, trying not to disturb him. He scooped them up as I walked away.

"What are you, a moron?" he asked. "This is printed single-sided. You can dock the wasted paper from your pay." He threw the papers in my face and watched them land all over the floor. "And pick up the trash on your way out," he said.

This is what I got for quitting waitressing to get a real job in the wine business. Or at least what I thought was a real job.

The Raging Corksucker, as he shall be known, was the owner and lead instructor of a wine education outfit he ran out of a shabby office, and to the outside world, he was a magnetic personality. The operation held its classes mostly in restaurants during off hours, overcharging finance types and collectors eager to learn about wine. His smile was wide, his jokes were perfectly timed, and he seemed to know everything about wine. So when he offered me a job as his assistant, I felt lucky to be chosen to bask in his glow.

It took me far too long to figure out that the halo was actually noxious gas, though there were plenty of warning signs from the start. The Corksucker was blind cc'ed on every email sent and received in the office—every employee email. And unchangeable settings on our computers meant that when-ever he sent any of us an email, an obnox-iously loud "PING" would go off, letting us know the Corksucker had sent a message that demanded immediate attention.

PING: "Did you call this person? [No such instructions were given.]

PING: "Why would you tell them we are paying for their dinner?? [His previous email said we were paying for their dinner.]

PING: "Are you so old that you don't know how to use your brain?" [To my co-worker in her fifties.]

For the better part of two years, I put up with long hours followed by late-night texts informing me of the various ways I was an idiot, with being verbally attacked for being a few minutes late in the morning or not eating lunch at my desk, and with the always-hovering threat of being fired for some unforeseeable infraction. He was the kind of guy who seemed happiest when he was crushing happiness in others. He was also the kind of guy who called his mom by her first name (huge red flag). And when that sweet woman, who'd often come by the office to help her son out, wasn't around, he'd say things like, "She's an old dog who needs to be put down." His own mother.

Once, after an event at one of the city's most revered French restaurants, he was sitting at the bar with the chef-sommelier when I walked up to check-in and he began to drunkenly scold me about forgetting to give someone a gift bag.

"Are you so fucking stupid that you can't remember to do something that simple?" he asked, with his face throbbing like a zit. "No, tell me, are you that stupid?" The chef-sommelier who had been listening with his eyes politely averted intervened. "That's enough," he demanded.

Everything came to a head one late Friday night at the office, thanks to a bottle of Champagne—but not the way you're thinking. I had stayed to count bottle inventory, and there was a huge rack that was dangerously rickety (I had complained about it several times). As I counted, I liked to touch each bottle to make sure I didn't miss any, and one tap shook the rack so violently it brought several bottles crashing down. One of them fell directly on my head and knocked me out. Luckily, another employee was working late, too, and was there to help.

The Corksucker first tried to blame me, then sent his now former wife to sweet talk me, presumably because he was afraid of a lawsuit. (At the time, she was his go-to gaslighter, although it appears she tired of the position.) Maybe it was the head trauma, or the fact that I didn't fear her the way I feared him, but I finally stood up for myself and called her husband out for his behavior.

On the way to work the next morning, I called my father and admitted I didn't have the will to fight, nor the guts to quit. "I think the best thing that could ever happen to you is that you get fired," he said. And as if ordained, I walked in and was fired on the spot.

Shell shocked, I left the office and wandered until I found myself outside my friend Morgan's surf shop, Saturdays NYC.

(As it happens, Morgan was also buddies with the co-writer of this book, though Adam and I wouldn't meet until years later.)

"What happened?" he asked, seeing the devastation on my face. As I started to tell him, he told me to go get my laptop and come right back. Then he helped me write an email graciously thanking anyone I had worked with over the last few years, letting them know that I was moving on and would be in touch about where I landed. Over doughnuts and wine we drank from paper coffee cups, we sent it out to every contact I had. "Never say a bad word," he said. "People will know the truth without you having to tell them."

A few hours later, I got an email from California. It was the manager of one of Napa's greatest wineries, whom I'd met several times at events and seminars. "I'm not surprised by your news," she wrote. "You were so sad when I saw you last time." The note overflowed with kindness and support and a promise to call when she was back in New York. "Question," she asked. "Would you ever consider a job in sales?"

Within days she had reached out personally to the head of the biggest wine distributor in New York to say there was someone she wanted him to meet. And within weeks, I had a new job in wine sales.

Though it sounds perfectly trite, what I learned from eating so much crap is that bad bosses can only beat you if you let them. I would never allow myself to be mistreated again. And even more importantly, I learned to listen to the people who love you. Your friends, your parents, they know, even if you think they don't.

Around every Raging Corksucker who stands in your way lies great opportunity. Sometimes you just need a little wine with breakfast to see it.

# Honey Nut Cheerios
## & MENDOZA CHARDONNAY

It's hard to believe that less than fifty years ago, few people outside of Argentina had ever tried Argentine wine, let alone heard of it. Now the ubiquitous name of Mendoza Malbec calls out from almost every wine list and store shelf you come across. It's become what California Merlot was to the nineties.

But did you know that Mendoza makes grapes beyond Malbec, and that they're seriously good and also stupidly cheap for the quality you get? My personal favorite is the Chardonnay. And this is a good moment to point out that as often as I say look for lesser-known grapes when you want bang for your buck (see pages 121–122 for more on finding good deals), there's also another way. If you just can't part with your beloved Chardonnay but don't always want to pay Celine Dion prices for your favorite Napa or Burgundy bottlings, look for a place that's known for quality wine production but not necessarily the specific grape you love.

Because it's usually planted in cooler areas of what is already a mountainous climate, Mendoza Chardonnay is surprisingly mineral driven for a New World wine. While it still has a toasty fleshiness that you'd expect from the Americas, it also has a bright appley, meloney, sea-shell saltiness that leans more toward Chardonnay's homeland of Burgundy than the wines from California and other parts of the New World.

The part-salty, part-sweet earthly treasure that is the Honey Nut Cheerio, on the other hand, needs no introduction. (And I have to ask, does anyone really prefer Original over Honey Nut?) Interestingly, Honey Nut's "almond" essence is derived from natural flavors in peach and apricot pits. Add your favorite milk, whether it be almond, oat, coconut, or cow, and the creamy-sweet effect is the same. Smoky-smooth Mendoza Chardonnay resonates with a similarly creamy viscosity. All that honeyed nuttiness at the bottom of the bowl chimes the bell of stone fruit and mineral saltiness in the wine. And makes you wonder why you didn't pair Argentine wine with your breakfast cereal sooner.

*$ Alta Vista "Classic" Reserva Chardonnay* ✳

*$$ Luca "G Lot" Chardonnay* ☀

*$$$ Catena Zapata Adrianna Vineyard "White Bones" Chardonnay, Gualtallary* ☀✳∭

## Lumberjack Breakfast
### & MOSCATO D'ASTI

The lumberjack breakfast is a brawny combination of eggs, ham, bacon, sausage, and pancakes, suspended in butter and maple syrup. It's all the comforting flavors, textures, and smells of the all-American diner right there on a single plate. And you can eat it any time of the day.

But please do not drink a mimosa with your lumberjack breakfast—you're better than that. And the lumberjack breakfast is better than that, too—show it some respect. You want a special something that's light, fresh, and sweet for your sugary protein and carb blowout, and that's Moscato d'Asti. It's a wine from the town of Asti in northern Italy made with the Moscato grape, and the Moscato Bianco in particular is exemplary, packed with citrus and floral elegance. These wines are fermented to be lightly sparkling and low in alcohol—about 5.5 percent—which also makes them particularly ideal for day drinking.

Because your plate should be swimming in syrup, sweetness is a key factor. Foods with higher sugar content tend to make wines taste more bitter than they are. To counteract that, you need a wine that's just as sweet, if not more so. Sweet whites always work well with savory foods—especially pork—to create that craveable balance of sugar and salt. And Moscato's fizz works to make sure the yolky heft of your eggs gets whisked away with each sip. The fluffiness of the pancakes is elevated by the crispness of the wine, and the doughy flavors are lightened up by the freshness of its fruit. One thing to watch out for with Moscato d'Asti is the big difference in quality between bottles that come from bulk producers and those that have been shown more care. Luckily, the prices are never outrageous, so you can enjoy this wine in combination with one of life's most satisfyingly simple feasts whenever the mood strikes.

*$ Michele Chiarlo "Nivole" Moscato d'Asti* ☀

*$ La Spinetta "Biancospino," Moscato d'Asti*

## Krispy Kreme Glazed Donut
## & CRÉMANT DE BOURGOGNE

If you want good bubbles without the Champagne price, it's time to dig into the world of Crémant. They're sparkling wines made in much the same way as Champagne (i.e., the Traditional Method) but with different aging requirements, and they're produced in nine different regions of France (and Luxembourg). Each is named for the place where it's created and is comprised of the same grapes used for still wine production in that area. So Crémant d'Alsace and Crémant de Bordeaux are both sparkling wines made the same way that come from two different places and grapes.

When the "Hot Now" sign is on, the classic Krispy Kreme donut is announcing it wants a bottle of Crémant de Bourgogne. Zesty and crisp, these wines can be made from Chardonnay and Pinot Noir as well as Gamay, Pinot Blanc, Pinot Gris, Aligoté, and Melon de Bourgogne. And because Burgundy is so close to Champagne geographically, the two often share similar characteristics, though the former is never quite as layered or complex due to shorter aging times and the more southerly latitude. But when you bite into that doughy sweet puff of glazed heaven, you want simple and affordable. And precisely because of those less strenuous aging requirements, Crémant de Bourgogne is a straightforward delight that's light on the wallet.

$ *Louis Bouillot Crémant de Bourgogne Perle de Vigne Grande Reserve Brut* ☀

$ *Domaine Celine et Laurent Tripoz Crémant de Bourgogne Nature* ☀☙

$$ *Bailly-Lapierre "Vive-la-Joie" Brut Crémant de Bourgogne* ☀

## Chocolate-Chip Pancakes
## & SPARKLING SHIRAZ

"Sparkling" and "Shiraz" are two words you may have never seen together. Or, if you have, maybe you turned your nose up accordingly. But however strange it still may be to think about Australian red wines having bubbles, they've actually been making them in Melbourne since the earliest days of the Victorian Champagne Company in 1881. And for anyone who's missed them entirely, there's never been a better time to give them a chance.

Typically found in a wine region on the bottom of the continent called South Australia, sparkling Shiraz comes from a number of subregions within a truly massive area. Until recently, most have been consumed domestically, and while they're still on the fringe, as their popularity has increased, so have their exports. Just like regular Shiraz, the wines are brimming with inky fresh blackberries and violets, but the sparkling kind has a pop of ebullience that will appeal to exactly the kind of person who likes chocolate chips in their pancakes.

The sweetness levels typically range from just off-dry to fully sweet, and there's (annoyingly) no clear way to know unless you look up the

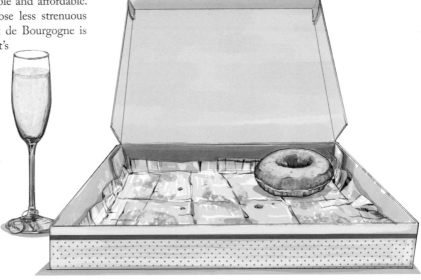

specific producer or lean on the help of a steward or wine shop employee. In this case it won't matter, because the sweetness of the pancakes and syrup will soften out any variations of sweetness in the bottle (when it comes to sugar-on-sugar overload, the mouth only has so many sensitivity settings). As a counterbalance, the moderate acidity will keep the chocolatey stodge moving. But the secret to this bubbly pairing is the touch of tannin you get from the red grape, which gently accentuates the bitter side of the chocolate chips, providing this bonbon of a breakfast just the bit of temperance it needs.

Tip: Sparkling reds shouldn't be served as cold as their pink or white brethren. The tannins introduce an element that makes wine feel strange texturally when too frigid. Just give it a little chill right before you drink it—a straight-out-of-the-cellar temp of 50 to 55°F (10 to 13°C) is perfect.

$ *Bleasdale Sparkling Shiraz, Langhorne Creek*

$$ *Mollydooker "Miss Molly" Sparkling Shiraz, McLaren Vale* ⁞❋ 🍂

$$$ *Rockford Sparkling Black Shiraz, Barossa Valley* ❀❋

# BEC
## & SANTORINI ASSYRTIKO

Perhaps the greatest aspect of living in New York is our superior breakfast sandwiches. It's a fact that New York's bodegas make the best bacon-egg-and-cheeses in the world, and while some people order their BECs as morning fuel, just as many of us order them at the end of a long night. There's no reason they can't also be a thing you pair with wine, especially if that wine is Santorini Assyrtiko.

Along with mildly important things like democracy and philosophy, the Greeks are responsible for bringing wine to the modern world. Santorini, one of the country's better-known islands, produces white wines from a grape called Assyrtiko (a-SEER-tee-ko) that's as beautiful as the land where it's made.

Santorini is a special place because the soils are a mix of volcanic ash and rocks that never allowed the root louse phylloxera to encroach on its vineyards. This wingless insect that feeds on the roots of grapevines hitched a ride to Europe in the 1860s. Unlike their American cousins, Old World vines had not developed a defense against this tiny assassin and were destroyed at devastating speeds. Scientists finally found salvation in grafting—taking the rootstock of an American vine and splicing it onto a European variety. Today, more than 85% of the world's wine comes from grafted vines. But, in Santorini, the mean little buggers never got a foot-hold, making these plants some of the oldest ungrafted vines on the planet. Wines from these vines are often described as more concentrated, complex, and pure—something you'll want to try for yourself.

The main grape, Assyrtiko, makes a naturally rich wine with a round, full body that wraps itself around a BEC as snugly as the foil. Santorini's version has the ripe citrus and fruit to cut the oozy cheese, while the bacon finds a co-conspirator in the saline minerality that's a classic characteristic of these wines.

$ *Santo Wines Santorini Assyrtiko* ❀

$$ *Domaine Sigalas Santorini* ❋

$$ *Hatzidakis Winery "Familia" Santorini* ❋⁞ 🍂

# Eggs Benedict
## & MACEDONIAN MALAGOUSIA

Dating back to the Roman and Byzantine Empires more than two thousand years ago, Macedonia has a long history of wine production, yet it remains one of the last traditional areas that's still largely undiscovered by the West. Staying true to their (actual) roots, they have continued to focus on locally native varieties of grapes, and most of them have names that intimidate all but the Balkan linguists among us. But don't let the lack of familiarity put you off. As more and more people seek to explore every corner of the wine world, exports of these wines are growing fast.

The mountainous areas of Greek Macedonia give us intriguing white wines made from grapes like Malagousia, a variety that has been cultivated here since its early viticulture history. It was believed to be extinct until it was resurrected in the seventies by a lone farmer who made it his mission to bring it back from the brink. I'm not sure how you find a grape in the backyard after it's been missing for twenty generations, but I'm sure glad he did.

Malagousia makes wines that can range in color from pale to deep straw (depending on whether they were oaked) and are always heavy on aromatics. They offer an interesting array of ripe peaches and honey interwoven with the pyrazine characteristics (winespeak for green notes ranging from grassiness to herbaceousness to spicy peppers) of green bell pepper and basil, which are brought together with a pinch of salt at the finish, making these wines a maddeningly good compatriot for eggs Benedict. You sometimes find Malagousia on its own and sometimes blended with Assyrtiko grapes indigenous to Greece. (Both the monovarietal and blended versions will do the trick here.)

Malagousia is a fuller white wine with moderately high alcohol that has enough density and roundness to match the hollandaise for richness. The oaked versions have a creamy texture, which provides them with a smooth disposition for meetings with the umami-rich yolks of perfectly poached eggs. Its almost Mediterranean-style freshness underpins the English muffin and Canadian bacon, and its storied character all but guarantees it will be your most interesting brunch guest.

*$ Wine Art Estate "Plano" Malagousia*

# Croque Monsieur
## & CHÂTEAUNEUF-DU-PAPE

Châteauneuf-du-Pape, or "the Pope's new castle," is an area in the southern Rhône Valley of France famous both for its wine and for being the relocated seat of the papacy for much of the fourteenth century. It's a name that just sounds expensive. And while bottlings here can start in the mid $50s and go way up from there, it's one of those places that has fully earned the right to charge a premium to revel in its delights. If you're a California wine lover looking to dip your toe into the vast and deep waters of French wine, this is a great place to start.

There are thirteen grapes approved for use in this appellation, which is way more than most, and if you count the white-gray-black mutations of the same grapes, that number climbs as high as twenty. Wine geeks love this fact, almost as much as they do the running debate among producers over whether the purest expression of Châteauneuf-du-Pape is achieved using 100 percent Grenache Noir, the backbone grape of the appellation, or by using all thirteen varieties, even if it's just in token amounts. While small and rarefied quantities of CdP Blanc are produced here (and if you venture into this realm please invite me over), more than three quarters of it is made from black grapes.

If Dionysus had ever made his way to southern France, he definitely would have ordered some CdP Rouge, the very embodiment of opulence, sex appeal, ageability, complexity, and unapologetic pleasure. Always broad-bodied and full of crimson red fruits like strawberry and raspberry, the Borgia-grade luxury of Châteauneuf makes sinners of us all. Its plummy and leathery aromas are followed closely by a stinky gaminess and brash herbaceousness (the French call this heady brew of sage, rosemary, and lavender *garrigue*) that are far more irresistible than they may sound. The personality is as big and extraordinary as the alcohol and tannins.

Although "croque monsieur" has always sounded to me like it should be the secret password to a swinger's dungeon, as you probably know, it is the best version of breakfast you can eat any time of day. Butter-fried ham and crispy bread teeming with melted Gruyère and béchamel, the classic Croque's liaison with Châteauneuf-du-Pape Rouge is truly *dangereuse*. Its high alcohol and generous body, born of sunny southern France, swarm the protein and dairy, and the fruits make it swoon. Traditional producers make a style using little to no new oak that's darker and spicier, while the CdP Rouge from more modern producers tends to be softer and riper. They both bring bliss to the croque monsieur, depending on your mood.

$ *Domaine du Vieux Lazaret Châteauneuf-du-Pape (375 ml)* ❄ 🥂

$$ *Domaine de Cristia Châteauneuf-du-Pape* ☀ ✳ 🥂

$$$ *Château Rayas Châteauneuf-du-Pape* ☀ 🍷 ✳

# French Toast
## & DEMI-SEC CHAMPAGNE

French toast is a debauched dish that requires a French Champagne of similar moral character. When you take sliced bread and soak it in eggs and milk, fry it, and drench it all in syrup, fruit, and whipped cream, you're obliged to pop a bottle of Demi-Sec Champagne. It's a category of bubbles with medium-level sweetness that's underappreciated, partially because it tends to walk the tightrope between refreshing and saccharine, like a Cirque du Soleil act. It has all the classic elements of a drier Brut Champagne, like the toasty croissant, zesty citrus, and fine-grade bubbles, but with increased sugar levels that add mesmerizing florality, rich fruit compotes, and a feather-light fluffiness as the wine passes through your palate. The bubbles act as an effervescent courier for this caloric bacchanal, so the eggy slabs of sugar toast feel a little less heavy.

$ *Veuve Clicquot Demi-Sec (375 ml)* ✳

$$ *Laurent-Perrier "Harmony" Demi-Sec* ✳ 🥂

$$$ *Armand de Brignac Demi-Sec* 🍷

# DRY SPELLS

On the front or back label of every Champagne, there is a word or set of words that always tell you how sweet or dry it is. Because of the specific way Champagne is made, any sweetness in the bottle was added at the very end of the winemaking process, before it was put under cork. There's so much acid in a bottle of Champagne that a small amount of sugar is needed to soften the sharpness even at the Brut, or dry, level. It's a little complicated, but in the case of super-high-acid wines like Champagne, it's all about how our mouths perceive the feeling of dryness. In a wine, if the sugar and acid are close enough in ratio, the sweetness reduces the sensation of acidity, without actually making the wine taste sweet. Think about a lemon and Coca-Cola. They have similar pH, which is how acidity is measured, but because the soda has so much more sugar, it doesn't taste sour. It's only when the sugar far outpaces the acidity that we are able to notice sweetness. Don't confuse this concept with a wine that smells sweet because it has ripe fruit aromas but is actually dry with no residual sugar. One is about how our noses can deceive us and the other is about how our tongues can do the same. Here are the names you see on a label and the corresponding sugar levels in order of driest to sweetest. For reference, g/L is short for grams per liter, and the average bottle is 750 milliliters, which is three quarters of a liter. The categories below are used specifically in Champagne but are usually very similar, if not identical, to the sweetness tiers used in other sparkling wine regions around the world.

## SPARKLING WINE SWEETNESS SCALE

| | | |
|---|---|---|
| Driest | 0–3 g/L | Brut Nature or Brut Zero |
| ↑ | 0–6 g/L | Extra Brut |
| | 0–12 g/L | Brut |
| | 12–17 g/L | Extra Dry |
| | 17–32 g/L | Dry |
| ↓ | 32–50 g/L | Demi-Sec |
| Sweetest | 50+ g/L | Doux |

# CHAPTER 7

# Trader Joe's: A Love Story

### SAVORY SOULMATES *for the* GROCERY CHAIN WEIRDLY CLOSE *to* YOUR HEART

**C**hances are good that you've never picked up a bottle of wine on your way home and thought to ask yourself how it wound up

at the store. But I can tell you that thanks to an archaic set of laws left over from Prohibition known as the three-tier system, the answer to that question is far more complicated than it should be. In the United States, wineries can't sell their products directly to stores, bars, or restaurants outside of the state they make their wine in. They can only sell them to suppliers, and those suppliers can't sell directly to those retailers either. They have to sell to distributors, who then sell the wine to your local shop or restaurant, and those distributors are the only ones allowed to actually deliver that wine in trucks to the stores and restaurants you buy them from.

Critics of the system don't like that each tier takes a cut along the way. Its proponents argue that it allows for rare and coveted bottlings to be more fairly dispersed to retailers and restaurants across the country, instead of all the inventory being controlled by a select few.

As a sales rep for a distributor, you're given a "book," which is the inventory you're tasked with moving, and a "run" of accounts, which is your assigned territory. My run consisted of restaurants and hotels, and my job was to reach out to those accounts, track down the buyers, and convince them to buy the wines in my book over someone else's.

The distributor I worked for was and still is the largest and most powerful distributor in New York State. Because of the major brands they represent on the spirits side,

which include pretty much every vodka, gin, bourbon, rum, and tequila you've ever heard of, they're kind of like the Amazon of alcohol, able to dictate terms and impose fees that restaurants and retail shops have no choice but to put up with. For this reason, they've earned the label—which I'm changing ever so slightly here—of the "Death Star."

When I first started as an eager young sales rep at the Death Star, it didn't take long to realize that even on the fine wine side of the company, where we had none of the power of the big liquor divisions, that reputation would proceed me every time I walked through a door—if I could actually get someone to agree to meet me.

My second day on the job, after a fruitless morning of phone calls trying to land my first in-person appointment, I reached a beverage director at a hot restaurant in Chelsea. I got about halfway through introducing myself before he cut me off.

"Look, I don't know you from a hole in the wall but let me be clear," he said. "I think your company and anyone who works for them should be drawn and quartered, and dragged through the streets. Never call here again." He hung up before I had a chance to exhale.

I thought for sure I was on my way to being fired. But when I told my boss Frank, he shrugged. "I probably should've warned you about him. There are a few more on your list like that. Don't let it phase you."

In my first year as a sales rep, I was called a cockroach, a leech, and even shit on someone's shoe, but I quickly developed skin as thick as a plump Syrah. I'd bounce back every day to put wine "in the bag," our term for the thirty-pound suitcase you wheel around the city for miles at a time, in snow or sweltering heat, filled with wine samples for your buyers. They might not like a single thing you bring them, but you still have to find a way to be charming and knowledgeable—and hope that the sweat from carrying that damn bag up the subway stairs isn't showing.

The head of the company, David, noticed my early success as a rep, and when I asked if there was any way to get some employer assistance to pay for my sommelier education, he said there wasn't, but he'd figure out a way. It

learned about wine, the easier it was to talk to sommeliers, and the more my confidence grew. And the more wine I sold, the more respect I earned, and the better my client list got, until I was regularly dealing with the best restaurants and somms in the city and winning Sales Rep of the Year. Before long, no one was calling me shit on a shoe. And the guy who wanted to drag me through the streets? He became one of my best clients.

As a sales rep, I worked on 100 percent commission. I ate what I killed, which in the early days wasn't much. Trader Joe's was my lifeline. As tough as the job was then, I loved it. And that's because I worked in an environment with great bosses from top to bottom. After four rewarding years, I started feeling like I had peaked in the position and needed

## Quirky, confusingly cheap, and consistently delicious is a combination that's hard to beat.

made me want to work ten times as hard and do ten times as well, which I did. Over time, I figured the whole sales thing out, breaking through on prestigious accounts that hadn't always wanted to do business with us. Formalizing my education played a big part in it. I took as many classes as I could through the Wine & Spirit Education Trust, graduating from one level to the next until I eventually made it to the fourth and highest level, which takes several years, five written exams, multiple blind taste tests, and a thesis to complete. On top of the wine schooling, I also learned that I worked for a good company, and that the axiom "big is bad" isn't always true. It's the people that define a place.

Along the way, what started out as a hostile, uphill battle hawking cases for a company everyone called the Death Star turned into a rewarding mission. The more I

to move on, and when I told David, he was instrumental in helping me find the job I wanted—at a different company.

By the time I left for Maisons Marques & Domaines, which became my second home for the next six wonderful years, I was doing well enough that I didn't need to rely on Trader Joe's purely for survival, but my love for it has never waned. You can always find some cauliflower rice and mandarin orange chicken in my freezer. There's a reason Trader Joe's is everyone's favorite grocery store. Quirky, confusingly cheap, and consistently delicious is a combination that's hard to beat. And while I can't make any promises about their Two Buck Chuck (the wine they can sell so cheap because you never know what vineyard it's from) I can guarantee that you won't do better at home for the price than these surprisingly good TJ-inspired matchups.

# Cauliflower Gnocchi
## & LANGHE NEBBIOLO

The first three times I tried to buy this insanely popular item, the neat little freezer row it was supposed to be stacked in was empty. When I finally scored a bag and prepared it with brown butter and sage, it was obvious why they can't keep this stuff on the shelves—and so was what I needed to drink with it: Langhe Nebbiolo.

A large sub-region of Piedmont, Langhe contains within its borders exalted areas making celebrated wines, such as Barolo and Barbaresco, from the grape Nebbiolo. But these wines are very tannic and take a tremendous amount of time to come around to being ready to drink. A more accessible version, in both price and readiness, is a designation called Langhe DOC. The wines are still made from Nebbiolo and they have the same emblematic truffled sage and dried rose petal bouquet—except with even more sass and freshness, because they aren't aged for as long in oak, if they are aged at all. The tart cherry fruit and sizzling red licorice are the counterstrike to the indulgent pasta side of this mostly healthy cauliflower dish. But since even unoaked Nebbiolo has enough astringency to strip a rusted griddle back to its original luster, the stubborn bits of gelatinous residue stuck in your mouth from this gooey gluten-substitute will be polished clean with each sip.

*$ Produttori del Barbaresco Nebbiolo Langhe* ✳

*$$ Giuseppe Mascarello e Figlio Langhe Nebbiolo* ✳✳✳

*$$$ Giovanni Rosso Ester Canale Rosso Langhe Nebbiolo* ✳ ♀ ✳

# Eggplant Cutlets
## & NAOUSSA XINOMAVRO

Eggplant is one of those rare vegetable-fruits with a meaty enough texture that you really can interchange it for animal protein in a recipe without losing any of the satisfaction. The cutlets from TJ's are so thin, the eggplant never gets soggy, and the crust becomes the main event, which is pretty much what everyone wants from fried eggplant. They even retain that hint of sweetness you get from fresh eggplant, without the hour of prep and cook time you need to actually make eggplant cutlets from scratch.

They tend to take on the flavor of whatever you're serving them with, so while dishes like eggplant Parmesan might call for a leaner, more tart wine like Chianti, when you're eating the cutlets more or less unadulterated, you want Naoussa Xinomavro.

It's all Greek to me, too, so to break it down: Naoussa is the appellation in northern Greece. Xinomavro is the grape; *xino* means sour and *mavro* means black, and it's pronounced "ksee-noh-maw-vrow." In Naoussa, which is a Protected Designation of Origin, or the Greek version of a French AOC appellation, it's the only grape allowed. With the Xinomavro grape, Naoussa grows one of the great challengers to Barolo's Nebbiolo, with wines that have a similar medium-full body and tannins chewier than jerky. It even has the same aromas of anise, dark plum, and tobacco and rivals Barolo's ability to age. But the very best bottles barely scratch the $50 mark, meaning you can go top-shelf for what would be the bargain basement of the Italian version. The wine has tannin to

spare for the crust and the layer of meaty eggplant inside, with enough plump, crimson, southern Mediterranean fruit to bring the mild aubergine sweetness to life from the frozen depths.

*$ Thymiopoulos Vineyards "Young Vines" Xinomavro Naoussa* ⁂❋

*$$ Dalamára Naoussa* ❋⁑⁌❋

## Cauliflower-Crust Pizza
## & ROMANIAN FETEASCĂ REGALĂ

If you're like me and walk the fine line between hedonism and respectability, cauliflower crust was made for you. Sprinkle some nut-cheese, a few veggies, and a little hot sauce on top and you have a healthy version of your favorite cheat food. Or just get it over with and drown it in mozzarella and marinara. Either way, Romanian Fetească regală (fey-teska rey-gala) will be a good-time buddy, and it's up to you how much of it you drink. They might not be in every wine shop, but you can find them online, and they're worth the effort—particularly if you like tasty wine at TJ's prices. They're often dry and strongly fragrant, like someone washed the dishes with Mrs. Meyer's hand soap and left just a hint of it in your glass. But their lower acidity keeps them soft, just like the veggies on your crusty pizza.

*$ Jidvei "Clasic'" Dry Fetească Regală, Tarnave Region*

## Mandarin Orange Chicken
## & CLARE VALLEY RIESLING

The Mount Lofty Ranges in South Australia have to be one of my favorite names for a wine zone. Just how lofty are they? Well, they make dry Rieslings that soar—and in the region called the Clare Valley are among the best Rieslings in the world. These wines have exotic citrus fruits and fragrant floral blossoms that are riveting, and a mineral spine with acid for miles. Wines from Clare Valley start on the inexpensive side, and even the best of them won't cost as much as the equivalent Rieslings from Germany. High-quality producers make versions that can age as long as some of the greatest red wines. That's convenient for TJ's sweet-and-tangy chicken, which can age in your freezer until you're ready to eat it, and tastes like it's straight out of the wok—for less than the cost of a Chinese delivery tip. Pop it in the skillet for a few minutes and you get crispy little orbs of juicy meat in a surprisingly tasty orange sauce, which goes down like a mountain stream with the Riesling's fresh citrus, minerals, and acid.

*$ Pikes "Traditionale" Riesling* ⁑⁌

*$$ Grosset "Polish Hill" Riesling* ❋❋⁌

# WHY DECANT YOU LISTEN

The vast majority of wine doesn't need to be decanted. In fact, decanting unnecessarily can have detrimental effects on a wine by oxidizing it too quickly before you can drink it, dulling its freshness in much the same way a sliced avocado loses its luster and goes a little brown when left out on the counter too long. Most wines are ready to drink when they arrive, so pop the cork and get down to it. The simple act of pouring it in a glass will give it all the help it needs to open up.

## When to Decant

Exceptional wines, like the very best Super Tuscans, Vintage Ports, and Bordeaux, are prime candidates. If you're popping a higher-end wine that was designed to age before it has reached its "peak expression"—the high point of flavor that often requires years or decades of aging—decanting it can help release more of its smells, tastes, and textures through the introduction of oxygen. It also helps remove unwanted sediment from older wines (in younger wines, the particles that form sediment have often yet to lose suspension). Because a wine that's opened early in its life has had less time to evolve, a decant usually gets you closer to seeing what it would taste like with more time left to its own devices. It's impossible to know the exact right time to open a precious bottle, but some wine publications keep track of vintage charts that offer general recommendations.

## When *not* to Decant

Don't automatically assume older wines need to be decanted. The longer the aging process, the closer a wine has gotten to where it's going—before it starts to turn and head to vinegar town. Decanting a wine that has already fully evolved just pushes it over a cliff of oxidation before you've had a chance to enjoy it. Always taste the wine first, even if you've had it before, because every bottle is different. Does it hit the front and back of your mouth and seem to weirdly skip over the middle? That means the wine isn't fully "open," and you should decant. If it hits all three points, it's ready to go: Put that decanter down. And if you're worried about sediment (which is harmless), you can use a sieve or pour the wine gently so the bits get trapped in the shoulder of the bottle.

## How to Decant

It's as simple as pouring the whole bottle into a container with a wider surface area, exposing more of the liquid to oxygen. Decanters come in all shapes, sizes, and prices but the form is usually secondary to the function. I'm a sucker for a hand-blown crystal sculpture of a decanter, but a plain-old plastic tea pitcher will get the job done just as well. The time a wine needs to spend in a decanter can range from a few minutes to a few hours, but the most important thing is to enjoy the wine's evolution as it changes from your first glass to the last.

## Black Bean & Jack Cheese Burrito
### & RIBERA DEL DUERO

TJ's manages to turn what could be a grim, gas-station packaged meal situation into a genuinely tasty little lunch pill you wish you had doubled up on. Behind the surprisingly thick and flavorful flour-cloaked veil, the black beans are earthy, the cheese has a lovely melted zing, and there's a mysterious sauce with a faint sweetness that gives it another gear.

When it comes to Ribera del Duero, you have to roll your *R*'s so you can let every syllable of this sensual region come in contact with your tongue. I've described these wines as "sex in a glass." From one of the most prestigious wine regions in Spain, the greatest examples are revered with the same affection (and price) granted to first-growth Bordeaux and the cult wines of Napa. Made primarily of Tempranillo grapes, they're the color of deep, opaque garnet with construction-man tough tannin, and are a mouthful when they're young. There can be grapes like Cabernet Sauvignon, Merlot, Malbec, and Garnacha blended in with the Tempranillo as well. All things black, from mountain cherries to mocha to truffle, dominate these wines with the kind of fresh-tilled earth people roll around naked in. Although the blue-chip offerings are what make the headlines, there are plenty of stunning options for $25 and under. Even at the entry level, there aren't many dogs from this region, making it a fun place to start without worrying about the variance between bottles.

Wines from RdD tend to be more robust than those from the neighboring Spanish region of Rioja, which are also based on Tempranillo. This works out for your burrito because the dark cherry, dried fig, and blackberry fruits that are the hallmarks of Tempranillo are even riper in RdD, and primed to take on the hearty mud of the black beans and the mildly sweet snap of the Jack and sauce.

$ *Bodegas Emilio Moro Ribera del Duero* ✳

$$ *Familia Fernández Rivera Tinto Pesquera Reserva Ribera del Duero* ❀ ✳ 🌾

$$$ *Vega Sicilia "Único" Ribera del Duero* ❄ 🍴 ✳

## Dark Chocolate Peanut Butter Cups
### & OLOROSO SHERRY

My best piece of advice is to lock them up or share them if you don't want to eat every single cup in one sitting. Beyond that, you're on your own with your willpower.

With sherry, there are a number of styles that range from desert dry to sticky sweet. Some are fresh and smell like a bag of raw, unsalted almonds. Others are oxidized and packed with a nuttiness similar to the roasted candied nuts you get from street carts. Names like "fino" or "oloroso" are telling you the style that's in the bottle (see page 117). The lighter ones are usually consumed before dinner as an aperitif, while the oxidized styles go with dessert as a digestif.

$ *Emilio Lustau "Solera Reserva" Dry Oloroso Don Nuño* ✳

$$ *Valdespino Oloroso VOS Sherry "Don Gonzalo"* ❀

$$$ *Equipo Navazos #74 Oloroso Montilla* ❄ ✳ 🌾

116

# SOLERA POWER

The finest versions of sherry come from years of fractional blending, which adds intriguingly unique textures, flavors, and panache over long periods of time. It's a complicated process meant to maintain style consistency and quality from one year's bottlings to the next, and it's achieved through what's known as a solera system. No, not a solar system. It's essentially a room full of very carefully stacked barrels organized sequentially by age into rows, with the youngest harvests added in small portions to barrels that contain blends of blends of every previous harvest and the blend before that—with some going back decades.

This insanely complex system is the reason it's impossible to know the exact age of a sherry, so the oldest systems approximate the average age of all the combined levels of the solera system. Some are centuries old, like the one at Gonzalez Byass, which started in 1847, or the one now housed at Osborne, which dates back to an incomprehensible 1792.

## Sherry's Not So Scary if You Know Your Styles

Lightest Body ← → Fullest Body

### DRY

**MANZANILLA**
The lightest and driest style; it's aged under a natural yeast seal called *flor*, which keeps the wine from oxidizing. When you smell it, you might think someone poured the Mediterranean into your glass (without the fish).

**FINO**
Still dry and light, still aged under *flor*, it's fresh with a smidge of funk and raw almonds.

**AMONTILLADO**
If halfway through the aging period a fino loses its *flor* (either naturally or intentionally), it becomes an amontillado, taking on a little more body and saltiness and a cashew-driven framework with a candied lemon vibe.

**PALO CORTADO**
Halfway between an amontillado and an oloroso, it's a weird but scrumptious style you don't see often. In these rare cases, the *flor* has died in an unexpected way and rather mysteriously developed a finesse and richness that's as coveted as it is difficult to replicate.

**OLOROSO**
A sherry that never gets its *flor*; it is oxidized from the get-go. Spicy and packed with a walnut signature, it's usually dry but also so rich that it can trick you into thinking there's sugar present.

### SWEET

**CREAM**
An all-encompassing category that includes pale creams, medium, and full creams, these wines can have sugar added so they aren't always naturally sweet. They can also be made a gazillion different ways, but at their core, this is a blend of a sweeter style with a drier style.

**MOSCATEL**
Naturally sweet, the wine is on the syrupy side and made from a type of grape called Moscatel de Alejandria that provides its hallmark *Sound of Music*-style hillside chorus of floral notes.

**PEDRO XIMÉNEZ**
Also naturally sweet, PX, as it is known by industry folks, is inky dark and maple-syrup thick. It can have around 300–400 grams per liter of sugar (there are around 100 grams per liter in Coke). So intense and so delicious.

# NETFLIX *and* CHILLED

## Binge-worthy Showstoppers for Your Next Streaming Fix

Just as there's a wine for every food, there's always a perfect bottle for whatever you're binging on-screen. Dystopian visions of the future call for pours with ancient complexity (try *The Handmaid's Tale* with Italy's Lacryma Christi, the "Tears of Christ"), while laugh-track sitcoms demand a more crowd-pleasing grape (*Friends* goes down like dental gas with Pinot Grigio). If you're revisiting *Orange Is the New Black*, try making your own pruno, the fermented fruit wine also known as prison hooch—all you need is some live yeast, crumbled bread, fruit, juice, sugar, and a toilet (though a one-gallon plastic jug will do). And the only thing to drink with *The Crown*? Her Majesty's favorite Bollinger. The right wine can pair with your latest streamer like an oenophilic soundtrack.

### KILLING EVE
### & Russian Krasnostop Zolotovsky

Krasnostop Zolotovsky is a Russian red as big and chewy as a Cabernet Sauvignon, as green-bell peppery as a Cabernet Franc, and as violent as TV's most endearing sociopathic Russian assassin, Villanelle, with all the nail-biting tension of a game of cat and mouse with MI6.

*$$ Domaine Burnier Krasnostop Zolotovsky, Natuchajevskaya, Russia*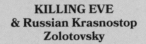

### STRANGER THINGS
### & Blue Wine

For eighties sci-fi fantasy, try a porthole to the upside down world of blue wine—the Demogorgon of the wine world—made by filtering white wine through the pulp of red grape skins. Mostly from Spain, the wines are a shade of Cookie Monster formaldehyde and among the stranger things you will ever drink, with a mild, sweet taste fit for Eleven.

*$ Marqués de Alcantára Blue Chardonnay, Spain*

## PEAKY BLINDERS
### & Egri Bikavér
### (Bull's Blood of Eger)

The darkest, thickest, bloodiest red wine produced today should only be consumed with the darkest, bloodiest show still on television (it also goes great with *Game of Thrones*, if you're one of those holdouts still waiting for the right moment). Hungarian Egri Bikavér, or Bull's Blood of Eger, is a spicy, crimson-hued ferocity of a wine named for the unlikely victors of a medieval battle whose intimidated foes surrendered after mistaking all the red stuff around their opponent's mouths as evidence of a blood sacrifice (they were just drunk). Like the Shelby brothers, it's scary good.

*$ St. Andrea Áldás Egri Bikavér*

## SUCCESSION
### & First Growth Bordeaux

As cousin Greg might say on Logan Roy's yacht, when you've got fuck-you money, the only wine worth drinking is First Growth Bordeaux, preferably with at least twenty years of age. Left Bank Bordeaux has five top ranks of quality called growths, and the first—and best—of them consists entirely of the legendary elixirs of the global elite known as Lafite-Rothschild, Latour, Margaux, Haut-Brion, and Mouton-Rothschild. They'll cost you significantly more than an HBO subscription, but probably not your soul.

*$$$ Château Lafite Rothschild, Pauillac* ❦ ♔ ✹

## NARCOS MEXICO
### & Mexican Wine

As hot as it is, Mexico still sits geographically just below the 30th parallel, right at the edge of quality wine production on both sides of the equator. It's a great place to grow Tempranillo that manages to smuggle flavors like dark chocolate, burnt espresso, and charred beef into the same bottle with stewy black fruits, scratchy tannins, and full-on black pepper.

*$ L.A. Cetto Sierra Blanca Tempranillo, Valle de Guadalupe*

## EUPHORIA
### & Skin Contact Wine
### (Orange Wine)

Racy HBO teen dramas are the province of skin contact, or white wines fermented on their skins, a process usually reserved for reds. These copper-tinted rule breakers are commonly known as orange wines, and they're full of tannin-charged emotions and sensuous, fleshy flavors like ripe apricot and exotic oolong tea.

*$$ Joško Gravner Ribolla Venezia Giulia, Venezia Giulia, Italy* ❦❦ ✹ ✿

## THIS IS US
### & Côtes du Rhône

As beautifully mixed as primetime's most diverse family, these wines can officially be made with twenty-one different grapes, which range in color from black to white to pink, and they waft with peppered blackberries, electric violets, and every herbal soap at L'Occitane. They're as cockles-warming as the Pearsons, without all the tears.

*$ Chateau de Saint Cosme "Les Deux Albions"* ❦ ✹ ✿

## SATURDAY NIGHT LIVE
### & Col Fondo Prosecco

Col Fondo, or officially *Rifermentato in Bottiglia*, is sour beer in wine form, which sounds laughable, and that's mostly the point. But there's something giddily drinkable about this natural wine from Prosecco with more tarty cheek-suction than Keira Knightley. Made in a similar method to *pét-nats*, they also have a little less fizz than typical Proseccos, making it a bit easier on you if they happen to go up your nose.

*$ Ca' dei Zago Col Fondo Prosecco, Veneto, Italy* ❦❦

## THE MARVELOUS
## MRS. MAISEL
### & Kosher Wine

It's actually a bottle of Kiddush wine that starts it all, the night her husband leaves her on Yom Kippur. Midge polishes it off in the subway on her way to revealing her inner funny woman (and boobs) onstage for the first time. Kiddush wines, meant for blessings and breaking fast, can be a bit sweet for most wine drinkers, so for a meeting with Mrs. Maisel that won't give you a sugar hangover, go with a wine that's simply kosher. Wineries the world over are now producing serious bottlings that are plenty dry and just happen to satisfy the requirements of Jewish law. Many come from Israel, but great versions are also made in places like California, Spain, and France.

*$$ Hagafen Cellars Prix Reserve Merlot Napa Valley, California* ❦ ✿

# CHAPTER 8

# Secrets of the Bargain Basement

*The* FOOD-LOVER'S COMPANION *to* CHEAP WINE

**T**he inconvenient truth about most wines you've actually heard of that cost less than $10 is that they're loaded with artificial enhancers like flavor additives, color dyes, and a surprisingly creepy list of other lab-manufactured plonk. But I promise there are wines out there with good ingredients at a bargain price point. Just like you have to rifle through the sales rack to find a decent pair of spats or culottes, you sometimes have to do a little work to find them. And they're rarely your standard mass-market Cabs or Chards. But if you're willing to embrace the unfamiliar, you can scoop up some beautifully made, lesser-known treasures for a comparative song.

It sounds counterintuitive, but when it comes to wine, cheap and obscure is almost always a better bet than cheap and familiar. That comes down to the many factors that ultimately determine how much a wine costs to produce, from the price of the land and labor, the yields at harvest, and the decisions made during the winemaking process, to the weather in a given year, the amount of money spent on marketing, and how far it will have to travel. But the most crucial factor? Popularity.

If you're trying to mass-produce a wine from a popular grape in a popular and expensive wine region—for example, California—and you want to get on the shelf for under $10, you have to use every drop you produce, not just the top-quality juice. Then you have to do some hefty manipulation to get your wine tasting good enough for people to want to drink it. Larger producers even have what are known as "sensory insight labs," where they tweak mass-produced wines to be just the right flavor, color, and smell to appeal to the broadest possible audience.

And it doesn't just stop at the two-buck mystery stuff. This kind of engineering with additives is rampant across the inexpensive tier of wines that retail for less than $10. Wines that are super fruity or inky red sell better than wines that have more translucent color or vegetal smells.

Imagine you've used all the fruit you harvested and ended up with a thin, watery concoction, because to keep volume up you didn't sort any of the subpar fruit out. So you just filter everything out of it, make it as neutral as possible, and then add the cosmetic colors, aromas, and flavors that you think will sell best. Since sugar and "oak" (the adjunct kind like chips, shavings, or even powder, not real oak barrels) can hide a lot of flaws, you can essentially put a fake wine out into the market with the average consumer having no idea how heavily adulterated it is. When that dark and fruity profile from a well-known place and grape is available for $8 a bottle, it most likely wasn't possible without manipulation.

To be clear, not all additives are bad. Some, like small doses of sulfur, are essential to a wine being stable enough for aging and transport and have been used safely for centuries. It's the ones like Mega Purple (a superconcentrate that adds color and flavor) and Velcorin (a hazmat-level microbial) that feel so far from natural they might as well be leaking from an alien probe.

Most people are surprised to learn that unlike food and medicine, alcoholic drinks aren't regulated by the FDA in the United States (with the very strange exceptions of wine with less than 7 percent alcohol and beer made from grain other than malted barley). There are currently more than sixty different chemicals and additives approved for use in wine, but producers don't have to disclose any of them on their labels—no nutrition facts, no ingredients. Ironically, the only thing they do have to disclose are sulfite levels above ten parts per million, which is pretty much the last thing most people need to worry about—dried fruit has about one thousand parts per million. Sulfites are a natural antimicrobial, and less than 1 percent of people in the world are actually allergic to them.

One safe bet is to simply pay more for good wine, and wouldn't it be nice if we were all Beyoncé, summoning rare magnums from our wine helicopters. But the rest of us seeking value have to do the regulating ourselves. To be clear, my gripe is with the lack of information us wine drinkers are privy to, not which fermented grape juice floats your wine boat. It's also important to note that big doesn't always mean bad, and expensive doesn't always means good. There are companies out there making tasty and honest wines at an everyday price point, and there are high-end producers that secretly doctor their wines with all sorts of additives, profiting in the shadows with little chance of exposure, since there is no label transparency or market accountability. You're never really going to know what's in that bottle, but when you're paying less than $20, there are a few general things you can do to be proactive.

It sounds obvious, but **choose a bottle from a winery with a real-sounding name**. Bulk producers often sell their wines under different labels for different demographics, but the base juice always comes from the same bulk vat. Avoid wines that only have fantasy names like "Sexy Beast" or "Funbags" on the label and no actual producer name. They are mostly inventions of marketing and almost certainly manipulated to fit the desired taste profiles of a target audience.

When you google a wine, the language you might find on that maker's website has likely been polished to oblivion, with claims that almost always sound great. Look on the back of the label to see who imported it, then **google the importer** instead. You'll be able to tell pretty quickly if that importer is quality minded and cares about responsible farming practices or is one of the baddies pedaling gimmicks by liquid volume. Even most domestic wines will have an importer or supplier listed on the back.

When in doubt, **ask for help**. Whether it's Total Wine or your neighborhood local, there's usually someone working who can speak to the wines they carry and the philosophy of the producers on the shelves. If they don't seem to know or care, it's a bad sign and probably time to find another wine shop.

Still, the best way to ensure you're getting a quality wine at a bargain price is to **take a leap outside your comfort zone**. Wines from places or grapes you don't know well, like Portuguese Touriga Nacional or an Arbois Rouge, can be just as scrumptious and responsibly made as the famous ones; they're just produced at a fraction of the cost. So if you love Chardonnay from Napa but don't always want to spend $40 for the good stuff, try Chardonnay from the Columbia Valley in Washington State. All you need to avoid the cheap swill is a little taste for adventure.

## If you like
## Classic French Champagne, try
# Brut Cava
## & FRENCH FRIES

It's often said that Champagne and French fries are a pairing worthy of a last meal. The grease with the acid, the bubbles with the salty fried crunch—these are life or death combinations. And I'd argue that Spanish Brut Cava and fries could just as easily stake that claim, except in this case, they don't have to, because you can afford this killer pairing anytime. Try a much higher quality Cava for the price of any entry-level Champagne and you might just see those Gallic sparklers blush.

Cava stands out in the inexpensive effervescence category because its second fermentation happens inside the bottle you drink it from, just like Champagne. It's a method of making sparkling wine that yields a finer, more integrated bubble, which is one of the crucial components for high-quality sparkling because it allows suds to stay sudsy longer. Even though the aging requirements aren't as stringent as Champagne's (if they were, they'd have to charge more), these wines still maintain those bready and yeasty notes you get from autolytic winemaking, with all the bristly, tightly woven fizz that's synonymous with much pricier bubbly.

*Cava* means "cellar" in Spanish, which is a reference to the French tradition of aging their Champagnes in caves beneath the ground. In the 1960s, the Spanish even tried to call their sparkling wine Champaña, but the real Champenois to the north weren't so keen and sued. Ironically, the case brought the Spanish region more attention than it ever had before—250 million bottles of Cava are now

sold each year around the world, compared with the 40 million that were sold annually before the lawsuit.

Agustí Torelló is a family winery that has become a shining star in a region known mostly for its large-scale producers. The wines have value at every tier, from the entry-level "Mata" to their bizarre, amphora-shaped vintage bottling "Kripta."

But Cava is more than just a cheap version of Champagne. It's its own unique sparkler, consisting of three Spanish grapes: Xarel-lo, Parellada, and Macabeo. Because the growing region is warmer than Champagne, they taste even riper than the French stuff, with all the acid. Brut Cavas offer a honeyed and earthy citrus vibrancy that makes crisp, golden fries snap to attention—and seem even crispier. Because they come from coastal areas, their natural salinity also works on fries as beautifully as a sprinkle of sea salt.

## If you like
## Northern Rhône Syrah, try
# Moroccan Syrah
## & BEEF LASAGNA

One great way to get more for less is to follow a renowned producer from a region you love to another place in the world where they're experimenting with the same grape. As the producer of coveted Crozes-Hermitage, Alain Graillot is one of the most revered winemakers in France's northern Rhône Valley,

where he built a reputation for exuberant Syrahs after starting his own domaine in 1985. But on a bicycling trip through the Zenata wine region of Morocco, the Syrah Whisperer realized what the rest of the world soon would: Morocco has some of the best potential for quality wine production in all of North Africa. Not only does the area have nights cold enough to offset its hot days, there aren't any polluting industries operating anywhere close by, so the kind of organic farming Graillot strives for is achieved that much easier.

He partnered with Ouled Thaleb, the oldest continuously operating winery in Morocco—which is saying something, because wine has been made in Morocco for at least two thousand years—and started producing mesmerizing Syrah. Despite the legal restriction prohibiting the sale of alcohol to Muslims in the country, of the forty million bottles it produces annually, 95 percent are consumed domestically, mostly by tourists. Because he exports his product, labeled "Syrocco," Graillot made it easier for a lot more of us to get a tasty peek behind Morocco's wine curtain. And if you hadn't ever heard someone compliment a Syrah for its sandalwood, tarragon, and sweaty leather riding chaps, now you have.

What that curious combination demands is beef lasagna. Graillot's Moroccan Syrah has the tannins for the meat, the red fruit for the red sauce, and finesse for the tomato acid, with enough pungent wet earth to withstand melted mozzarella and Parm. There's also a peppery roughness that grinds against thick layers of béchamel or ricotta, making each bite that much silkier.

## If you like
## Châteauneuf-du-Pape, try
# Minervois Rouge
## & PAD THAI

Besides Bordeaux and Burgundy, Châteauneuf-du-Pape, or CdP, is the most famous red wine in all of France. Unfortunately, it's as robust in body, flavor, and alcohol as it is in cost. The wines of Minervois in the Languedoc region of southern France are based on similar grapes (Syrah, Mourvèdre, and Grenache) and they can satisfy the urge to treat yourself to a good CdP without the financial sad trombone. Many farmers in the area sell their grapes to local co-ops to survive, but Château d'Oupia managed to prove itself as the little winery that could, breaking free as a generational family business that grows and bottles its own wares to fanfare worldwide. These reds are supple and sensuous enough to take to bed with you, which is also one of the best places to enjoy them, alongside a giant carton of Pad Thai.

Noodles, protein, cilantro, bean sprouts, eggs, and peanuts with fishy soy sauce, brown sugar, and a paste made from dark and sticky sour tamarind—there are so many flavors and textures in this South-Asian mainstay that your wine partner requires serious firepower. Brash Minervois Rouge takes up that call to arms with a battery of Châteauneuf-style powder.

## If you like
## Left Bank Bordeaux, try
## Bekaa Valley
## Bordeaux Blend
## & ROSEMARY CRUSTED
## LAMB

The *Vitis vinifera* grape has been cultivated in Lebanon for more than five thousand years, beating Alexander the Great by about three millennia. You might think it's too hot for grapes, but the Bekaa Valley has elevations that make it perfect for vines. The grapes grown here are similar to those in Bordeaux, and though the Lebanese wine industry is long established, political tumult tends to make any given year a wild card. Periodic violence in the region has been known to hinder distribution and the ability to hire harvest workers—or to even harvest at all.

Chateau Musar is the most famous of these wineries, with a back vintage catalogue as great as any fabled Bordeaux château for a price that's usually one or two digits less. (Their entry tier, Jeaune, which comes from younger fruit, can be had for less than $25.) To give you an idea of how wildly dedicated this winery is to its craft, the 1984 was harvested at the height of the Lebanese Civil War, with bullets flying as they picked grapes. Only two vats were produced, and other than a few bottles that were sold to private collectors in 2013, they've never seen the light of day. (If you have one, call me anytime.)

Bekaa Valley Bordeaux blends are not only uncommonly good, the stories they carry make them more fascinating than almost any other wine produced today. They contain all the wonders of classic Left Bank Cabernet Sauvignon–based Bordeaux with the added intoxications of Mediterranean herbaceousness and earthy rusticity, both of which are a lock for lamb with an aromatic rosemary crust. All the dried herbs and tilled soil neutralize any mild gaminess, while the vivid concentration of dark berries helps animate the juices in what tends to be a tougher, drier meat. You get tannins that are round and forward but not overwhelming, unlike the sticker shock on a remotely comparable Bordeaux.

## If you like
## Brunello di Montalcino, try
# Rosso di Montalcino
## & SEAFOOD GUMBO

Another way to find value is to look for the entry tier wines in a high-quality European region you already know and like. Rosso di Montalcino is made with the same Sangiovese grapes used to produce the Italian region's much more famous Brunello di Montalcino—often from the exact same vineyards. Yet without the fancy oak and intense fruit selection that drives the ageability and price way up on Brunello, the Rosso can be had for far less. (When you're looking for bargains, you don't need ageability because you'll be drinking them young.) Castiglion del Bosco, a winery in the remote, wooded northwest of Montalcino, has been producing wine since 1100 (yes, almost a millennium). Today, the organic estate-grown bottlings are among the best qualitative values in the region. These are spicy wines with bitter cherries and tannins as expressive as the local hand gestures. As it happens, their gnarly fruits and bold tannins travel remarkably well to Louisiana, where celery, onion, and bell pepper form the "Holy Trinity of vegetables" that make up gumbo. Sangiovese's buoyant textures and jazz-worthy verve fit the Big Easy's most celebrated dish like

a beaded necklace. Whether your spices skew Creole or Cajun, it's always Fat Tuesday whenever you introduce a glass of Rosso di Montalcino to the dark roux and savory shellfish of any New Orleans gumbo.

## If you like
## California Bubbly, try
# New Mexico Bubbly
## & CHEESE FONDUE

New Mexico's Gruet Family Winery has increased production one hundredfold since its founding in the early 1980s. That's because the Champenois father, daughter, and son team who decided to move to this unforgiving climate to plant vines knew what they were doing. The wines they produce defy the odds in both quality and style, with a ripeness that rivals California's and a freshness that can only be achieved through the Traditional Method. Compare Gruet with the more expensive sparkling wines coming out of California—they're mostly just as good.

Whether you're dipping into your cheese with veggies or bread, these acid-forward New Mexico bubbles cast a spell on tiny cauldrons of molten fat and grease. Best to leave them to it.

# THE CHEAP WINE CHEAT SHEET

The more familiar the name, the less you get for your money. So when you're looking for value, you can't afford to be a label queen. But inexpensive can still be delicious. For marquee label quality at never-heard-of-it prices, take a break from the usual and try these wallet-friendly alternatives instead.

| IF YOU LIKE . . . | TRY |
|---|---|
| Chablis | Alsatian Pinot Blanc |
| White Burgundy | Margaret River Chardonnay |
| Napa Chardonnay | Columbia Valley Chardonnay |
| Sancerre | Quincy |
| Marlborough Sauvignon Blanc | Italian Verdicchio |
| Left Bank Bordeaux | Lebanese Bordeaux Blends |
| Right Bank Bordeaux | Buzet |
| Napa Red Blends | Stellenbosch Bordeaux Blends |
| Rioja | Navarra |
| Priorat | Montsant |
| Willamette Valley Pinot Noir | Patagonia Pinot Noir |
| Red Burgundy | Central Otago Pinot Noir |
| Central Coast Pinot Noir | Bierzo Mencia |
| Argentine Malbec | Chilean Carménère |
| Châteauneuf-du-Pape | Minervois |
| Northern Rhône Syrah | Moroccan Syrah |
| California Syrah | Hawke's Bay Syrah |
| California Zinfandel | Italian Negroamaro |
| Brunello di Montalcino | Rosso di Montalcino |
| Chianti Classico | Mondeause Noir |
| Barolo or Barbaresco | Langhe Nebbiolo |
| Champagne | Cava |
| California Sparkling | New Mexico Sparkling |
| Sauternes | Pacherenc du Vic-Bilh |
| Vintage Port | Late Bottle Vintage Port |

# HAVE WINE, WILL TRAVEL

## *THE BYOW FIELD GUIDE*

There are plenty of restaurants without liquor licenses that allow you to bring your own wine. There are also just as many restaurants with wine lists that let you do it, too. When you BYOW with a group of friends who all bring something different, everyone gets a chance to try that many more pairings. And when you do it right, you also get to drink great wines you otherwise wouldn't have ordered off the menu—because no one wants to be that group-dinner monster who orders the $150 bottle of wine.

I assure you the sisterhood of the traveling bottles is very real. And the uninitiated always seem to have the same questions. Matthew Conway is a veteran New York City somm who is deeply accomplished in the art of BYOW. As the beverage director and general manager at Marc Forgione in Tribeca, he runs the globally renowned wine program for the Michelin-starred Iron Chef who gives the restaurant its name. And back when he was one of Zagat's 30 Under 30 sommeliers, he taught me that bringing your own wine is not only encouraged, it's also something of an open secret within the industry that everyone is doing it. Conway BYOWs at least two nights a week dining out at restaurants across the city, and he also actively encourages people to B their own Ws to his own restaurant. On the following pages, he breaks down the rules of your new favorite pastime.

## Why BYOW?

Usually it's because the restaurant doesn't have a wine list or offers only a very basic one. Or you might have a special bottle from a birth year or anniversary you want to drink for sentimental reasons, or simply something you've been saving. In all scenarios, the goal is to drink "better" than you would if you ordered from the list.

## Does every restaurant do it?

Many casual spots allow it for small per-bottle fees of $10 or $15 with no quantity limitations. Some higher tier restaurants don't permit corkage at all, but most will with some limitations like bottle maximums and fees as high as $150 per bottle. These are usually places that have extensive wine cellars and staff purely dedicated to wine service, so fair enough. Eater provides a good list of BYO-friendly establishments in most major cities.

## What to bring

If it's a group, I always try to think about what might be the most memorable bottle of the night. I also make sure someone is bringing Champagne, because if everything goes south and the wines just aren't showing up, Champagne solves all the problems a day could throw at you. I also often bring Syrah from the Northern Rhone because it's my jam.

## What not to bring

Bad wine. You shouldn't bring bad wine anywhere. Heavily manipulated and bulk produced? Don't put that down your throat. There are oceans of inexpensive, flavorful wines out there that respect the Earth and are made by small farmers who would love your support. Most restaurants don't allow you to bring a producer that they offer on their list. But why would you want to bring something they already have? Nobody shows up to Morton's with a filet mignon in hand. It's about enhancing the experience, not just saving money, so don't buy a bottom dweller at a retail store to save coin. You're better off with the least expensive bottle on a decent wine list.

## Call ahead

It's good policy to let fine-dining establishments know what you're bringing in advance. They'll tell you their corkage fee and how many bottles they allow. If you're bringing high-quality wine to a restaurant that doesn't serve wine, be prepared to bring a bottle opener and maybe even glassware. Just make sure they're OK with it beforehand. Most places will get you something that can be used as an ice bucket if you ask nicely.

## How many bottles can you bring?

Two per person should be the max in any scenario. If you have six people and ten bottles, it's always nice to order something off the list, too, and plan that into your night. If it's just you and your partner, bring a bottle and start with a cocktail or finish with an after-dinner drink. The idea isn't to be greedy or take advantage.

## Don't complain about corkage fees

Restaurants are businesses that run on much smaller profit margins than most other industries. They need to make money to stay open, and allowing you to bring something that they aren't making money from isn't a good business model. Also, nicer restaurants still take the time to open and serve your wine, and time is money when the sommelier could be at another table selling wine rather than opening the bottle you didn't pay for.

## What do you do with the bottles you bring?

On the casual end, bring the bottles with you to the table and let the server know what you plan on doing before you start opening them or pulling out glassware. On the higher end, take them to the maître'd, who should already have notes that you are bringing wine because you called ahead.

## Offer a taste to the staff

You should never bring a bottle to a good restaurant that's opening and handling your wine without expecting them to taste it. If you'd like to share more than that taste and they accept your offer, ask them to bring you an empty glass and pour it for them. (It's awkward to expect a sommelier to pour for him or herself, no matter how genuine your intentions.) I love it when people bring wines that are very special and share them. It gives me and my staff an opportunity to learn about wines we might otherwise not be tasting.

## Be polite and overtip

It's always nice to say thank you to the people who served the wine and to tip them well—say, 25 percent—when the corkage is reasonable. If they waive the fee and do all the service, make sure to tip accordingly, or slip the team some cash on the side. You can also tip on what the bottle would have cost if you had ordered it from a list.

# WINES THAT BRING IT

While they might not work for every dish, here are some safe wine bets for most casual restaurant fare to keep in your back pocket.

### Thai and Vietnamese

*Go-to: German off-dry Riesling and Beaujolais*

Spicy foods like Thai and Vietnamese need lower alcohol so the wines don't aggravate the heat. Wines with more perfumed aromas also swell nicely around dishes with a lot of pungent ingredients in the same bite, from chiles and curry to lemongrass and mango. And you'll want enough acidity for all those supercharged contrasts in flavor and texture.

### Red-Sauce Pasta and Pizza

*Go-to: Piedmont Arneis and Tuscan Sangiovese*

Arneis has an herbal gusto that allows fresh basil to sing, and Sangiovese has an unmistakable profile of tart cherry, red pepper, and ripe tomato that will leave you wondering where the wine ends and the sauce begins. One of the most obvious examples of "what grows together goes together," red sauce and red fruit have been walking hand in hand since Roman times.

### Indian and African

*Go-to: Alsace Gewürztraminer or*
*Australian Shiraz*

While their spice influence is as diverse as the world of wine is wide, the two cuisines share a similar heat and smoke profile—one that was made for wines that aren't truly sweet but have a ripeness of fruit that conjures the softness of sugar, along with an equally spice-rich profile to complement the vibrancy of the seasonings.

## Sushi and Japanese

*Go-to: Austrian Grüner Veltliner and
Oregon Pinot Noir*

Soy and umami are behind much of Japanese cuisine, which can be fried or raw and everything in between. Sake is an obvious choice, but there are many great options if you stick with wines that are lighter in texture and body with more acidity and plenty of herbal and flinty savory notes.

## Chinese

*Go-to: New York Riesling and
California Zinfandel*

In Europe, food and wine have evolved in tandem over thousands of years, but you don't find the same "like with like" symbiosis in Asia, where traditional alcohols like baijiu are mostly grain based. You'll need to head back to the USA to find a great match for Chinese cuisine. New York Riesling has the fruit pucker and low alcohol; Cali Zin has even riper fruit, restrained acidity, and big body. Both profiles work just as well to keep sweet and spicy flavors jiving without magnifying any currents of heat. (Chinese wines, particularly from northern Yunnan and Ningxia, are starting to gain global attention and distribution, and I encourage you to try them, too.)

## Mediterranean and Greek

*Go-to: Greek Moschofilero and Agiorgitiko*

A style of cuisine so clean and fresh deserves an equally vibrant and crisp wine. Whether it's grilled vegetables, hummus, or lamb, nothing goes better with Greek than a wine from the same country. The food and wine also have a shared herbaceousness that makes them natural companions.

## Burgers and Bar Bites

*Go-to: Argentine Torrontès and Malbec*

Pub fare is primarily defined by its grease and heaviness, which call for wines that are big on flavor, body, and alcohol so they don't get buried in the starch-and-fat groundswell.

## French and Bistros

*Go-to: Côtes de Gascogne Blanc and
Gaillac Rouge*

Sure, the French love their classic regions, but they also love their secret everyday pleasures, most of which come from South West France. Elevated and delicious at forgiving café prices, these popular French table wines are sophisticated enough for haute cuisine but go just as well with bistro fare.

## Seafood Shacks and Clam Bakes

*Go-to: Chablis and Provence Rosé*

Fish and shellfish preparations, from grilled to steamed to fried, have differences you could parse for days, but they all share a softer texture and ocean core that always answer to the seabed minerality of these two wines.

## Spanish and Tapas

*Go-to: Spanish Godello and Jumilla Monastrell*

It's all sensuality and lower-lip biting temptation here. I'd bathe in these wines if the mood struck and someone was willing to fill the tub. With staple ingredients like olive oil, garlic, and ham, Spanish cuisine needs wines with freshness and power to run with the flavor bulls.

# CHAPTER 9

# Crave the Date

ONCE-A-YEAR COUPLINGS
WORTH WAITING FOR

**B**oth my grandfather and my grandmother were Southern Baptist ministers. When I was growing up, no one in my house drank alcohol; nor did anyone in my extended Kentucky family. Needless to say, it was a very big deal when I decided to go into the wine business. For the first few years, every time I talked to my grandmother about my job, she would cry. She thought I was getting drunk for a living.

A few years back, the grandkids staged a mutiny. All of us drink, and we'd been hiding it for so long at family gatherings it became an open joke well into adulthood that our Solo cups were full of "Coke" and "iced tea." By the time my youngest brother, Garrett, was of legal drinking age, we had decided enough was enough. We may have still been sitting at the kids' table, but we were big kids now.

So we finally put the bottles on the table and poured them into proper wineglasses. As our grandparents gawked, my parents shifted uncomfortably, stuck in the middle of their parents and their children, while all of the cousins toasted our silent rebellion.

There have been some awkward moments, but I have some pretty incredible grandparents. They've come around to thinking that maybe this could be a worthwhile calling, this drinking for a living, because they see how happy it makes me.

When I came home to visit later in the year, we were sitting around the kitchen table and my grandfather, whom we call Hootie, asked me about wine. He said he felt like he was watching this thing that I was so passionate about from the outside, and that he didn't really understand it all, and that this made him sad.

Hootie had a simple request. For Christmas, I was to bring home a bottle of wine for him and my grandmother to try. My dad almost fell out of his chair. My shocked grandmother yelled, "Oh! Harold!" It was an amazing moment. My grandparents had made it to their eighties without ever tasting a drop of alcohol, and here we were, jaws to the floor—no one could believe it.

A debate started at the table: What should I bring?

"Champagne!" insisted my cousin Megan. "Really good Sauvignon Blanc," chimed in my stepmom, Diane. "Whatever will get them the drunkest," joked Garrett. "Are you sure?" was all my dad could muster, staring at his father in disbelief.

When I got back to New York, I polled some wine friends, all of whom had different ideas: aged Burgundies, rare Bordeaux, fruity Napa Cabs, Vintage Champagnes, light rosés. But the more I thought about it, the more I remembered that when I first tasted wine, I found it bitter and only put up with it because I was interested in the end result. My grandparents wanted to try wine to share the experience with me, and I wanted them to like what they tasted.

After much fretting, I decided on a Moscato d'Asti. Moscatos have about 5.5 percent alcohol, so it wouldn't make them too woozy, and they're also sweet and fizzy, kind of like the soda pop we grew up drinking. I found a good bottle and packed it in my suitcase.

**The experience of tasting and sharing together at the table, bringing people and generations together, is one of the most beautiful things about wine.**

When the big moment came, I poured each of my grandparents a small glass. My grandmother, Granzie, took a sip and pretended not to like it (southern women are complicated), but then gave a silent nod of approval with her second taste. My grandfather, on the other hand, finished his glass before I could even explain what was in it. "If I have a second glass, will I get drunk?" The whole family burst out laughing, and I quickly refilled him. "No, Hootie, you'll be fine!"

From that moment on, wine has become a fully integrated part of our family gatherings, whereby at the end of the night, several empty bottles are usually found across the table and everyone's curious about what I'm pouring next. On holidays like Christmas and Thanksgiving, even my grandparents will have a nip.

The experience of tasting and sharing together at the table, bringing people and generations together, is one of the most beautiful things about wine. And after you try these special-occasion pairings, you won't want to wait a whole year to try them again.

## Thanksgiving Leftovers Sandwich
### & CHINON

If you're like me, you have stuffing on the brain. Thanksgiving is the meal I most look forward to all year, and that's largely because of the leftovers sandwich that comes the next day. In my house, we go classic: toasted white bread, turkey, cranberry sauce, stuffing, a crucial layer of mayonnaise, and a touch of black pepper. It's the best sandwich of the year, and it's critical to honor it with the right drink: Chinon Rouge.

Chinon is a region in the Loire Valley that yields some of the world's best Cabernet Franc. It's related to the more widely known Cabernet Sauvignon, but the grape is relegated to second-fiddle status in blends in places like Bordeaux. Thanksgiving, and especially the day after, is perhaps the best time to give Cabernet Franc its due.

The loudest flavor in any Thanksgiving leftovers sandwich is cranberry sauce, so you want a wine that has enough acid to play along with that trumpet. Chinon also has enough fruit and structure to buttress the gravy and mayo. And Cab Franc's tannins are softer than those in Cab Sauvignon, so when they bond with your protein as you swallow, the bird's even milder next-day flavor won't get snuffed out. The hallmark of Cabernet Franc is its pyrazine aroma, which in this case is a very good thing, since every leftovers sandwich is better with a few grinds of pepper. The earthy notes of the stuffing also help to amplify the wine's natural herbaceousness, which means both the sandwich and the wine get knocked into a higher bracket when you drink them together—something for which even the pickiest family member can give thanks.

*$ Marc Brédif Chinon*
*$$ Olga Raffault Chinon "Les Picasses"*
*$$ Domaine Charles Joguet Chinon "Clos de la Dioterie"*

## Potato Latkes
### & GOLAN HEIGHTS SPARKLING

I've tried a hundred takes on latkes. They've been flat and latticed and thick and husky, and I've yet to meet one I didn't like. This has everything to do with the fact that they're all pretty much grated potato crisped in fat. The flavor is deep-fried and savory, which is what distinguishes these golden disks of starchy contentment from their pan-fried hash brown brothers.

Like the multifarious latke, winemaking traditions in the Middle East are both young and old. Vine cultivation in the area dates back millennia, but mostly ceased during the Ottoman Empire. The contemporary torch was picked up by Baron Edmond de Rothschild, owner of the legendary Bordeaux estate Château Lafite-Rothschild, who started importing grapes to what was then Palestine from France, establishing a winery in 1882. Today in Israel there are five main wine regions and more than three hundred wineries, many of which are producing very legitimate juice. In the Golan Heights, a subregion of Galilee, sparkling wines are being made that are not only kosher, but insanely good with traditional potato latkes, whether at Hanukkah or any other time of the year.

On display here are the same winning acid-and-fried-potato fundamentals that make French fries and Champagne so irresistible. And while these Israeli sparklers all have the classic markers of Traditional Method bubbles, I recommend the blanc de blancs, which are 100 percent Chardonnay, lending them a singular lemoniness that puts a zesty bow on any creamy horseradish sauce you're adding.

*$$ Golan Heights Winery "Blanc de Blancs" Brut Galilee* ☀☷ ✳

# Pumpkin Pie
## & RUTHERGLEN MUSCAT

Pumpkin pie might be responsible for creating a cottage industry of pumpkin-spiced shamelessness, but when that pumpkin and the corresponding spice are left where they belong—in the pie—is there any better way to end an imperialist Pilgrim feeding frenzy?

There actually is, and it's to eat that pumpkin pie with some rare Rutherglen Muscat. It comes from the tiny town of Rutherglen in southern Australia, known for gold mining long before it was famous for its wine. Today, a handful of producers have put it permanently on the map with some truly lust-worthy dessert wines. The grape they use is called Muscat à Petits Grains, meaning "Muscat with little berries," but the local wine growers use a name that's more to the point, Rutherglen Brown Muscat, which is exactly the color of wine this very specific grape produces.

Once the juice has been fermented into an unctuously sweet wine, it's fortified with a neutral grape spirit to halt the fermentation and retain the naturally high sugars of the grape mixture. This is an old French method known as mutage that produces a style called Vin Doux Naturel (see page 88). Once fortified, these wines can age as little as three years, but in the finest cases, they're aged more than one hundred years before

bottling. This makes for one magnetically complex, nectarine-driven dessert wine that I like to call "holidays in a bottle."

Rutherglen Muscat is one of the few wines that can do justice to all the deep pumpkin pie flavors of toffee, caramel, vanilla, butterscotch, and sweet baking spices, with a corresponding note of each. The amber-hued Aussie also has the nutty, buttery, candied fruit smells produced by rancio oxidation (see page 65), which will amplify the same in the filling and the crust.

*$ R.L. Buller Wines Fine Old Muscat Rutherglen (375 ml)*

*$ Campbells Rutherglen Muscat Victoria* ✳☷ ⚘

# Powdered Jelly Donuts
## & WHITE ZINFANDEL

I've loved powdered jelly donuts my whole life. It wasn't until I moved to New York that I learned about their connection to Hanukkah. The oil the donut is fried in is an homage to the small amount of oil that is said to have burned miraculously for eight days in the ancient temple in Jerusalem. Filled with jam and topped with sugar, the *sufganiyah* is a natural for White Zinfandel. And before you roll your eyes, hear me out. White Zinfandel of yesteryear was bulk produced and tasted like mediocre sugar water. And yes, some of them still do, but there's a new guard of quality producers in California who've resuscitated the category.

The saviors of this love-to-hate-it pink drink decided to apply the same principles the French do to produce their famous dry rosés, and it worked wonders on American Zin. They are dry—hear me when I say dry—and packed with juicy citrus, and they range in hue from

fluorescent fuchsia to soft salmon. They have a mid-palate that's bursting with every berry of the rainbow, which feels like an extension of the jelly in your donut. And the pleasingly tart finish dispatches with the dough just in time to do it all again. If you're still in doubt, it may be of comfort to know that Bill Murray has been spotted drinking White Zin, so even if you need to do it ironically, you're covered either way.

*$ Monte Rio Cellars Dry White Zinfandel, Suisun Valley* 🌼 🍃🕊

*$ Turley Wine Cellars White Zinfandel, Napa Valley* 🌼 ☀ 🌿 🍃

# Peeps
## & FRANCIACORTA

We all know what Peeps taste like, but in case you forgot, they're the semi-edible marshmallow-adjacent sugar turds you start seeing at Easter, most often in the shape of chicks or bunnies, with the consistency of spray-foam insulation. The colors vary; the flavor less so. But the good news is that they can survive a nuclear winter, which may or may not be a true Peep fact. But I swear the rest that follow actually are . . .

The life of a Peep begins with a boiling batch of sugars and corn syrup. Gelatin and vanilla extract are then added before the mix gets put through the Depositor, a top-secret machine that has reduced the once twenty-seven-hour Peep-shaping process to six minutes flat. The final flourish is the addition of the infamously indestructible eyes, which scientists at Emory University have determined are actually made from a non-toxic edible wax called carnauba that can survive not only boiling water but also acetone, sulfuric acid, and phenol (found in household disinfectants). They haven't tested fallout radiation on them—yet.

The Depositor can make three thousand five hundred Peeps per minute, five million Peeps per day, and more than two billion Peeps per year, or enough to go around the Earth twice. Seven hundred million of them are consumed annually in America alone, although just who exactly is eating them remains a mystery. Some of the most popular ways to consume Peeps are "stale" (seriously, 25 percent of them, according to the company itself, though it prefers the term "aged"), microwaved, frozen, roasted (for s'mores), and, most troublingly, as a pizza topping.

The greatest thing about Peeps is that you can find one in just about any color for any holiday, and all of them go remarkably well with a sparkling wine called Franciacorta.

The sparkler from northern Italy deserves just as much attention as the froufrou Frenchie in Champagne. The two bubblies have plenty in common, most notably in the grapes that make them, which in both cases are primarily Chardonnay and Pinot Nero (Noir), and occasionally Pinot Bianco (Blanc). Both are made in the Traditional Method. Both have long histories of quality wine production. And both produce age-worthy styles, with mandatory requirements for aging in cellars before they can be released to the market. And though they also both share similar veins of toasty brioche and layers of fresh fruit, only the Italian bubble can pull off the kind of zippy Vespa of citrus required to smash through the Peeps' shimmery sugar crust and imbue its (almost) marshmallow with fresh flavor. These wines turn your mouth into a private little bouncy castle, which is just about the only place for a Peeps show that's appropriate for adults.

$ *Bellavista "Alma Gran Cuvée" Brut* 🎋 🌿 ✳

$$ *Barone Pizzini Brut Nature* 🎋🌼✳

$$$ *Ca' del Bosco Annamaria Clementi Dosage Zéro Franciacorta Riserva* 🌼🎋✳🌿

## Honey Baked Ham
## & PASO ROBLES PETITE SIRAH

Harry J. Hoenselaar opened the first Honey Baked Ham Company store in Detroit in 1957, and he said the idea for his iconic spiral ham slicer came to him in a dream. He built the prototype using a tire jack, a pie tin, a washing-machine motor, and a knife. This was a man

dedicated to ham. The hunk of meat now synonymous with Christmas is smoked for twenty-four hours with hardwood chips, then spiral-sliced to the bone and covered in a sweet, crunchy glaze that frankly makes this southerner weepy.

Only a full-bodied red with high tannin has the richness to sashay with such sacchariferous swine. Dancing with sugar plums, dark chocolate, and black pepper, Petite Sirah cracks that porker right open. The grape, known as Durif in its home country of France, is a cross between a Syrah and another French grape called Peloursin. The vast majority of it is grown in California. With less than ten thousand acres (4,000 ha) planted globally, it's not the most common red, but it's still relatively easy to find.

Paso Robles is an AVA in Southern California that's about three times the size of its neighbor to the north, Napa Valley. It's known for a number of different wine styles, with varying microclimates that distinguish them, and some of the best Petite Sirah is grown here. The diurnal flux in Paso Robles is greater than in almost any other appellation in California, with hot days that allow the grapes to ripen in full and cool nights that keep the ripeness from getting out of control. The result is an inky black, boldly flavored red that will lift that succulent ham up with its dark fruit and body, and moderate the fat with its tannin. I also recommend a good tooth brushing afterward to avoid purple teeth.

$$ *J. Lohr Tower Road Petite Sirah* 🎋✳

$$ *Turley Wine Cellars "Pesenti Vineyard" Petite Syrah* 🌼✳🎋🌿

# Birthday Funfetti Cake
## & ROSATO SPUMANTE (PROSECCO ROSÉ)

Funfetti cake has always been one of the world's great inventions, even if its newfound ubiquity on Instagram has pushed it to the brink of overexposure. That's because it is impossible to say, eat, or even think about Funfetti without smiling a tiny bit. Funfetti cake—any confetti cake, really—is a party unto itself, but you can put even more fun in your 'fetti with a chilled bottle of spumante rosé from Prosecco in northern Italy.

You've had Prosecco. You crave it. You drink it in Aperol spritzes. But few people know how Prosecco differs from other sparkling wines, particularly Champagne. It's made through a bulk process called Charmat in a large tank instead of in individual bottles as it is for Champers, giving it softer fizz (see page 62 for more on how sparkling wine is made). Many people also might not realize there's a rosé—or rosato—version, because pink wines can't be labeled "Prosecco," due to the grapes that need to be used (though that may be changing soon, with so many producers now in the blush game). Most Prosecco producers label the pink bottlings "spumante," the Italian term for sparkling wine.

Even though these spumante rosés have similar levels of sugar to Champagne, the wines often taste sweeter because the grapes used, which run the gamut from Pinot Noir to the little-known Raboso Veronese, give riper fruit flavors and have less acidity. They're really good with Funfetti cake for a few reasons. The Charmat Method results in delicate bubbles that aren't as sharp as Champagne's, which helps make the cake feel even lighter and airier. And the wine's fruity, floral flair and vanilla-bean highlights are a birthday wish granted for the Funfetti's Technicolor sweetness and sprinkles.

$ *Mionetto "Prestige Collection Gran Rosé" Spumante Extra Dry* ☀ ✳

$$ *Altaneve Spumante Rosé* ✳

# Gingerbread
## & PASSITO DI PANTELLERIA

Whether your holiday gingerbread house is a fixer-upper or a confectionary Versailles, the experience of building it while drinking dessert wine is all that really matters. Your scaffolding should be the Italian kind made from the grape Zibibbo di Pantelleria, which I'm not even going to sound out for you. Just drink a bottle and roll a few *R*'s somewhere and you'll be close enough.

Pantelleria is a tiny little volcanic island that's actually closer to Africa than it is to Sicily or mainland Italia. It's a bizarre black rock eight miles tall and five miles wide in the middle of the Mediterranean that doesn't have any beaches—just grottos steaming with hot springs warmed by the volcano that gives it its name. The island itself is just the part of the volcano's tip that's above water. There's a wind called the sirocco that's so strong it regularly rips across the island at sixty miles per hour, grounding all planes, reducing visibility to almost zero, and forcing everyone to shelter indoors until it's gone. And this is where one of the best unknown dessert wines in the world is made.

Zibibbo is the local name for the ancient grape of Muscat of Alexandria, one of the oldest genetically unmodified varieties on earth (Cleopatra was an actual fan). Extreme viticulture gets its name here on this island, where they have to dig holes in which to plant the vines to protect them, then wall them inside stone enclosures to shelter them

even further. The grapes are put through the *appassimento* process (see page 87) and then vinified (fermented) into a wine that smells like the perfume section at Macy's. Which is to say the aromas are wild and all over the place and force you to keep going back to see what else you can find in the glass. The profile is lush with candied citrus zest, dried figs, honeycomb, balsamic reduction, Mediterranean scrub, and lychees. You can almost hear Charlize Theron throat-whispering its name in a fragrance commercial: "Zibibbo. From the Islands." The electric amber color comes with a bright palate and a finish that erupts with gusto, which is the only thing your sharp and toasty gingerbread will yield to.

*$$ Donnafugata Ben Ryé Passito di Pantelleria (375 ml)* ☀️ ⚜️

# Superbowl Nachos
## & CALIFORNIA CHARDONNAY

Whether you love football or hate it, root for a team or just wait for the halftime show, there's one thing about Super Bowl Sunday upon which almost every American can agree: Nachos are awesome. And though the pressure to enjoy them with beer may be strong, depending on how many sausages are in the room, you can and should reach for a wine stem—then fill it with good old-fashioned Mom Chardonnay from California.

California Chardonnay is the Yanni of the wine world: big in the nineties, largely ignored now, but in this case super popular with women over sixty-five. I'm here to tell you that they're better than you remember (Yanni less so). California Chardonnay was one of the first wines to prove America's wine-making prowess, but by the mid-nineties, producers had adopted a heavy, buttery, super-oaked style. It rode that fashion for a while, but many wine drinkers moved on to other, more interesting things. These days, California Chardonnays are much more balanced and less heavy handed, and they're not just for girls' weekends in Sarasota anymore.

There are a number of appellations making great Cali Chard today. Notable are Napa Valley, Sonoma, and Anderson Valley for richer (but still elegant and balanced) styles and Carneros and Santa Barbara for wines that are a little leaner.

These contemporary, more sophisticated styles also tend to maintain the higher alcohol content that's one of the trademarks of Cali Chard. In the same way that higher acidity can help amplify flavors and textures in food, so too can the presence of more alcohol. When mixed with the fatty cheese and guac, that extra alcohol enhances the sensation of umami, which also bolsters the savoriness of any black beans you might add. Chardonnay's natural salinity squares up like a linebacker with the chips, and its mild tannic grip does right by pork or beef. But even better, thanks to a winemaking process called malolactic fermentation, which makes wine seem richer and creamier (and yes, often buttery), that Cali Chard completes a smooth fade to the end zone of melted Monterey Jack and sour cream.

*$ Nielson Santa Barbara County Chardonnay* ⚜️

*$$ Chateau Montelena Chardonnay Napa Valley* ☀️ ⚜️

*$$$ Aubert Wines Larry Hyde & Sons Vineyard Carneros Chardonnay* ⚜️ ☀️

# THE JUDGMENT OF PARIS

California wine was long considered a joke to Europeans, who assumed correctly for the last thousand or so years that they had the market cornered on the world's greatest wines. When the modern winemaking era began to develop in the mid-twentieth century, what they didn't realize is that American domestic soils contained some of the most robust terroir on the planet, and it would only be a matter of time before the generational winemaking knowledge gap closed. Their rude awakening came on May 24, 1976, a day that will live in wine infamy. It's what's known as the Judgment of Paris, and it marked a revolution in the industry.

Organized as a publicity stunt by a British wine merchant who only sold French wines, the event consisted of two seemingly innocuous blind tastings judged by top sommeliers, winemakers, and critics in Paris. One tasting would decide the world's best Chardonnays and the other would pit the red wines of Bordeaux against the Cabernet Sauvignon blends of California. It was orchestrated under the pretense that the French wines would win easily against the arrivistes from California. Rugged wines from poor vintners, the thinking went, made in a place no one had ever achieved anything notable, simply couldn't compete with the greatest examples of the craft known to man and beast.

*Time* magazine's Paris correspondent attended the event as a favor, although he and everyone else assumed the David and Goliath setup would be a nonstory. The big twist, of course, was that the California wines handily swept both the red and white categories, beating all the French competition.

Because the tasting was blind, the judges only had their misplaced confidence to guide them—one famously sipped a California wine and sighed, "Ah. Back to France." The final scores awarded top marks to the 1973 Chardonnay from Chateau Montelena and the 1973 Cabernet Sauvignon from Stag's Leap Wine Cellars, both in Napa Valley. Some of the judges were so shocked and angry that they demanded their scorecards back, afraid that anyone would ever find out what they marked down. A bottle of each now lives at the Smithsonian in Washington, DC.

"The Judgment" helped pave the way not only for U.S. wines but also for the rest of the newly emerging wine world—Argentina, South Africa, Australia, and beyond. It was the moment the doors swung open and oenophiles everywhere realized that great wines could be produced anywhere, not just the classic regions that had claimed dominance for so long. Forty years later, the styles have changed some, but American wines aren't just delicious; they're a global market force. As generation after generation of what were once considered young wineries have matured and multiplied, they've acquired the institutional knowledge required to compete on a global stage, which can only come from experience.

CRAVE THE DATE

# TRICKS *for* TREATS:
## *HALLOWEEN CANDY TO TRY WITH YOUR BOO!*

Certain combinations of wine and candy can immediately lift your spirits, and the best of them most often involve dessert wines. A category that includes some of the most prestigious (and expensive) wines in the world, dessert wines can be still, fortified, or sparkling, very dry to very sweet, and everything in between—and most people know very little about them. The easiest place to start is with the flavor or texture that's the driving force behind the candy you want to pair. Many of those components—nutty, sweet, bitter—may overlap in the same treat (think Snickers versus a plain Hershey's bar), and this should not cause distress. Embrace the double dose—you can choose to zero in on your favorite flavor or try to find a wine that has all the notes you're looking for in one bottle, which is harder to pull off but also part of the fun.

## Bubble Gum

The style of wine you choose will be dictated by the flavor of the gum, and the simplest way to prevail is to match like with like. For the classic bubblegum flavor, think about what pairs with that strawberry-banana profile: a pink and fruity wine like rosé Port. If your gum is blueberry flavored, find a blueberry wine, which really does exist. If it's a minty fresh chew, just spit your gum out. I'm not a miracle worker.

## Caramel and Toffee Candy

The interplay of salty and sweet make them natural candidates for fortified wines for the very same reason. Wines like Vin Doux Naturels from southern France and Montilla-Moriles from southern Spain are intentionally oxidized in the winemaking process, giving them that buttery depth of character that comes from playing both sides of the salty-sweet flavor line.

## Dark Chocolate

The dominant characteristic here is bitterness. And bitter rarely goes with bitter unless you introduce sugar to the mix. The sweetness acts as the binding seam between the tannins in both the chocolate and the wine, making some red dessert, fortified, and sparkling wines good options. It takes a unique bottle that's sweet but based on red grapes to maintain a bitter twinge, like a Barolo Chinato or ruby Port. If your dark chocolate has any other flavors you can focus on, like nuts or coconut, you'll have more options.

## Gummy and Taffy Candy

Chewiness begs for acidity. Something to clean off the gelatin stuck to your teeth. With their added $CO_2$, bubbles are the best assistant for a mouth washing. Because these candies are usually fruit flavored, find a similarly juicy, fresh, and fruity dessert wine. Styles based on white grapes with loads of acid and a soft touch of sugar, like Riesling, work well because they usually have a lot of berry and citrus flavors.

## Hard Candy

Even though they start hard, they slowly melt in your mouth, so you have a viscosity challenge similar to gummy candy, though not as extreme. Focus on the flavor of the candy itself, whether it's fruity, minty, or spicy. Fruity hard candies will pair well with juicy, concentrated wines like late harvest and ice wines. Candies that are spicy may need the added element of sweet baking spice, which can come from the grape Gewürztraminer or from time spent in oak, like in late-harvest Chenin Blanc.

## Licorice

Since real licorice isn't sweet, the lack of sugar creates a similar problem to that of dark chocolate but with a flavor more acute than cocoa. This is such a specific taste, the only thing you can do is find a wine that embodies comparable medicinal or intensely spiced flavors, like Brachetto d'Aqui, or pink versions of grapes like Cabernet Franc.

### Marshmallow or Nougat Candy

Embrace the fluff! Fortified wines are a great place to go with these candies, because the powerful body amplifies the puffiness and the acidity wipes it away. If it's coated in chocolate or nuts, head in an oxidized white wine direction, such as tawny Port. If it's coated in light sugar dustings, something fruity and bubbly like a Prosecco can also hit the spot.

### Milk Chocolate

Look for a wine with a similar balance of milder flavor and smooth texture. You want something that has cocoa-rich characteristics without being too intense in its flavor profile to overwhelm the chocolate. The added cream that softens the chocolate's bitterness opens more doors than pure dark chocolate ever will. From Italian Vin Santo to ruby Port to late-harvest red Zinfandel, there are plenty of easy paths to take.

### Powdered Candy

Since these are usually simple powdered sugars with fruit flavorings, like Pixy Stix or my childhood favorite, Fun Dip, choose a wine that has a little more complexity to ramp up the party in your mouth. Consider straw-mat white dessert wines like Muscat cultivated the world over, or, to be geekier, a Côtes du Jura Vin de Pailles.

### Nut-Based Candy

One cool thing about wine is how much it can display very specific nutty aromas, with all kinds of almonds, chestnuts, walnuts, hazelnuts, and peanuts. Try to suss out a wine that has been oxidized, which produces that nuttiness, and then try to sync up with the specific nut. Great examples are Zibibbo di Pantelleria and richer styles of sherry.

### Sour Candy

For the record, if you ever want to get on my good side, sour candy will do it. There's no better category. And when there's that much acid in your candy, you better have that much and more in your wine. Fruitiness and freshness must abound. I usually go for a sparkling or white dessert wine from grapes known for packing pop and tart, like Sauvignon Blanc or Riesling.

### Spicy Candy

When you add heat to a food, sugar is the best way to provide contrast to soften the spice. These candies often have cinnamon, so seek out wines with a similar cinnamoniness. This is a characteristic naturally conjured in grapes like Gewürtraminer or Pinot Gris but can also be accomplished with oak, as with sweet botrytized wines like Barsac.

### White Chocolate

We won't hold it against white chocolate that it isn't actually chocolate (it's made with cocoa butter). Its suave, gentle sweetness and hint of vanilla fall into its own lane. You'll want a dessert wine that has floral and baking spice notes to enhance the best parts of the candy and subtle sweetness to match. Still and sparkling made from the Muscat grape are willing partners, as are fortified whites like Port.

# SWEET SURRENDER

There's a very special dessert wine waiting out there for every candy in the land.

**100 Grand** TOURIGA NACIONAL PORT *Yakima Valley, Washington* / Fortified Sweet Red

**3 Musketeers** LATE BOTTLE VINTAGE PORT *Douro Valley, Portugal* / Fortified Sweet Red

**5th Avenue** RIVESALTES GRENAT *Rhône Valley, France* / Fortified Sweet Red

**Airheads** RIESLING LATE HARVEST *Long Island, New York* / Dessert Sweet White

**Almond Joy** ZIBIBBO DI PANTELLIERA *Sicily, Italy* / Dessert Sweet White

**Andes Mints** LATE HARVEST SYRAH *Paso Robles, California* / Dessert Sweet Red

**Annabelle's Rocky Road Bar** DULCE MONASTRELL *Jumilla, Spain* / Dessert Charmed Red

**Apple O's** BONNEZEAUX (CHENIN BLANC) *Loire Valley, France* / Dessert Sweet White

**Atomic Fireballs** BARSAC *Bordeaux, France* / Dessert Sweet White

**Baby Ruth** RUTHERGLEN MUSCAT *Victoria, Australia* / Dessert Luscious White

**Big Hunk** VIN DE CONSTANCE *Constantia, South Africa* / Richly Sweet White

**Bit o Honey** HERMITAGE VIN DE PAILLE *Rhône Valley, France* / Richly Sweet White

**Blow Pops** SPÄTLESE ROSÉ *Burgenland, Austria* / Lightly Sweet Pink

**Brite Crawlers** RIESLING FEINHERB *Mosel, Germany* / Lightly Sweet White

**Bubble Tape** COTEAUX DU LAYON *Loire Valley, France* / Richly Sweet White

**Butterfinger** RIVESALTES AMBRÉ *Rhône Valley, France* / Fortified Sweet White

**Candy Cigarettes** MONBAZILLAC *South West France* / Dessert Sweet White

**Candy Corn** LATE HAVEST CHARDONNAY *Willamette Valley, Oregon* / Dessert Sweet White

**Candy Necklace** LATE HARVEST SAUVIGNON BLANC *Casablanca, Chile* / Dessert Sweet White

**Caramello** MOSCATEL DE SETÚBAL *Setúbal Peninsula, Portugal* / Fortified Luscious White

**Charleston Chew** TORRONTÉS LATE HARVEST *Mendoza, Argentina* / Dessert Sweet White

**Cherry Sours** MACVIN DU JURA ROUGE *Jura, France* / Fortified Lightly Sweet Red

**Chimes Ginger Chews** LATE HARVEST TRAMINAC *Danube, Croatia* / Dessert Sweet White

**Circus Peanuts** ORANGE MUSCAT *Santa Barbara, California* / Dessert Sweet White

**Clark Bar** RIVESALTES TUILÉ *Rhône Valley, France* / Fortified Oxidized Red

**Cow Tales** ZWEIGELT AUSLESE *Neusiedlersee, Austria* / Fortified Sweet Red

**Dots** WHITE ZINFANDEL *Napa Valley, California* / Lightly Sweet Pink

**Double Bubble Gum** ROSÉ PORT *Douro Valley, Portugal* / Fortified Sweet Pink

**Fun Dip** CLAIRETTE DE DIE *Rhône Valley, France* / Sparkling Dry White

**Gobstopper** RECIOTO DI SOAVE *Piedmont, Italy* / Dessert Sweet White

**Goobers** MANZANILLA SHERRY *Jerez, Spain* / Fortified Dry White

**Good & Plenty** SPARKLING SHIRAZ *South Australia, Australia*

**Gummy Bears** RIESLING KABINETT *Nahe, Germany* / Lightly Sweet White

**Gushers** LATE HARVEST SEMILLON *Mendoza, Argentina* / Dessert Sweet White

**Heath Bar** MAURY VIN DOUX NATUREL *Rhône Valley, France*

**Hershey's Kisses** ZINFANDEL LATE HARVEST *Lodi, California*

**Hot Tamales** PINOT GRIS SÉLECTION DE GRAINS NOBLES *Alsace, France* / Dessert Sweet White

**Jawbreakers** CHAMPAGNE EXTRA DRY *Champagne, France* / Sparkling Sweet White

**Jelly Belly** RIVESALTES ROSÉ *Rhône Valley, France* / Fortified Sweet Pink

**Jolly Rancher** QUARTS DE CHAUME *Loire Valley, France* / Dessert Sweet White

**Juicy Fruit** RIESLING ICE WINE *Finger Lakes, New York* / Dessert Sweet White

**Jujyfruits** MUSCAT DE BEAUMES-DE-VENISE *Rhône Valley, France* / Fortified Sweet White

**Junior Mints** BANYULS ROUGE *Roussillon, France*

**Kit Kat** VIN SANTO OCCHIO DE PERNICE *Tuscany, Italy*

**Laffy Taffy** LATE HARVEST GEWÜRTZTRAMINER *Gisborne, New Zealand* / Dessert Sweet White

**Lemonheads** RIESLING BRUT *Finger Lakes, New York* / Sparkling Dry White

**Licorice** BRACHETTO D'ACQUI *Piedmont, Italy*

**Life Savers** TREBBIANO VIN SANTO *Tuscany, Italy* / Dessert Sweet White

**M&M's** LAMBRUSCO AMABILE *Emilia-Romagna, Italy*

**Mamba's** VOUVRAY MOELLEUX *Loire Valley, France* / Dessert Sweet White

**Mars Bar** NERO D'AVOLA PASSITO *Sicily, Italy*

**Mike & Ikes** VIDAL BLANC ICE WINE *Niagara Peninsula, Canada* / Dessert Luscious White

**Milk Duds** LOUPIAC *Bordeaux, France* / Dessert Sweet White

**Milky Way** TAWNY PORT *Douro Valley, Portugal* / Fortified Oxidized White

**Mounds** SAUTERNES *Bordeaux, France* / Dessert Sweet White

**Mr. Goodbar** MARSALA MISTELLA *Sicily, Italy* / Fortified Sweet White

**Nerds** FREISA DI CHIERI FRIZZANTE *Piedmont, Italy*

**Nestlé Crunch** RASTEAU VIN DOUX NATUREL *Rhône Valley, France*

**Now & Later** SANTORINI VINSANTO *Santorini, Greece* / Fortified Oxidized White

**Pay Day** SERCIAL MADEIRA *Madeira, Portugal* / Fortified Oxidized White

**Peanut Chew** COMMANDARIA *Cyprus* / Fortified Sweet Amber

**Pez** TROLLINGER *Württemberg, Germany*

**Pixie Stix** CÔTES DU JURA VIN DE PAILLE *Jura, France* / Dessert Sweet White

**Pop Rocks** CHAMPAGNE DEMI-SEC *Champagne, France* / Sparkling Sweet White

**Raisinets** RECIOTO DELLA VALPOLICELLA *Veneto, Italy*

**Red Hots** JURANÇON MOELLEUX *South West France, France* / Dessert Sweet White

**Red Vines** CABERNET FRANC ICE WINE *Niagara Peninsula, Canada* / Dessert Sweet Pink

**Reese's Peanut Butter Cups** AMONTILLADO SHERRY *Jerez, Spain* / Fortified Oxidized White

**Riesen** COLHEITA PORT *Douro Valley, Portugal* / Fortified Oxidized White

**Ring Pop** 3 PUTTONYOS TOKAJI ASZÚ *Tokaj, Hungary* / Dessert Sweet White

**Rolos** VERDELHO MADEIRA *Madeira, Portugal* / Fortified Dry to Sweet White

**Runts** ROSÉ D'ANJOU *Loire Valley, France* / Lightly Sweet Pink

**Salt Water Taffy** GRAUBURGUNDER AUSLESE *Steiermark, Austria* / Dessert Sweet White

**Salted Licorice** CABERNET D'ANJOU *Loire Valley, France* / Lightly Sweet Red

**Shock Tarts (Chewy Sours)** TOKAJI ESENZIA *Tokaj, Hungary* / Dessert Luscious Sweet White

**Skittles** RIESLING SEKT B.A. HALBTROCKEN *Rheinhessen, Germany* / Sparkling Sweet White

**Skor** SAMOS ANTHEMIS *Samos, Greece* / Fortified Sweet Amber

**Slo Poke** CREAM SHERRY *Jerez, Spain* / Fortified Sweet White

**Smarties** VERMENTINO DI GALLURA SPUMANTE BRUT *Sardegna, Italy* / Sparkling Sweet White

**Snickers** OLOROSO SHERRY *Jerez, Spain* / Fortified Oxidized White

**Sno Caps** RUBY PORT *Sierra Foothills, California* / Fortified Sweet Red

**Sour Patch Kids** RIESLING SEMI-DRY *Finger Lakes, New York* / Lightly Sweet White

**Sour Punch Straws** CABERNET FRANC ICE WINE *Niagara Peninsula, Canada* / Dessert Sweet Pink or Red

**Sour Skittles** SAUVIGNON BLANC LATE HARVEST *Russian River Valley, California* / Dessert Sweet White

**Spree** SEMILLON LATE HARVEST *Columbia Valley, Washington* / Dessert Sweet White

**Starburst** MOSCATO D'ASTI *Piedmont, Italy* / Sparkling Sweet White

**Sugar Daddies** STRAW WINE *Swartland, South Africa* / Dessert Sweet White

**Swedish Fish** GAMARET *La Côte, Switzerland* / Lightly Sweet Red

**SweeTarts** RIESLING SPÄTLESE *Mosel, Germany* / Lightly Sweet White

**Take 5** ZWEIGELT SEKT *Niederoesterreich, Austria* / Sparkling Sweet Red

**Tootsie Rolls** SAGRANTINO DI MONTEFALCO PASSITO *Umbria, Italy* / Dessert Sweet Red

**Twix** MAVRODAPHNE *Pátras, Greece* / Fortified Sweet Red

**Twizzlers** CAVA ROSATO EXTRA-SECO *Penedes, Spain* / Sparkling Sweet Pink

**Vanilla Midgees Tootsie Rolls** PEDRO XIMÉNEZ *Jerez, Spain* / Fortified Luscious Amber

**Warheads** GEWÜRTZTRAMINER VENDAGE TARDIVE *Alsace, France* / Dessert Sweet White

**Wax Coke Bottles** BOAL MADEIRA *Madeira, Portugal* / Fortified Sweet White

**Werther's Original** PEDRO XIMÉNEZ MONTILLA-MORILES *Andalucia, Spain* / Fortified Luscious Amber

**Whoppers** MALAGA MOSCATEL *Andalucia, Spain* / Fortified Sweet Amber

**York Peppermint Pattie** BAROLO CHINATO *Piedmont, Italy* / Fortified Sweet Red

**Zero Bar** WHITE PORT *Douro Valley, Portugal* / Fortified Sweet White

# CHAPTER 10

# Dinner Party Duets

## PERFECTLY PASSABLE BITES

V anessa!" screamed the scraggly voice on the phone. "You've got to get over there! Do you hear me? Get over there now!"

The growling bear on the other end was my frenzied but lovable co-worker Jerome, who was feeding me one of his long-shot leads, and not the good *Glengarry* kind. There was a new restaurant opening in my neighborhood, and I needed to be the first to talk to the owners if I'd have any chance of landing the account. Such is the life of a wine sales rep—when you get the call, you stop whatever you're doing and go, even if your mom happens to be in town visiting from Kentucky. Nine-to-fivers don't last long.

Jerome was a liquor rep in his mid-sixties whose age and wisdom had never quite spilled over into patience or calm. He'd tell me stories about his days as a hoodlum in the Irish gangs of his youth back in Queens and Brooklyn, when things in his vicinity had a tendency to fall off the back of trucks. It was endearing, but also a reminder that he was, at least back in the glory days, not someone you messed with. Now he wore wingtips and three-piece striped suits. He was, like so many in the wine business, a self-made, colorfully shady character—one who had chosen the sale of legal substances over the illegal kind.

His frantic call also came with an agenda. As a rep in the liquor division of our company, Jerome was in constant competition with reps from smaller distributors who had both wine and liquor in their portfolios. Many restaurant buyers love the convenience of one-stop shopping, where they can order their booze and wine from the same person.

So by tag-teaming with me on the wine side, he knew he'd have a much better chance of landing their account. To help me was to help himself, and he knew that as a hungry pipsqueak sales rep, I'd take any table scraps he was offering.

That day, my mother and I had been planning a leisurely afternoon of window shopping, but she was a good sport and agreed to walk over with me instead. The place was tiny and the location seemed cursed—at least three restaurants had crashed and burned in the same space. On its face, it looked like this one wouldn't be any different. I smiled and introduced myself, and the owner, Dean, popped his head out of the kitchen. "You're the wine expert, right?"

"Kidding," he said after reading my face. I couldn't tell if he was kidding.

Dean and his wife, Maya, were the proprietors of Jack's Wife Freda, a casual cafe with ambitious hybrid cuisine adapted from their home countries of Israel and South Africa. Dean's father happened to be visiting from Johannesburg that day, and he and my mother sat and chatted as I got to know Maya and Dean. At the end of our long conversation, they said they loved that I was a neighborhood local with a passion for wine. Then they told me they wanted to keep their wine list small and interesting, and if I was up for it, they'd like to give me a shot at putting it together for them. In the industry, it's what we call "writing the list," and it's a job usually reserved for an in-house beverage person or seasoned wine consultant.

It's almost unheard of for a sales rep to be tasked with creating an account's entire wine list. As first-time restaurateurs themselves, Dean and Maya said they understood what it meant to take a risk. They just had no idea how big of a risk they were taking. At the time, I had five years under my belt in the industry, but I had never written a wine list and was just completing my formal somm education. I had read plenty of wine lists. I had talked about plenty of wine lists. I had certainly drunk from more than my fair share of wine lists. But no one had ever thought to trust me with writing one—I was thrilled.

It would only be a modest one-pager of straightforward wines, but I treated it with the kind of care and obsession you might expect from a surgeon preparing for a triple Michelin bypass. That meant agonizing for weeks over the choices, how they'd work with an eclectic and unfamiliar range of dishes like shakshuka, rosewater waffles, and Peri-Peri chicken (dry-rubbed with Mozambique bird's-eye chili), and for even longer on how to describe and categorize them. The psychology of menu writing is a very real thing, and how you present your selections on a wine list can make or break it. Just as importantly, what do the wines cost to buy and how much should they be sold for? (Inside tip: Because so many customers erroneously assume the second most expensive wine on a list offers the best quality for the money, it always sells the most—so it's actually the biggest opportunity to plug in a bottle with a higher profit margin.) A wine list is only successful if it actually makes money for the restaurant.

The day the restaurant opened was also my birthday, so I got to celebrate two milestones—making it to age twenty-eight without owning a properly fitted bra, and the thrill of having vaulted headfirst into the biggest challenge of my professional career and Kerri Strug-ing the landing. With three locations and counting, Jack's Wife Freda is now a downtown institution. And eight years on, I still have the privilege of writing their wine list.

The one thing I figured out in those early days curating wines for such unique flavor profiles was that trial and error is the only way to learn—and the error part is best done at home among friends. My tiny apartment on Broome Street became my lab. And the experiments were driven by what my roommate took to calling "the Monster," the ever-growing stockpile of wine that lines my walls in racks and overflows in loose stacks across my floor, accumulated over years. Back then the Monster was even more aggressive, with cases of samples arriving by the week; it was not uncommon to trip over one of its tentacles on your way to the bathroom at night.

Because I grew up in a home where the front door was always open, I tried to institute the same philosophy in my first-floor apartment, which turns out to be a very popular policy when it involves free wine. All my friends know they can pop by anytime for a bottle on their way somewhere else. And it's never difficult to find willing guinea pigs for my human trials . . . er . . . dinner parties. Of course, living the dream of overpaying for a cramped New York City apartment means you often don't have room for an actual dining table (particularly if half the usable space is overtaken by wine). Easy, shareable finger-and-napkin couplings pair well with good friends huddled awkwardly around small couches, floor pillows, random chairs, and tiny coffee tables.

# Shrimp Cocktail
## & VALDEORRAS GODELLO

Godello is the name of the white grape and Valdeorras is the name of the appellation in Spain. Areas like Bierzo, Monterrei, and Ribeira Sacra also produce wines from this grape, but as the most well-known and respected for quality, Godello is the big *V*. It was a grape that faced near extinction before impassioned vintners in the area picked up the torch just a few decades ago, and we are grateful. This is an example of how conscientious farming, gutsy vision, and serious winemaking prowess can create a beast of a white wine that isn't prohibitively expensive.

With their combination of grapefruit and lemon, along with a crush of acid and gravelly minerality, Valdeorras Godellos can be a near dead ringer for Sauvignon Blanc. What makes them distinct is that they have higher alcohol than your typical Sauvignon and a saline drag that begs for food—specifically the sea and finger kind. Shrimp cocktail obliges Spanish Godello in kind, with its mild ocean flavor and sharp cocktail-sauce tang. Both are invigorated by Godello's opulent, briny edge. And the cost of pairing with this mid-level white never gets jumbo, so you can always be the host with the most shrimp.

*$ Bodegas Valdesil "Sobre Lías" Godello* ☀ 🦪🐚

*$$ Bodegas Avancia "Avancia" Old Vine Godello* 🌿☀🐚🦪

*$$ Rafael Palacios "As Sortes"* ☀✳

# Prosciutto & Melon Sticks
## & CARTIZZE PROSECCO

There is Prosecco and then there is Cartizze Prosecco, the rarefied jewel in the crown. It's still made in the Charmat, or Tank, Method, just like every other version of the Italian sparkler, but this one is particularly special. The long name is Valdobbiadene Superiore di Cartizze DOCG, which is a mouthful, but what it's telling you is that the fruit came from a tiny area of about 264 acres (107 ha) just outside the well-respected region of Valdobbiadene. It's known as the finest land for growing Glera, the main grape used to make Prosecco, and the category represents the very best and smallest amounts of Prosecco produced anywhere. It's an instant upgrade for salty, razor thin prosciutto and ripe melon, which are transformed by Cartizze from an easy antipasto staple into something truly memorable.

*$ Adami Prosecco di Valdobbiadene Superiore di Cartizze Dry* 🌿🦪

*$$ Villa Sandi Superiore di Cartizze "La Rivetta"* ✳🌿🦪✳

153

# IT'S NINE P.M.
## *Do You Know Where Your Wine Is?*

# HOW TO STORE YOUR WINE SAFELY

Wine is a living, breathing thing that requires very precise conditions in order to age. The delicious liquid in that bottle right now is at just one life stage on the pendulum swing between grape juice and vinegar. How long it stays that way depends on how it's stored, and also whether it was intended to age in the first place.

A wine fridge is called a cave (pronounced "cahv," in the French way) because it simulates the natural conditions of underground caves, which have been used to store wine properly for thousands of years. It also just sounds a lot sexier than wine refrigerator. The optimal conditions they mimic are a constant, cool temperature of 55–60°F (13–16°C) with 60–70 percent humidity. The requirements for fine wine storage are as long as Mariah Carey's green room rider—everything has to be just so, and if the terms aren't met, the wine may refuse to sing or turn nasty. But very few bottles in the world are worthy of the diva treatment.

The vast majority of wine is not made to age and should be consumed soon after you buy it. It's only the small percentage of wine that gets better with time that requires regulated storage. That percentage varies by wine-making region, but most experts agree that less than 10 percent of wine improves after a year of coming to market and less than 1 percent improves after five to ten years.

How do you know what bottles can age? Most of them already have age when they're released to the market. For example, Brunello di Montalcino, a famous red wine appellation in Italy, is required by law to age for five years in the winery before it can be sold. Since the current offering from the winery will already have at least five years of age when you buy it, you can safely assume they made that wine with aging in mind and took the time and care to treat it accordingly. Its price tag will reflect those years of effort. On the other hand, an inexpensive Sangiovese, which is the same grape used to make Brunello, will likely only be a year old when it becomes available for purchase and was not made to age.

If you're like most of the world and plan to drink your wine in the next six months or so, storing it on a rack in your pantry or a kitchen counter is perfectly fine—just keep it away from the stove (and the cabinet above it). You'll wind up cooking your bottles along with your food.

# The Big *Don'ts*

### *Don't* store bottles with corks standing up.

It dries out the cork, which allows oxygen to seep into the bottle, and it will eventually make your wine undrinkable.

### *Don't* let the light in.

The reason so many wine bottles are made with dark-hued glass is because UV light breaks down wine in the same way it does anything that spends too much time in direct sunlight. The colored glass acts like sunscreen for the wine, but no amount of sunscreen can protect it from a few weeks on a windowsill.

### *Don't* expose it to temperature fluctuations.

When it's warm, wine expands, which pushes the cork out of the bottle. When it cools, wine contracts, pulling oxygen into the bottle. Neither of these things is good.

### *Don't* store good wine in a food refrigerator.

The humidity is too low. It dries out the corks, which prematurely oxidizes your wines. I always feel bad when people tell me that they've had special bottles lying in their food fridge for months or even years. That wine is no bueno. If you're one of those people, I'm so sorry. Go open it right now and hope for the best.

### *Don't* toss a bottle unless you really know it's gone bad.

Even if a cork has started to pop out or the temperatures in your home have shifted greatly, it's never a guarantee that the wine is a goner. The only way to know for sure is to try it. Some of the best wine I've ever had has come from bottles that appeared to be in very poor condition when I was only using my eyeballs. Even if the color is scary, wine isn't harmful as it turns, so always give it a sip before you give it the dump.

## Risotto Balls
### & BRUNELLO DI MONTALCINO

Of all the iterations of Sangiovese that Tuscany produces, Brunello di Montalcino is the most well-known, and it's one of those wines that has earned its stellar reputation. Brunello is the local name for Sangiovese, and Montalcino is the town, and the wines that come from this place-grape combination are big in body and tannin. Yet they still manage to maintain an acidic framework that gives them a power and precision to bowl you over when you drink them young—and maybe even make you a little misty by the time they get older.

The currents are cherry, savory herbs, and dried leather, and as they age they develop aromas of dried saddle, dried rose petals, and rich cinnamon. One of the first a-ha moments I ever had with a wine was with an older Brunello. It was a 1975 Biondi Santi Riserva, and if only I had known at the time what a piece of history I was drinking. Even a young one that's not as rare or expensive goes amazingly well with risotto balls. The tannin of such a powerful wine brings clarity and finesse to doughy, yeasty rice amalgamations of the starchiest order. The sharpness of the Brunello's acidity barrels through any marinara you're dipping them in like a rodeo bull, and its dense red fruit and herbal core blanket the sauce's spicy edge.

*$$ Castiglion del Bosco Brunello di Montalcino*

*$$$ Conti Costanti Brunello di Montalcino*

*$$$ Biondi-Santi Brunello di Montalcino Riserva*

## Pigs in a Blanket
### & MARGARET RIVER CHARDONNAY

Let's be clear. You're free to get as fancy as you want, but the only true pig in a blanket in this world starts with a Hebrew National mini-frank and ends with Pillsbury Crescent Roll crust. All other versions are mere pretension. Since the beginning of time, these two crucial components have achieved that juicy-hot, flaky, buttery, and scrumptiously dippable bite every time. Margaret River, located in the south-western corner of Australia (opposite side of the continent from Sydney), produces some of the best versions of the world's most ubiquitous white, Chardonnay, even though it has scarcely fifty years under its winemaking belt.

The top wines from this region can age as long as white Burgundy, yet still have more approachability in their youth, when white Burgs can be austere and unapproachable. So they are easier to drink young and still able to go the distance—just the kind of bewitching characteristics that might convince you to break up with your steady Old World Chardonnays (or at least consider an open relationship).

Margaret River's zesty freshness creates a fulcrum with the fat of the frank and the flake of the dough, and its savory profile works in tandem with the protein. The saltiness of both lingers softly, just long enough to leave you salivating for another bite and sip.

*$$ Robert Oatley Vineyards "Signature Series" Chardonnay*

*$$ Vasse Felix Heytesbury Chardonnay*

*$$$ Leeuwin Estate "Art Series" Chardonnay*

## Classic Crudités
## & VERMENTINO DI SARDEGNA

It's known as Vermentino in southern Italy, but this white variety gets around. You'll see it as Pigato in central Italy, Favorita in northern Italy, and Rolle in France, and it has at least fifty other names beyond those, depending where in the world it's grown. These wines are what I like to call tweeners, because they're halfway between Sauvignon Blanc and Chardonnay, with medium body, acidity, and alcohol. They can be found all across the Mediterranean, from Provence and Corsica to coastal Tuscany, but the version that comes from an appellation on the island of Sardinia called Vermentino di

Gallura has distinguished itself above the rest. Locals claim it has been grown on this tiny patch of land since the fourteenth century, and while both oaked and unoaked styles are made there, I prefer the unoaked versions of Sardinian Vermentino with my freshly cut veggies. Like a new bag of sour patch flavors, these wines have every tart fruit you could want, from lime and grapefruit to green apple and white peach, followed by a hallmark bouquet of daffodil and almond. When your crudités include everything from mild and nutty cauliflower to sharp radicchio, this Leatherman of wines has all the tools you need to open them up.

*$ Argiolas Costamolino Vermentino di Sardegna*
*$ Monteoro Vermentino di Gallura Superiore*

# Jalapeño Poppers
## & SPÄTLESE RIESLING

Germans being Germans, they're so precise in their winemaking that they're able to make as many as six passes through the same Riesling vines at different points of ripeness during harvest time to make six entirely distinct styles of wine, all with different levels of dryness or sweetness. They even have specific words to convey these different ripeness levels on their labels, which also describe the style of the wine. The system is as immaculate as the wines it produces, although the verbiage can be difficult for mere non-Germans to understand.

Thankfully, they spell it out for us; we just need to learn a little wine-German. Each level has a name, and they ascend in the order in which they're picked, from driest to sweetest: Kabinett, the reserve quality to be kept in the winemaker's "cabinet," is picked first, then comes Spätlese (late harvest, and while you might think late harvest is last, strangely, it's only the second of the passes), followed by Auslese (select harvest grapes), Beerenauslese (select harvest grapes made from dried berries), Trockenbeerenauslese (select harvest grapes made from select dried berries), and Eiswein (made from frozen grapes that are picked last).

Anytime you have spice, meat, and fried greasiness all in the same mouthful, Riesling with a touch of residual sugar is a great compromiser. Sugar softens spice and Riesling has its own savoriness to match the cheese and heat-packed stuffing, along with acid to counter the grease. Spätlese Riesling is usually off-dry and picked a week or so after the first harvest, which gives them a touch more residual sugar in the finished wine. They're full-bodied and searingly rich without being sweet like dessert varieties.

*$ J & H Selbach "Saar" Riesling Spätlese, Mosel*

*$$ Joh. Jos. Prüm Reisling Spätlese, Mosel*

*$$$ Egon Müller Scharzhofberger Riesling Spätlese, Mosel*

# Artichoke Dip
## & OREGON PINOT GRIS

Artichoke dip satisfies our deep yearning for healthy-sounding things that aren't, which may explain its universal popularity. Earthy, nutty, good-for-you artichoke soaked in creams and mayos of varying thickness, with melty, salty Parmesan cheese, the dip is a study in duality that Pinot Gris from the Dundee Hills of Oregon comfortably abides.

Located half an hour south of Portland, and completely contained within the larger and more famous Willamette Valley AVA, the Dundee Hills are a wine region that embraces Pinot in all its forms. The red (Pinot Noir), the pink (Pinot Gris or Pinot Noir), and the white (Pinot Noir for bubbles and Gris for still) are all nurtured with care here, but the most underrated value among them is the Pinot Gris. An Alsatian transplant, this immigrant grape has made a happy landing in the Pacific Northwest. Because wines labeled in the New World as Pinot Gris (instead of Pinot Grigio) have also been produced in a style that has marked acidity and a weighted mouthfeel like its Alsatian relatives, the crispness helps your taste buds reset, so you can forget what you've just done and hit that dip again. The style is also aromatically intense with lime citrus, pea shoots, sea grass, kiwis, and a rich spiciness that amplifies the muted artichoke flavors and fleshes out the mid-palate before the stony, bone-dry finish— all the Portland-style weirdness you need for one sinfully dressed-up vegetable.

*$ King Estate Willamette Valley Pinot Gris*

*$$ Bethel Heights Vineyard Pinot Gris*

# IS PINOT GRIGIO
# THE SAME AS PINOT GRIS?

The simple answer is almost. Pinot Grigio means "gray pinot" in Italian and Pinot Gris means "gray pinot" in French. Genetically, they're the same grape with two different names. But once geography comes into play, the gray ladies diverge. In northeastern Italy, the style of Pinot Grigio is light, dry, citrusy, and crisp. They are often pale and lemony in color. In northeastern France, the Pinot Gris has more body, richness, spiciness, evident acid, and sometimes just a touch of sweetness. They tend to have a golden color when they're young that can progress into a deep ambered hue with age. Producers growing this grape outside of France or Italy can choose to label their wine with either name, depending on the style. So if it's full and ripe, it's labeled Pinot Gris. And if it's light and fresh, it's Pinot Grigio. With the exception of those produced in France, most of these wines are fermented completely dry, meaning there's no sugar left in the bottle, no matter which name appears on the label, unless otherwise noted with indicators like "late harvest."

## Seven-Layer Dip
## & SALTA MALBEC

Mendoza Malbec is everywhere you look. From $5.99 grocery-store bottles to wood-aged versions going for triple digits on menus, these Argentine wines are as easy to find as California Cab and just as wide ranging in quality. But there are plenty of regions in Argentina other than Mendoza making really good Malbec, with identities all their own. One of my favorites is Salta, an appellation that's home to some of the most spectacular vineyards in the world.

At 10,207 feet (3,111 m) above sea level, Salta can also lay claim to the second-highest-elevation vineyard on the planet (there's one higher in Tibet), with less rainfall than the Sahara Desert. The vines are so far up that on most days there simply aren't any clouds to shield the grapes from the beating sun, but Salta's extreme altitude produces temperatures cold enough to counteract the intense solar exposure. It's a bit like the difference between a bad burn and a nice tan.

The area is so remote it wasn't exposed to the phylloxera louse that devoured the vines almost everywhere else in the world, meaning some of its grapes are still on ungrafted rootstock. Some argue this gives the wine a purer flavor and vibrancy; others think it's marketing. I think it doesn't hurt, so why not?

Salta produces only about 1 percent of Argentina's wine, but it's worth the effort to find a bottle, especially if you're making seven-layer dip anytime soon. Refried beans, sour cream, cheddar, guacamole, tomatoes, green onions, and black olives on a tortilla chip confront you with so many textures and flavors, only the high-altitude moxie of a Salta Malbec will do. Salta differs from the Argentine Malbecs you might be used to because its grape skins are so much thicker, making for chewier tannins that have enough might for dishes with texture overload and a thicker, fleshier wine that requires a few more chomps to take down. The juice inside is roaring with acidity, which gives the tomatoes a bit more salsa. And the dark magenta color and concentrated structure produce wafting fruits that are almost as black as the olives.

*$ Bodega Amalaya, Calchaqui Valley* 
*$$ Bodega Colomé "Auténtico" Malbec, Salta*

# CHEESE *and* MEAT PAIRING: THE RULES

### 1

The color of the cured meat is a good indicator of the type of wine that will pair well with it. The lighter the meat, the lighter the wine. The darker the meat, the fuller and deeper-hued the wine.

### 2

Pair wine and cheese by flavor intensity, keeping age in mind: Young cheese tends to be milky and delicate; aged cheese tends to be drier and more savory because the moisture has evaporated, which concentrates flavor. Pros call this *affinage*. Wine is similar to cheese in that young wines tend to be fresher and more lively, with fruit that's very primary and straightforward. Aged wines have more concentration and nuance, and they become more complex and savory with time. So young cheeses require a juicy, fruity, vibrant partner that can often be found in unoaked whites, dry rosés, and reds with big fruit and fresh acidity. Older cheeses do better with bigger-bodied wines that have been barrel aged or have developed oxidative notes.

### 3

The principles of contrasting and congruent pairings apply for cheese and wine: Sometimes you want to go same-same and sometimes opposites attract. And sometimes they both work well, and it's fun to offer each type and let your guests experiment. This also works for texture, where you might pair a rich creamy cheese with buttery, oaky wine or sharp bubbles. They provide two different, equally wonderful sensations.

### 4

Most cured meats and cheeses are high in fat or salt or both. You want to look for styles with higher acidity (try cooler-climate versions of the grapes), because salt softens acidity, and fat needs the acid to refresh the palate. The rule of salty and sweet also applies. Most sweet wines do well with most cheeses for this reason.

### 5

Tannic wines tend to do better with aged cheeses and meats that have fatty crystal deposits because the two bond together to create harmony. If you want to drink red with a younger cheese, pick a lighter, low-tannin version.

### 6

You can always default to the most fundamental rule of them all: What grows together goes together. An easy google search of the best cheese, meat, and wine from a single dream destination will yield plenty of exciting suggestions.

### 7

The sauces and spreads you serve will have a large impact on the wine. Try to pair lighter fruit jams with whites, darker fruit jams with red, and sweet or spicy sauces and honeys with wines that have some residual sugar.

### 8

Fruits, nuts, herbs, spices, jams, marmalades, honeys, balsamics, and pickled veggies are charcuterie mainstays because each brings out the flavors in the other, along with the meat and cheese. Half the joy is in the discovery—so don't get bogged down in strict pairing recommendations. Mixing savory and sweet and tangy and buttery for all the potentially delicious and weird combinations is why we love to eat.

# CHART-CUTERIE

## How to Pair the Classic Meat & Cheese Plate

These tried-and-true combinations will get you started. I've included some very popular cheeses and others that I simply love, and there's plenty of room for creative license once you figure out what works for your own palate.

| Cheese | Type | Meat or Bread | Serve with | Wine |
|---|---|---|---|---|
| Asiago | Firm to semi-soft cow's milk | Peppercorn salami | Toasted crostini, cherries, walnuts | Sangiovese |
| Brie | Soft cow's milk | Mortadella | Water crackers, figs, honey-roasted pecans | Brut Sparkling |
| Camembert | Soft cow's milk | Smoked ham | Strawberries, raspberry jam, almonds | Cabernet Sauvignon |
| Cheddar | Semi-firm cow's milk | Summer sausage | Whole-grain crackers, grapes, almonds | Merlot |
| Chèvre | Soft goat's milk | Salami | Baguette, dried apricot, almonds | Sauvignon Blanc |
| Comté | Semi-firm cow's milk | Cured ham | Wheat crackers, roasted garlic, toasted hazelnut, rosemary | Little to No-Oak Chardonnay |
| Cottage Cheese | Curdled cow's milk | Whole wheat toast | Pineapple, canned peaches, fresh ginger, honey | Chenin Blanc |
| Edam | Semi-firm cow's and goat's milk | Speck | Super seed crackers, apricots, peach | Pinot Gris |
| Epoisses | Soft cow's milk | Crusty baguette | Candied orange rind, honey, rosemary | Marc (eau de vie) |
| Feta | Soft sheep's and goat's milk | Pita chips | Olives, roasted red peppers, pine nuts | Pinot Grigio |
| Fondue | Melted Swiss cheeses (cow's milk) | Soft pretzel | Granny Smith apple, cornichons, fresh endive | Off-Dry Riesling |

| Cheese | Milk | Meat | Accompaniments | Wine |
|---|---|---|---|---|
| **Gorgonzola** | Blue, soft cow's milk | Prosciutto | Nut bread, raisins, cashews | Gewürztraminer |
| **Gouda** | Semi-firm cow's milk | Capocollo | Nutty crackers, grapes, walnuts | Malbec |
| **Gruyère** | Semi-firm cow's milk | Salami | Whole grain bread, figs, pecans | Pinot Noir |
| **Halloumi** | Semi-firm goat's and sheep's milk | Chorizo | Pita, grape tomatoes, black olives | Zinfandel |
| **Manchego** | Firm sheep's milk | Serrano ham | Crusty bread, green olives, spiced almonds | Garnacha |
| **Mascarpone** | Soft cow's milk | Prosciutto | Crostini, cantaloupe, basil, sea salt, pine nuts | Dry Riesling |
| **Mimolette** | Aged firm cow's milk | Terrine | Crusty bread, cherries, blackberries | Mourvedre |
| **Monterey Jack** | Semi-firm cow's milk | Sobrassada | Anchovies, pimentos, caper berries | Tempranillo |
| **Mozzarella** | Soft cow's milk | Prosciutto | Breadsticks, sun-dried tomatoes, and green olives | Greco |
| **Parmigiano Reggiano** | Firm cow's milk | Prosciutto | Sea salt crackers, balsamic sage jam, pistachios | Dry Lambrusco |
| **Pecorino Romano** | Firm sheep's milk | Coppa | Italian bread, pickles, pine nuts | Montepulciano |
| **Provolone** | Semi-firm cow's milk | Brine-cured turkey | Butter crackers, tomato, and basil | Dry rosé |
| **Raclette** | Melted Swiss (cow's milk) | Cured ham | Boiled potatoes, cornichon pickles | Gamay |
| **Ricotta** | Soft cow's, goat's, sheep's, Italian water buffalo's milk | Smoked duck slices | Sea salt crackers, sage, honey, pine nuts | Syrah |
| **Robusto** | Semi-firm aged cow's milk | Speck | Dried fig, dark chocolate, and macadamia nuts | Nebbiolo |
| **Roquefort** | Blue semi-firm sheep's milk | Smoked pork loin | Whole grain crackers, dates, pecans | Ruby Port |
| **Swiss** | Firm cow's milk | Smoked country ham | Rye bread, pickles, spicy mustard | Viognier |

# CHAPTER 11

# Boring but Beautiful

HEALTHY CAN *also* MEAN HAPPY

The ageless angel-creature emerged suddenly behind us in the clearing, dressed in Lycra as white as the sun. "Do you guys know where the yoga class is?" it spoke, as our eyes adjusted to the temporary blindness. All we could offer was a shrug. And as quickly as she had appeared, Christy Turlington was gone.

We caught up with her and about fifty other models, It girls, and beauty influencers as they were preparing their mats in a remote field for a celebrity yoga class being held at the Wölffer Estates, a picture-perfect vineyard in Sagaponack known for its "summer in a bottle" rosé.

The event was organized to promote the opening of an intimidatingly exclusive new private health club in Manhattan called the Well to the Hamptons crowd, and as my friend Michelle and I joined the perfect humans who had gathered among the vines, it became pretty clear that the cool yoga outfits we had meticulously planned were trash.

There's chic and then there's the Well, where the kind of flawless rich people who only exist on Instagram actually exist in real life, in Tuesday-afternoon yoga outfits that cost more than your car. It's the kind of gym that makes Equinox look like a YMCA in Secaucus, with actual medicine doctors on staff, and "meditation domes" and "reflexology lounges"—where if you own Goop products it means you probably don't take wellness seriously enough.

I'd been practicing yoga for a long time and knew all the advanced moves. If my outfit didn't impress, my poses surely would, and I was determined to show them off.

This is a good time to mention that I was born with a severe misalignment in my legs. I was the kid with the Forrest Gump leg braces, and my knees have been prone to dislocation all my life. It's something I have to be aware of, especially in hot environments. And on this particular day, I obviously ignored the warning about the heat wave that would push the "feels like" temperature to 110°F (43°C).

So there we were, in the middle of a vineyard with no sun cover, about to take a hardcore yoga class with the High Priestesses of Wellness. When the world-famous yoga instructor started us off with a meditative practice, the birds were chirping, the vines were rustling, and the sun was beating so hard I was already gushing with sweat. By the time we got up from the mat to actually start moving, I was a human Slip 'N Slide.

When we got to the advanced moves—and everyone knew them better than I did—I tried my best to keep up. The instructor announced that we were going to twist ourselves into an inverted position by pivoting off of our right foot. And as my body turned where I wanted it to go, my foot and shinbone did not. The next thing I knew I was on the ground screaming like a poltergeist. I saw my thighbone go one way and my shinbone go another, and the pain was so pronounced I lost my grip on space-time.

Up until this moment in life, my knee had always popped right back in. And yet here I was unable to push it back, and the searing torture had me verging on blackout. The fifty Insta specimens all turned at once to see who was murdering a racoon, and when they saw what was happening, they began gathering around, unsure of what to do or how to muffle its screams.

"Call an ambulance!"

"What happened?"

"Who is she?"

"What is it?"

I heard another voice, calm and gentle, come behind me and place a hand on my head. He appeared to be some kind of suspiciously handsome healer, making mumbo-jumbo words about my sympathetic nervous system and shock. Whatever they were, they started to relax me. And the pretty people took a deep breath. But then my calf muscle twitched and the pain went supernova and my howls reached an octave I've never achieved again. I can't even imagine how upset Christy Turlington must have been.

Flanked by two gorgeous celebrity trainers, I was lifted up and carted off into the winery where, to almost everyone's horror, I refused to get into the ambulance, determined that with some coaxing, my knee would eventually snap back into place. If you've never dislocated a knee, I can tell you the agony on a scale of one to ten is a twelve, but as soon as you pop it back in, you're basically fine. And that's what happened a few minutes later. All that remained were my stained leggings and pride. Everyone was so damned kind and caring, it only made the humiliation worse.

Of course, being healthy doesn't need to be something people see you doing, or cost thousands of dollars a month—you do it for yourself. In college, I was the walking cliché who gained forty pounds, and it took me years to eventually lose the weight and keep it off. It wasn't rocket science or the work of a miracle nutritionist; it was learning to make simple diet and exercise rules and follow them. I hated working out, so I found ways to exercise that I actually looked forward to, like yoga and running. (Some see those activities as punishment—that's how I feel about spin classes.)

But my biggest secret was finding two ways to make healthy food taste better: wine and hot sauce. Always hot sauce.

# Impossible Burger
## & MARLBOROUGH SAUVIGNON BLANC

The term "veggie burger" covers pretty much anything with a plant-based patty that's served between two pieces of bread. And it's usually all a die-hard meat eater needs to hear before they say "pass." But lately, the category has expanded and improved in so many ways, even the beef people are getting curious. Of the veggie burgers that try to re-create the experience of eating meat, none does so more successfully than the Impossible Burger. And while I still love a patty that embraces its vegetal nature, the Impossible is a modern food miracle that manages to be everything great about fast-food burgers *and* vegetarian food.

It even bleeds and sizzles like real meat when you cook it, due to an iron-packed compound called heme that's everywhere in nature, including plants, but particularly prevalent in animal muscle. It's got meat texture and plant-based umami taste with a hint of coconut oil, a novel hodgepodge of flavor and mouthfeel that would seem to present a pairing challenge. But particularly for those who dress their burgers with the classic lettuce, tomato, pickle, onion, and cheese, the riddle is easily answered with New Zealand Sauvignon Blanc.

Like veggie burgers, New Zealand Sauvignon Blanc is a catchall category of its own. When trying to get a handle on these wines, it helps to understand that there are a number of regions on New Zealand's North and South Islands that produce different styles. The benchmark comes from a region called Marlborough on the northern tip of the South Island, which produces wines that are intensely aromatic, zesty, and often fierce on the palate. Marlborough is the region that put New Zealand Sauvignon Blanc on the map for most

Americans in the late nineties and early aughts, but these days, if you look beyond the biggest players, some wineries are changing the perception of what Sauvignon Blanc from the area can taste like.

The most interesting producers are making something less heady and more food-friendly, which is more difficult than it sounds. Sauvignon Blanc is a grape that is naturally rich in aromatic character with a big herbal impact, and Marlborough's wines have pyrazines to spare. People often associate them with notes of "bell pepper" or "grassiness," but they can also remind you of things like tomatoes, green beans, and jalapeños. Then there are the fruit notes, like grapefruit, lime, mango, pineapple, and gooseberry. The best Marlborough wineries manage to marshal all these disparate elements to achieve cohesion. To go with all of these beautiful smells is an immodest amount of acidity, which butts right up against the sear of the veggie patty, the richness of the bun, and the tart of the pickles.

Marlborough Sauvignon Blancs also have a good amount of what's called mid-palate texture, where you feel a lot happening in the middle of your mouth that can leave behind a tactile residue that's silky or waxy. This coating effect works to balance the Impossible textures and flavors of the burger itself. How much, or how little, of the pairing's success is owed to the mysteries of heme, I'll leave to the scientists.

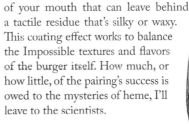

$$ *Dog Point Vineyard Sauvignon Blanc* ❀ ⚘ ✳

$$ *Greywacke Wild Sauvignon Blanc* ❀ ⁑ ✳

## Every Sushi Takeout Place Ever
### & GRÜNER VELTLINER

While I'd prefer $700 omakase prepared by seven-hundred-year-old sushi masters, my constant craving for the stuff—at least three times a week—means I can only afford to order the regular-person kind that comes with the green plastic fence. But I make sure to have a few nice bottles on hand to upgrade the experience. And when the order involves a California roll or two (which is always), Austrian Grüner Veltliner always comes next.

While it's never been as famous as its wine-producing European counterparts, Austria has a winemaking history just as long. Because of its cooler climate, its best wines tend to be white, and the most ubiquitous and revered white grape in Austria is Grüner Veltliner. It can be made in a variety of styles from super light and crisp to full, rich, and dense, but no matter the rendition, the wines are pure and vibrant, with a bursting expression of minerality.

That's a delight for California rolls. The wine's crispness has a way with the flavor and texture of imitation crab and real crab alike. The minerality is nicely complemented by the seaweed and sesame, while its monster acid gets an assist from the vinegared rice. The often lower alcohol content of Grüner Veltliner also ensures the lightness of the sushi doesn't get blown away by too much body.

*$ Weingut Fred Loimer "Lois" Grüner Veltliner, Kamptal* ☀ ✳ 

*$$ Sohm & Kracher "St. Georg" Grüner Veltliner, Leithaberg* ✳

*$$$ Schloss Gobelsburg "Ried Lamm 1 ÖTW" Grüner Veltliner, Kamptal* ✳

## Broccoli and Tofu Stir-Fry
### & LONG ISLAND MERLOT

When you get to the last fifty miles of Long Island, it splits into the North Fork and the South Fork. Both produce wine, but the north has the bulk of the vineyards. The Forks are an unforgiving place to grow grapes, because in the fifteen miles of width that stretches from north to south, there's climate impact from an ocean, a bay, and a sound. The tip of Long Island can have aggressively cold winters and summers with consecutive days as hot as parts of the Sahara. Winemakers also have to contend with mildew, rot, drought, floods, and every disease you can think of. Yet they still do it—because Long Island is a place that makes (gasp) really good wine that's too often spurned for its more glamorous American competition on the West Coast.

Merlot is one of the most planted varieties on Long Island, which is its own AVA. With loamy, well-drained soils, some of these vineyards are producing wines delicious enough to be confused with bottlings from their Old World counterparts in Bordeaux and coastal Tuscany. On my first trip to the North Fork, I visited Macari Vineyards and tasted offerings from super light and dry to ice-wine sweet, and they were all lovely, but I was struck by just how excellent the Merlot was. It had depth and tension that owner Gabriella Macari explained to me was owed to that crazy list of climate factors that can only be found here.

Long Island Merlot has tannin that's as velvety plush as a fluffed-up hotel pillow and an earthy mineral thread that's distinct to the east end of New York. There are few places in California where Merlot is grown with so much unique terroir identity. You get the classic vein of plum that you might expect from Merlot intertwined with semisweet licorice and a crush of acid that the West Coast simply can't match. Your healthy stir-fry is lucky to have such a Strong Island beauty by its side, as there's a good kind of green pepper in the Merlot that helps support the sautéed broccoli (or any other green you want). Tofu is always more textural than it is flavorful, but that sharp bite and savory element to the wine bring out all the soy and sesame you can get from the sauce. The lower alcohol won't Buttafuoco your veggies, and the "taste of the wok" will shine against the tar, earth, and mushrooms these wines can embody. So be sure to serve your next stir-fry with the right Fork.

$ *Palmer Vineyards Merlot, North Fork*

$$ *Macari Vineyards Reserve Merlot, North Fork*

$$$ *Wölffer Estate "Christian's Cuvée" Merlot, South Fork*

## Avocado Toast
## & RUEDA VERDEJO

Rueda is a region in north-central Spain that produces some of the tastiest and most affordable quality white wines that the land of the matador offers today. The main grape grown here is called Verdejo, and when the wines made from them are young, they smell like someone muddled a bunch of grapefruit and lime and threw in some fennel and white peach. The best versions from older vines are capable of age, and they have all the sangria-like fruitiness of an almond dipped in orange-scented candle wax. But that fruity nose is deceiving, because these wines aren't sweet—they're temptingly dry and salivating for your next avocado toast.

If you like Sauvignon Blanc, Rueda Verdejo is just as light in body and high in acidity, and that's precisely the equation you need for creamy mashed avo. The wine's herbal element acts in concert with the bread, which is usually a whole grain. And if you're smart enough to add a sprinkle of sea salt, your bite will detonate with Verdejo's slight salinity and a bolt of acid for every taste bud. If you're being strict on your calorie count, search out the lightweight verdant options that are 12 percent abv or less.

$ *Marqués de Caceres Verdejo Rueda*

$$ *Belondrade Rueda "Belondrade y Lurton"*

## Sweetgreen Harvest Bowl
## & BORDEAUX BLANC

Unless it's something as delicious as a large box of pizza, which is totally worth the fleeting shame of getting eyeballed carrying solo into your building by the Action Jackson in gym clothes on her way out, there's nothing better than a meal that makes you feel morally superior walking home. The Sweetgreen Harvest Bowl does that job admirably, and what it lacks in pizza's craveability, it makes up for in wild rice, a bitter leafy something, a little fruit for sweetness, goat cheese and sweet potatoes for a creamy effect, with a grilled chicken anchor. It's a gastro-combo built on the premise that opposite flavors and textures attract, and there's a white blend out of France that operates much the same way.

A blend of grapes with wildly different styles, white Bordeaux, or, if you want to be chic, "Bordeaux Blanc," is a wine born of competing forces. There are three grape varieties used to make it: Semillon gives the wine a round waxy body and a touch of honey; Sauvignon Blanc works as the antagonist with a grassy, sharp edge; and Muscadelle, which not every château chooses to use, works as a supporting character, adding pronounced floral and grapey aromas. The traction these three pull together as a unit covers every angle and texture that your big bowl of designer nutrition can deliver.

$ *Château Tour de Bonnet, Entre-Deux-Mers*

$$ *Château Carbonnieux Blanc Pessac-Léognan*

$$$ *Château La Mission Haut-Brion Blanc*

# Simple Grilled Chicken
## & JURANÇON SEC

Jurançon is a winegrowing region in southwestern France known for grapes no one has ever heard of. The dry style is mainly made from Gros Manseng with a touch of Petit Manseng and a few other white grapes in tiny quantities, and they range from light and crisp to round and waxy, depending on how ripe the grapes are when picked. Some producers choose to use oak and others use stainless steel, which means the differences in texture and body can be even more pronounced. But what they all share in common is a deep golden color and an exaggerated aromatic profile that hits every mark, from spice and fruit to mineral and floral and back again. They can sometimes smell oxidized, but don't be afraid—these wines were meant for food.

There's so much going on in Jurançon Sec, you won't even notice how plain your grilled chicken is. The voluptuous body has enough extra juice to make up for any lack of flavor in the meat. If you squeeze a little lemon or lime on the chicken, you can magnify the impact of the wine tenfold, bringing out the concentrated quince, apricot, and honeysuckle. The wines are yet another example of styles that can smell sweet when you first nose them, but as long as the word "Sec" is on the label, they are indeed dry, so you're not drinking any residual sugar. If you don't see a Sec, watch out—Jurançon produces a sweet wine from the same grapes that's not so diet friendly.

$ *Domaine Cauhapé Jurançon Sec* ❋☀

$ *Domaine Bru-Baché Jurançon Sec* ❋

# Strawberry Sorbet
## & CAVA ROSADO

Trying to keep it healthy doesn't mean accepting you will never enjoy eating again. I like to choose a sorbet when I'm in the mood for a sweet treat, because you can indulge without all the fat. (Yes, we know there's still sugar, just let us live!) I confess I don't know if it's the flavor or the pretty pink color, but I go with strawberry every time. And if I'm going pink, I'm going all in.

In the Penedès region of northeastern Spain, sparkling wines are made the same way as Champagne, with two separate fermentations, the second of which happens in the bottle you drink it from. Here they call it *método tradicional*. The aging requirements are not as stringent as they are in Champagne but the quality can still be exceptional. Even at the sub-$15 mark, there are some excellent wines I would happily imbibe. Smelling the pink ones is like inhaling a rainbow of electric raspberry, strawberry, and blueberry notes topped with a lemon-lime Care Bear. Take a sip with strawberry sorbet and it's a slushie ride to a land of hearts and unicorns.

In addition to the three main grapes used for regular Brut Cava—Macabeo, Parellada, and Xarel-lo—the *rosados* must consist of at least 25 percent red grapes. One of my favorites is Trepat, which is a little-known red grape indigenous to Spain. I'm as much a sucker for its neon pink hue, which matches the sorbet, as I am its sparkle. The strawberry-meets-strawberry double dare strikes just the right balance between indulgence and simplicity, whether you sip the wine separately or pour it over the top of your sorbet. And because Traditional Method sparklers tend to be low in both alcohol and carbohydrates, you can mostly check your guilt at the door.

$ *Segura Viudas Cava Brut Rosado* ❋

$ *Raventos i Blanc Conca del Riu Anoia Espumoso Rosado "De Nit"* ☀❋

$$ *Gramona Argent Rosé Brut Nature* ☀

WINESPLAINING

BORING BUT BEAUTIFUL

# WHY IS MOST WINE
## NOT VEGAN?

**A**s weird as it sounds, the vast majority of wines are not vegan friendly for anyone adhering to the strictest principles. Yes, wine is made from grapes, but there are two ways to filter wine, and one of them uses animal products. After the initial fermentation, there are small solid bits that make a wine hazy. Some winemakers give the mix enough time to clarify itself, allowing all the solids to slowly fall from suspension and sink to the bottom of the barrel or tank. These wines are bottled unfined or unfiltered (and sometimes say it on the label). But that process is sluggish and imperfect, so most wines are fined or filtered with substances that function like a magnet, moving through the wine and pulling out the unwanted stuff along the way. Winemakers often use a fish gelatin called isinglass, egg whites, or casein, which is a dairy protein, to accomplish this. At one time, ox blood was also used, but it's been outlawed in the United States and Europe since 1997. Once the fining agent has done its job, it's removed along with the gunk it's collected, which is why you don't ever see it listed as an ingredient (in the rare cases when ingredients are actually listed).

There are some wineries that do follow vegan practices, and they use ceramic filters or a type of clay called bentonite, which work the same as the animal options but at about three times the cost. Some wineries, like Querciabella in Tuscany, have even employed vegan principles in their vineyards, including using plant compost instead of animal compost and advocating for the change of biodynamic certification guidelines to allow ceramic substitutes for previously required animal-based methods.

171

# SNACK WELL
## *THE RIGHT STUFF*
## *for the LIGHT STUFF*

Erica Cerulo and Claire Mazur are two women I deeply admire for their ability to balance serious careers with a commitment to health and wellness. Co-founders of the late, great fashion and lifestyle site Of a Kind, co-authors of a wonderful book about female partnerships, *Work Wife*, and co-hosts of the podcast *A Thing or Two*, they're also best friends and business soul mates who define what a healthy work-life relationship can mean for success. We met through my co-writer, Adam, who counts himself lucky to be their friend and biggest fan. As an experiment, we asked Erica and Claire to curate a list of their favorite healthy snacks, and then I paired them with wines—for those Friday afternoon meetings when coconut water simply won't do. Here's what they had to say about their four P.M. pick-me-upgrades.

## THE SNACK:
# BjornQorn

*Claire & Erica:* Remember that moment in 2013 when everybody was like, "Nutritional yeast! It's just like cheese but healthy!"? And you were like, "Says who?!" Well, says BjornQorn, a company that's managed to coat satisfyingly crunchy popcorn with a mysterious mixture of nutritional yeast and salt in an extremely addictive way that tastes genuinely cheesy and nutty and complex.

## THE WINE PICK:
# DOURO VALLEY BRANCO

*Vanessa:* The same grapes that make white Port—Rabigato, Arinto, Viosinho, and Folgasão—are also used to make dry white wines (Branco is Portuguese for "white"), and the best versions, which are labeled "Reserva," can age like fine white Burgundy. They can be cavernously layered and spicy, with white flowers and a sexy, woody spine.

## THE PAIRING:
*Claire & Erica's verdict:* This one feels like cocktail hour at a fancy bar with fancy popcorn—one of those spots that refills your dishes of olives and cashews without even asking. The wine has a richness that the popcorn lacks, which is almost like adding that extra shot of movie-theater butter on top. Olivia Pope made us think that popcorn only went with red wine, but wow, was she wrong.

*$ Duas Quintas Douro Branco* ☀✳❄

*$$ Quanta Terra Grande Reserva Branco*

*$$$ Niepoort "Coche" Douro Branco* ☀✳🥂

## THE SNACK:
# Moon Juice Chile & Lime Dried Mango

*Claire & Erica:* Think of them as adult fruit roll-ups—surprisingly juicy, sweet dried fruit balanced out by tangy lime and spicy chipotle.

## THE WINE PICK:
# CASABLANCA SAUVIGNON BLANC

*Vanessa:* Coastal Chile is where the mineral snap of Old World Sauvignon Blanc meets the bold ripe citrus of the New World. With breezes from the Pacific Ocean cooling the growing season temperatures, cold weather grapes like Sauvignon Blanc thrive in appellations like Casablanca (the other one). Racy lemon-lime and grapefruit arrive up front, followed by a stony, savory caboose.

## THE PAIRING:
*Claire & Erica's verdict:* Picture Romy and Michele on their way to that high school reunion, minus the fight and the whole thing about Post-It Notes. There's heat, there's tang, and there's so much camaraderie. And if you close your eyes, there's maybe a patent-leather dress and a pair of platform shoes.

*$ Prisma Sauvignon Blanc* ✳🥂

*$$ Concha y Toro Terrunyo Sauvignon Blanc* ☀✳

## THE SNACK:
# Seaweed Snacks

*Claire & Erica:* Seaweed snacks serve an express purpose in the snack ecosystem: When you're not actually hungry but need a hit of salty umami, you reach for these paper-thin flavor bombs. Like maki without the protein or the price tag.

## THE WINE PICK:
# CHABLIS

*Vanessa:* Chablis is an appellation that's part of the larger Burgundy region, but it produces a very different kind of Chardonnay. The style here is crisp and fresh, with very little use of oak. This is an area that practically defines minerality, and if you really want to understand that term, Chablis is a great place to start.

## THE PAIRING:

*Claire & Erica's verdict:* Claire did such a good job smelling this wine that she got it on her nose. This combo tastes like a cold beach day—when the season is over but you still head to the shore anyway (and look exceptionally cool in a sweatshirt and cutoffs). We're thinking that since this wine pairs so well with seaweed, it's probably also fantastic with sushi.

$ *Maison Louis Jadot Chablis*

$$ *Domaine Christian Moreau Père & Fils Chablis*

$$$ *Rene et Vincent Dauvissat Chablis*

## THE SNACK:
# Roasted Unsalted Almonds

*Claire & Erica:* Hands-down one of the most versatile and important foods in a healthy-snack arsenal. Eat them plain, bulk up your granola, add some heft to a smoothie, throw 'em on your cheese plate.

## THE WINE PICK:
# FINO SHERRY

*Vanessa:* The lightest and driest style of sherry, Fino's archetypical flavor characteristic is that of dry, unsalted almonds, and thus as congruent as it gets when paired with the real thing. The pale fortified wine is made from a grape called Palomino and aged under a yeast cap called *flor* (for more on this, see page 117) that keeps the wine from oxidizing. Along with the nut threads, they have sea-salt crunch and a bouquet of fresh Mediterranean herbs, fresh dough, and baked citrus.

## THE PAIRING:

*Claire & Erica's verdict:* In 2012, the two of us were on a real sherry kick, and we're remembering why. It's truly a shame that no one served it to us with almonds because we would probably still be beating that sherry drum hard. This is the sophisticated snack pairing you'd consume on your Mallorcan vacation—the sort of thing that would have you wondering why you make things so complicated at home. Next time you invite people over, you'll pull out this combo to impress them with just how easy and chill you are (LOL, you're not).

$ *Emilio Lustau "Solera Reserva" Fino Jarana*

$$ *Emilio Hidalgo "La Panesa Especial" Fino*

## THE SNACK:
# Daily Crave Lentil Chips— Smoked Gouda

*Claire & Erica:* These taste so good that it's hard to believe they're healthy. Imagine a Gouda-flavored Bugle, but unfurled and made out of lentils.

## THE WINE PICK:
# WHITE RIOJA

*Vanessa:* White wine once made up half the production in Rioja but now accounts for just a tiny minority. It's a shame, because while the reds made here are colossal, the whites, mostly made from Viura, are just as momentous. In some cases the whites can age for as long as the reds, if not longer. Honeycombed, nutty, and salty with a savory cheese-rind undercurrent, they're easy to pair with everything from cheese and chips to steak. At the reserva level, expect a little oxidized funk, which is intentional and more than a little indulgent.

## THE PAIRING:
*Claire & Erica's verdict:* Why did we think Rioja was a red?! Something we do know is that both this snack and this wine smell *good*. We probably could have eaten the entire bag of these chips, but we decided to take a pause and actually sip the wine. Our reaction: total fruit-and-cheese plate sensation when combined. The wine tastes more floral—in a good way—when you drink it after the Gouda goodness (the Gouda-ness?). It's like magic.

*$ Bodegas Muga, Muga Blanco* ☼⫶✳

*$$ R. López de Heredia Viña Tondonia White Reserva* ☼✳

*$$$ Remelluri Blanco* ☼🍂❧

## THE SNACK:
# Medjool Dates

*Claire & Erica:* We have long believed that dates would be the next big thing and now feel vindicated that our sneaking (and hoping) suspicions were right.

## THE WINE PICK:
# NEMEA AGIORGITIKO

*Vanessa:* With a winegrowing history dating back to the fifth century BCE, Nemea is one of Greece's most prestigious red-wine appellations. The main grape is called Agiorgitiko, which looks scary to pronounce, but just put a *y* everywhere you see a *g* and you'll be close enough. The styles made from it can be anything from light and sweet all the way up to seriously dry and full bodied. Most value offerings you'll find exported are round and plummy with silky-smooth tannins and a soft, dry finish.

## THE PAIRING:
*Claire & Erica's verdict:* Not sure what it is, but there's something about this wine that just washes a date down. It doesn't exactly diminish the sweetness so much as mellow it—and makes us want to grab another. One of the best dead-simple appetizer ideas we've ever seen (c/o cookbook all-star Julia Turshen) is to stuff dates with mascarpone, and something tells us this dry Grecian red would work equally well with that added dairy element.

*$ Boutari Nemea Peloponnese* ✳

*$ Gai'a Estate Agiorgitiko Nemea* ☼❧✳

# CHAPTER 12

# What to Pair with Greens

TURN YOUR WORKWEEK *into* SALAD DAYS

**M**y mom's mom, whom we call Me-mom, grew up on a tobacco farm in a town called Stop, Kentucky, because it's the last stop before you hit the Tennessee border. There, 30 percent of the population lives below the poverty line, and the other 70 percent uncomfortably close to it. My grandmother really was that girl who walked ten miles to a one-room schoolhouse, and she was the only female in her class to earn a high school diploma. Her family depended on the earth for everything—for sustenance, for economic support, for entertainment, even for health remedies.

Throughout her life, even after she moved to the big city, which in Kentucky counts as Louisville, she maintained her close relationship with the natural world. Growing up, my siblings and I would spend our afternoons with her as she tended to all the verdant things that grew on her property. It was strewn with magical green-leaf plants so tall and dense we could get lost in them, and flowers I learned later were rare variants she had managed to coax into flourishing against the odds. When we got sunburned, she didn't buy gel from the store; she walked out to the garden and cut an aloe leaf open and spread the sticky gunk all over us while we squirmed. She knew practical things about plants that are largely lost on my generation.

On a visit home, she overheard me on the phone giving an interview about biodynamics, which is a holistic approach to farming that's rooted in sustainability, natural inputs, and the lunar calendar. She asked me what I was talking about, and when I explained the method she smiled.

"Is this somethin' ya'll say is new?" she chuckled. "People been farmin' this way for centuries and lawnger. My mother planted everything by the signs. When she wanted to plant stick beans so the vines would run, she did it when the signs was movin' up."

Farming matters to the wine you drink for the same reasons it matters to the produce you eat, and maybe a little more. Making great wine requires a Memom-level connection to the land and plants, because the agricultural philosophy behind any given fermented grape juice directly impacts its quality and style. That's why so many farmers in the trade call themselves "winegrowers" and not winemakers. And the truth is that you can't make good wine from bad grapes. No amount of technological backroom manipulations can make subpar grapes great again. Of course, there are plenty of ways to make crappy wine from good grapes, but those who do don't tend to last long.

# WINEGROWING METHODS

**The four main buckets of cultivation are conventional, sustainable, organic, and biodynamic. You sometimes see them referred to on wine labels or in ads, and the vagaries can be confusing at best. Here's a simple breakdown on the most common farming methods.**

## CONVENTIONAL

Most modern commercial farming falls under this broad category, which involves using the most efficient means possible—namely, chemical fertilizers and herbicides—to promote larger yields and protect against diseases and pests.

It took a long time for producers to realize that all those cost-efficient chemicals were slowly turning their prized soils into dust devoid of nutrients, and producing wine that, despite its consistency, lacked the luster it once had. Happily, as the world has shifted toward environmental responsibility, more and more producers have moved away from heavy chemical use in favor of practices that are more natural and less harmful to the land. And making better wine for it. But there are still many bulk producers using conventional methods to farm their grapes, and it isn't always easy to tell which ones they are.

## SUSTAINABLE

The goal here is for the winegrower and winemaker to create a farming system that's self-sustaining. It's more of a mindset applied to specific issues in a winegrowing region (not everyone shares the same challenges) than an actual set of governing rules. That said, there are organizations that certify sustainable vintners, but it can be expensive to go through the process, and not every winegrower farming sustainably chooses to do it. There is currently no uniform set of laws that govern sustainability, but generally speaking, a few key goals are: leaving land fallow to regenerate, using natural composts and cover crops that assist in returning needed nutrients to the soil, recycling water and limiting drainage and runoff, recycling and reusing materials, using owls and hawks instead of sprays to eliminate pests, and employing renewable-energy power systems.

## ORGANIC

For the most part, organic farming is what all farming was before the birth of synthetic fertilizers and chemicals in the 1910s and 1920s. In the United States, there are strict controls on every step from seedling to bottle, and even how the bottle is stored. The rules apply to any wines produced domestically, as well as imports produced abroad, that want the USDA organic certification on their labels. Because it's a complicated and expensive process, not every winery that farms organically is certified, which can make the waters murky for consumers. The best way to determine if you're buying organically produced wine is to do a little research or find a retail store that's conscientious about what they sell. In my book, practicing is just as important as being certified.

## BIODYNAMIC

On a basic level, biodynamics sees the farm in the context of a wider pattern of lunar and planetary rhythms. Unlike organic viticulture, it is a closed, self-contained system, where the plants, animals, and earth elements all play a specific role. It goes beyond the idea of what you don't use to focus on what you create from your own land to use. The idea sprung from a desire to bridge the gap between the scientific, material, and spiritual worlds. For example, the lunar calendar is used to determine when to do just about everything on the vineyard and in the winery, including planting, pruning, harvesting, fermentation, and bottling. It may sound like hocus-pocus, but if the moon affects ocean tides and stabilizes the Earth's climate and seasons, is it so far-fetched to imagine that it might also affect living things like plants and their growth cycles?

Because biodynamically farmed land isn't immune to diseases and pests, natural methods are employed for different issues. Estuaries of lavender are planted between rows of vines to attract bees, which in turn pollinate other plants that give nutrients to the soil. Fertilizers come from animals indigenous to the area that spend their days grazing and pooping in the vineyards, while their hooves provide the natural machinery for tilling and replenishing the soil.

While it's not legally defined, biodynamic farming is impressively consistent around the world thanks to an independent agency called Demeter that certifies farms and vineyards. Getting the official nod isn't easy, and the actual farming itself is extremely laborious, with no fallbacks to modern technology or synthetic chemicals. When calamity strikes, biodynamic farmers can only rely on their diligent preparation work, and as a result some vintages risk devastating crop losses due to unpredictable weather or disease.

Next time you go through the fuss of preparing a healthy salad with all the expensive, responsibly sourced ingredients, you may want to pair it with a wine worthy of those blue-chip organic microgreens. Farming matters just as much to your fermented grapes as it does to anything else you eat.

## Cobb Salad
### & CROATIAN GRAŠEVINA

That boomerang symbol over the *s* in "Graševina" means you pronounce it "sh." More importantly, it's the most planted grape in Croatia and also the same grape genetically as Welschriesling. And though it has nothing to do with the Riesling you may know, it is a crisp and aromatic wine. The districts most well-known for Graševina have names that are tough to remember, like Hrnjevac, Ilok, Mitrovac, Venje, and Kutjevo, which all come in a range of styles. But the best dry versions have a little bit of oak aging, which shores up their body, making them a Balkan-good alternative to your favorite Chardonnay.

If Cobb salad was a dinner party, it would be a potluck at a senior center. But Graševina is just exciting enough to turn that big-button telephone of a salad into *Magic Mike* night at your local casino. It's got the architecture, from both the grape and the oak, broad enough to handle the boiled eggs, bacon, and chicken, and enough zest for the avocado and romaine, with a funky-freak finish that brings the house down on the blue cheese, Dijon, and red-wine vinaigrette.

*$ Enjingi Graševina, Kutjevo* ☀🍃

## Kale Caesar
### & NAVARRA ROSADO

Kale used to be the throwaway garnish *under* the things you'd actually eat from the salad bar. Now they're tossing it in blenders and charging perfectly rational people $12 to drink it with activated charcoal. At some point you say, OK, if I can't beat this rabbit feed, I might as well join it. And that's how the kale Caesar gets you. All that Parmesan, garlic, and crouton crunch makes for a weird but compelling combination with such bitter greens, leaving a lot of salty and sour without much reprieve. Yet for some reason, we keep coming back.

Spanish *rosado* (or rosé) provides just the right counterbalance. Navarra, a region in northeastern Spain that's a geographical kissing cousin to its more famous neighbor in Rioja, produces a *rosado* that's full of ripe strawberries, match-sparked orange peel, and exotic spices like cardamom. These pink Spaniards have bountiful body and gush with juice, which helps soften all the salt, garlic, and cheese, but also the ideal amount of prickliness to keep that bitter kale on its toes.

*$ Ah-So Rosado (It's in a can!)* ☀🍃

*$ Viña Zorzal Garnacha Rosado* ☀🍃

*$ Bodegas y Viñedos Artazu Garnacha Rosado "Artazuri"* ✳☀🍃

# Wedge Salad
## & GERMAN SILVANER

Although suddenly in vogue after years in the wilderness, the Tony Bennett of salads never really went away—it was just enjoying semiretirement at pretty much every steakhouse and country club in America. But the least nutritious "salad" there is has always been cool, crisp, and delicious. Its iceberg, creamy blue cheese, bacon crumbles, and diced tomatoes will be recognizable to most, but its German wine counterpart of Franken Silvaner (also spelled "Sylvaner") can be more of a head-scratcher to the uninitiated, mostly because of the oddly shaped bottle it traditionally comes in. Called a Bocksbeutel (Box-boy-tuhl), it looks a bit like someone compressed an apple and its stem to make a vessel that's short and circular and flat on the bottom with a small spout for a neck.

The Silvaner that comes inside is typically Badlands dry with a racy steel plate of minerality and earthy juju running through the middle, with firm, full body. Just like a really good trail mix, there's a salty-sweet appeal with this combination—a touch of fruit complements the tomatoes and chilled tiers of iceberg, and a savory streak folds right into the bacon and blue cheese.

$ *Weingut Juliusspital Silvaner Würzburger Ortswein Trocken* ⦙⃰ ✳

$$ *Weingut Rainer Sauer Silvaner Escherndorf Am Lumpen 1655 GG* ⦙⃰

# Greek Salad
## & GREEK MOSCHOFILERO

Growing up in Kentucky, we didn't have Greek salad. Or at least I didn't. Don't get me wrong, we had cucumber and onion salad, but with entirely different accompaniments. All that sharp and salty character with nothing sweet or gravy-like to soften it was a lot for a southerner to take the first time. Now I find that balancing act of feta and olives, oil and vinegar, and cucumbers, tomatoes, and onions so refreshing, I wonder how I ever lived without it.

I feel much the same about Moschofilero ("Moss-ko-feel-er-row"), the light-bodied Pinot Grigio of Greece. It's a budget-friendly porch pounder with citrusy freshness that ranges from perky lemon to sweet orange blossom, with yet more dimensions of melon and pepper. The best Moschofilero comes from Mantinia on the Peloponnese Peninsula of Greece, a cool, high elevation region where the grape has been planted since the time of Plato. And I can only imagine he was drinking it when he wrote the Allegory of the Cave. This is one of my favorite examples of the philosophy you now know, that what grows together goes together. It almost feels like those ancient Greeks must have made the salad to go with the wine—then screamed "Eureka!," as they were wont to do.

$ *Domaine Skouras Moscofilero, Arcadia* ⦙⃰

$ *Troupis Winery "Hoof & Lur" Moschofilero, Arcadia* ☼❦ ⦙⃰

## Spinach Salad
### & ITALIAN FREISA

Spinach is a green so strong that the Olympic committee has considered banning one of its chemical components (ecdysterone) because of its Popeye-style steroid effect on performance. Its flavor is equally strong, which is why so many good spinach salads rely on the sweetness of cranberries or strawberries to round them out.

For a wine that does the trick with just as much aplomb, look to the subregion of Langhe in the larger northern Italian region of Piedmont, known for its iconic Barolo and Barbaresco. Freisa offers fresh, easy-drinking wines that are a value alternative to just about everything else grown in these fabled hills. The grape itself can be polarizing, because the styles it makes range so widely, from slightly sparkling and sticky sweet to big, bitterly tannic, and dry. To find the still style that leans toward dry, look for Langhe Freisa. It has a piercing, red-fruit edge that channels strawberries, cranberries, raspberries, and cherries. It's also laced with a ring of tannins that can present as green olive, sage, and bitter green almond. Both the wine and the salad keep you constantly guessing whether the flavors are sweet or sour or bitter or all three, so you know it's a proper Italian love affair.

$ *Francesco Boschis Langhe Freisa Bosco delle Cicale* ☀

$ *G.B. Burlotto Langhe Freisa* ☀✳

$$ *Giuseppe Rinaldi Langhe Freisa* ☀✳

## Tuna Niçoise
### & ITALIAN PINOT GRIGIO

Pinot Grigio is to Italy what BBQ is to the south. It's everywhere, and every region has its own local spin. Unfortunately, much of what you find in the market today tastes like flavored water, but it doesn't mean you should dismiss the category wholesale. After it was introduced to the U.S. in the 1970s, Pinot Grigio became one of our top imports in less than twenty years, mostly because it filled a void in a white-wine world dominated at the time by buttery, overly oaked styles of Chardonnay. But all the success bred imitation, and pretty soon everyone wanted skin in the PG game, setting off a downward slide into bulk mediocrity and discount racks.

Though you'll have to navigate a minefield of bland duds at the inexpensive end of the spectrum, there are happily still many refined and refreshing bottlings out there for less than $25. You'll find most of them in Northeast Italy, where regions like Friuli-Venezia-Giula and Alto-Adige produce Pinot Grigio with love—the kind packed with lemon citrus, raw nuts, and sea-salt salinity. A good Niçoise has thinly sliced tuna that's barely seared at the edges and left mostly rare, and that's where this French classique meets the Italian nuovo. Despite its delicacy, great Pinot Grigio has the saltiness to manage the cooked eggs, but its herbal, verbena-like complexity also lends a freshness bright enough to slice through sensitive tuna like a laser.

$ *Attems Pinot Grigio Friuli, Friuli-Venezia Giulia* ✳

$ *Livio Felluga Pinot Grigio Colli Orientali del Friuli, Friuli-Venezia Giulia* ⁝⁝✳

$$ *Elena Walch Pinot Grigio, Alto-Adige* ⁝⁝

WHAT TO PAIR WITH GREENS

# YOU'RE HOLDING IT WRONG

If your glass has a stem, that's where you should hold it—keep those paws off the bulb! It helps keep the temperature of the wine where you want it, without your hands warming it up, and the glass doesn't get gross and grimy from your fingerprints. I love wine in a simple tumbler, but I save the stemless glassware for casual nights and casual wines. If the winemaker was serious about producing a high-quality wine and you were serious about spending the money to buy and maybe even age it, do the wine a service and give it a proper stem.

# WHAT EXACTLY IS "NATURAL" WINE, ANYWAY?

I take a deep breath every time someone asks me this question, because right now, there is no clear definition. And as the contentious term burrows its way further into public consciousness, there's a growing need to resolve its meaning and introduce some universal standards. In the meantime, in the simplest sense, the idea is that nothing is added or taken away, both during the grape-growing process and while the wine is being produced at the winery. In the vineyard, the non-interventionist approach typically entails grapes that are either organically or biodynamically farmed without irrigation and handpicked without machinery, resulting in smaller but more flavorful harvests. In the winery, it means no added sugars, foreign yeasts, or bacteria, no additives for color, mouthfeel, or flavor, no fining, filtration, or heavy manipulation, and (usually) no added sulfites.

Wines made in this method tend to have a very unique profile from year to year, because each vintage is intended to be an unadulterated expression of that particular harvest. Only with the least amount of human intervention, the thinking goes, can the truest flavor of terroir find its way into a bottle. Beyond a desire to farm and make wine responsibly, the movement is also a response to the homogenization of winemaking over the past few decades—the concern that too many wines taste the same.

But the topic is more controversial than you might imagine among wine people, with entrenched camps on both sides of the debate. True believers often cite the environmental benefits, the more interesting grapes, and the forgotten wine techniques that make for fascinating taste profiles unlike anything the traditional side can produce. And there's ample evidence to support those claims in producers like Joly in the Loire and Occhipinti in Sicily, which make some of the world's most delicious wines that also happen to be natural. But traditionalists point to the very real problem of volatility in natural wines, which are not stabilized, resulting not only in large variation in quality from bottle to bottle, but the fact that most can't age for more than a few years before they need to be consumed or thrown away.

Natural wine pushes us to be aware of how important it is to get rid of the garbage that mass production has introduced to the winemaking process. And some are delightful and wildly singular—there are plenty of natural wine producers I salivate over. But it can also be maddening when you buy a bottle, get it home, and realize volatile acidity or secondary fermentation has made the wine unpleasant, which happens more often than the style's proponents would like to admit. And because natural wines don't receive any treatments to enhance their flavor and texture, they are often much lighter and brighter—and a little funkier—than expected.

The word "natural" itself might be the biggest problem. As Ted Lemon, one of the most influential winemakers in California, puts it, "There's nothing natural about winemaking. You can't go find a glass of Chablis in the wild." To a certain extent, wine cannot exist without some human manipulation. You can't just smush some grapes and drop them in a hollowed-out tree trunk and expect them to turn into wine worth drinking. And when you get dogmatic about what method is natural and what method isn't, with no room for interpretation, you miss the bigger picture: all most of us really want is delicious wine that's free of artificial crap, responsibly farmed and produced without harmful chemicals, and as good for the earth as possible.

And contrary to what some of you might think, just because a wine is natural doesn't mean it won't also give you a hangover. Me—mom always said, "You wanna play, you gotta pay." Lest we all forget, alcohol is a poison—a delicious, tantalizing, deliberately intoxicating poison. If you overdo it, expect to pay the piper the next morning. No amount of natural can change that fact. Of course, the less "bad" additives in your wine (and the lower the alcohol content), the less severe the impact will be.

That said, the mere mention of the word "sulfites" tends to send certain people into a tizzy these days. And while many natural winemakers use sulfites sparingly, if at all, it's not something anyone should be getting too hung up on. The term refers to sulfur dioxide ($SO_2$), a preservative that is widely used in winemaking and has been for centuries. It has antioxidant and antibacterial properties that make it essential to maintaining a wine's freshness over an extended period of time, allowing it to age without spoiling. In this country, if wine contains more than ten parts per million of sulfites, the law dictates that the warning "Contains Sulfites" be included on the label. That's to pro-

tect the less than 1 percent of the population who actually have a severe sensitivity to sulfites. Are you OK with most condiments you get from the grocery store? Do you love a little dried fruit? If so, you're fine. These items contain more sulfites than the average bottle of wine. The truth about sulfites is that they are a natural by-product of winemaking, so there's really no such thing as a truly sulfite-free wine.

In one sense, natural wine is no different from any other category of wine: Some are good, some are less than good. When you do decide to give these wines a go—and you should—just keep an open mind. They are probably unlike any wine you've ever tasted. Some are going to be a little cloudy, others might taste strange at first and then grow on you, but you will find a bottle you love.

# CHAPTER 13

# The Standard Bearers

THEY'RE PAIRING CLASSICS *for a* REASON,
*but* THEY LOVE A GOOD TWIST

**T**he queen of Spain was two tables to our left. A senator was in the seat behind us. When the waiter came by to offer us complimentary oysters with pink Champagne, Colin, my best friend since second grade, sat across from me shaking his head. "What is this world you live in now?" he asked. I smiled and shrugged. It was just an average Tuesday at the Four Seasons, where my work in wine had turned me into a regular.

I still remember the first time I walked up those grand stairs into the famous Philip Johnson dining room and took it all in. The elegance of the women in their Louboutins, the pickled Wall Streeters in their bespoke suits, the unmistakable scent of global domination and Hermès. The term "power lunch" was specifically coined for this place, and I was enamored with the New York spectacle of it all.

Julian and Alex were the owners, and they welcomed everyone like friends. After I had put some time in and became a familiar face, they introduced me to all the daily fixtures at the bar, like the gold trader Chris, who had a corner seat and a Bloody Mary waiting for him every day at noon. Or Charles and his crew of spit shined private equity misfits, who would sidle up after work. Or, if you were lucky, Charlotte, a powerhouse of a woman whose occupation I never fully understood, who was always in the mood for smack talk with her best pal, Daniel, the general manager, after her first Negroni (all I needed to know was that when she spoke, everyone shut up). They were part of a revolving carousel of *Bonfire of the Vanities* characters who always seemed to be there with their Manhattans and martinis, hashing it out. Everything they ate and drank went to their house accounts, because no one should ever have to deal with something as vulgar as a check.

Right up until the end in 2016, when it closed, the Four Seasons felt like a parallel universe, where if you could afford it—or had the kind of expense account I eventually did—you could live inside a Slim Aarons photograph (or at least an Annie Leibovitz spread) for a few courses at lunch or dinner. Over its sixty-year run, its two dining rooms hosted everyone from Nixon and the Clintons to Jackie O and Princess Di, and on any given day, you could find Martha Stewart a table over from Anna Wintour or Warren Buffet. Before Marilyn sang "Happy Birthday" to JFK, they ate dinner at the Four Seasons. As Henry Kissinger eulogized, "The Four Seasons is an institution, not a restaurant. Its layout facilitates privacy. Its ground rules permit table-hopping. Its code of conduct imposes restraint. Half the guests come to be in familiar circumstances. The rest come to observe the regulars, who enjoy the clubby atmosphere and their function as an exhibit."

Among the restaurant's many milestone firsts, the most notable was a menu that actually changed with the seasons. James Beard, the chef whose name now doubles as the Pulitzer Prize of the food world, was a principal contributor to the development of that once groundbreaking concept. He even paired wines for each season, and he was the first to include American wines on that list.

In the end, when they auctioned off the Four Seasons' iconic mid-century contents, demand was so strong that it drove the bidding well north of $4 million, beating the highest pre-auction estimate by about $3 million. (To give you an idea of the nostalgia-fueled frenzy, four ashtrays went for $12,500.) Today, items of serviceware and furniture, including everything from champagne glasses to bread trays, are part of the permanent collection at the Museum of Modern Art.

After they lost their lease, Julian and Alex briefly reopened the Four Seasons in another space a few blocks away, but it closed in less than a year. And I'm still heartbroken for both of them. But this story has a happy ending, because if there was anyone up to the challenge of taking over the most historically significant dining space in America, it was the guys behind Major Food Group. The space—now called the Grill—couldn't have hoped for a better second act.

As it happens, the triumvirate that makes up MFG, chefs Mario Carbone and Rich Torrisi and their partner Jeff Zalaznick, got their start just a few blocks from my apartment in NoLita. Before they presided over their global restaurant juggernaut, which now stretches from Israel to Hong Kong, they had a tiny sandwich shop called Torrisi, where I had a front-row seat as the insanely good, semi-secret, set-menu dinners they hosted at night put them on the map.

So when it was announced that they would be taking over the storied Seagram Building space, it seemed meant to be—at least for me. And on the day the Grill received its first *New York Times* review, I got a cryptic email: "Ten PM celebration. Dress your best." I grabbed my roommate and bestie, Merri, and rushed uptown, and when we arrived, a train of waiters were bringing out massive 3-liter bottles of Champagne and magnums of 1942 tequila, and the place was overflowing with food. Then the ice luges got wheeled out, and the crowd of four hundred roared. By the end, people were dancing on tables. I've always imagined that this was the kind of party they're always talking about when they say they don't throw parties like they used to anymore.

At the Grill, the great and the good still get to take their victory laps in the same place they've been doing it since 1959. Under its new stewards, companies are still merged, divisions spun off, book deals signed, ideas financed, titans trampled, and third and fourth acts written. But now the food's better.

Just like America's greatest dining room, some things are so unimpeachably classic you can't mess them up, no matter how many incarnations you put them through. And the same goes for food and wine. These combinations are the cornerstones of wine pairing, and they've stood the test of time and geography because they're indisputably perfect—and instantly understood. (And not by coincidence, most also happen to be aphrodisiacs.) But they're powerful enough to accommodate almost any new twist you can cook up for them, as long as you stick to the principles that make them so great as pairings to begin with. So in the spirit of pumping fresh blood into old and revered institutions, I'm offering my own variations on the standards, with wines that do just as much for their respective dishes as the traditional standbys.

# Caviar
## & BLANC DE NOIRS CHAMPAGNE

Champagne is the tried-and-true method for washing down caviar, known for its ability to heighten the saline notes without overwhelming the dainty salt-cured roe. Some wines can leave an unpleasant tinny metallic aftertaste when consumed in combination with this delicacy, but Champagne successfully steps over this land mine, refreshing the palate between decadent bites (or bumps if you're bougie).

I'm not asking you to go too far off the beaten path, but I promise you won't regret a scenic detour into the niche category of Blanc de Noirs. The three main grapes of Champagne are Chardonnay, Pinot Noir, and Pinot Meunier. Both of the Pinots are black grapes. Most Champagnes are a blend of at least two of them, if not all three. On the rare occasions that only the black grapes are used, the label will say Blanc de Noirs, which means "white wine from black grapes."

If that's confusing, think about your Champagne. Ever seen a red sparkling Champagne? (The answer is no.) All Champagne is either white or pink. To make white wine from black grapes, producers employ a specific technique when the grapes come into the winery at harvest to be crushed. The grape juice is immediately separated from the skins before it can absorb any color—the juice inside is clear regardless of the skin's pigment, so if you take the two apart before they can mingle, the hue stays colorless. It is a very rare and highly coveted style, often described as having a distinct earthy quality and muscular power.

Of all the Champagne houses, Krug is one of the most famously paired with caviar because of its signature style, which is richer and more full-bodied than most Champagnes thanks to the oak they use during fermentation. But I dream about taking that creamy charisma one step further with their Clos d'Ambonnay Blanc de Noirs, one of the most revered in the category, which I imagine would be the ultimate partner for caviar, given the earthy effect of 100 percent Pinot Noir. It starts at around $2,000 a bottle, when you can find it. I'll bring the caviar.

In the meantime, there are plenty of other worthy Blanc de Noir options out there, and if you're like me and can't afford most Champagnes, look for bottles from the Aube, which is Champagne's southernmost subregion. It's known for high-quality Pinot Champagnes at a gentler price.

*$ Fleury Blanc de Noirs Brut MV, Aube (375ml)* ☀️🎐🥬

*$$ Eric Rodez Grand Cru Blanc de Noirs Champagne MV* 🌼☀️🎐

*$$$ Krug Clos d'Ambonnay Blanc de Noirs Brut* 🌼🍾☀️

# Steak au Poivre
## & POMEROL

The main river that feeds into Bordeaux from the Atlantic is called the Gironde, which wishbones into two smaller rivers called the Dordogne and the Garonne. The land on the southwest side of the Gironde is called the Left Bank, which is primarily known for Cabernet Sauvignon–based wines, and the northeast side is the Right Bank, known for Merlot and Cabernet Franc. While Cabernet Sauvignon and steak go together like peas and carrots, consider going for a Merlot, particularly one that comes from the most ravishing and unforgettable Right Bank Bordeaux appellation, called Pomerol.

Pomerol produces Merlot that smells like so many things at once it can leave you guessing for days. Start with black plum, black cherry, boysenberry, espresso beans, bay leaf, raspberry, blackberry, blueberry, fig, violet, iris, tobacco leaf, bay leaf, mint, red and black licorice, star anise, mushroom, truffle, forest floor, bitter chocolate, coffee, allspice, vanilla bean, and tart nectarines, to name a few. Depending on the producer, Pomerol ranges from medium-bodied and supple to big-bodied and bold, but every last one of its iterations is a cuddle puddle of lust for steak au poivre.

Filet mignon pan-seared to a state of peppery, crusty grace, sauced with butter, heavy cream, cognac, Dijon mustard, and more black peppercorns: Together with Pomerol, this, my friends, is the Immaculate Conception of wine pairings, the Orgasmatron of meat and grapes, the "You complete me" of pampered mouth holes. That first divine bite, so luxuriously potent and pungent, is the moment the glass slipper slides onto Cinderella's foot. It's all the reasons you bought this book—and almost certainly underpaid for it.

$ *Château Mazeyres "Le Seuil de Mazeyres" Pomerol* ☀☀🕊🌿

$$ *Château Bourgneuf, Pomerol* 🌿☀

$$$ *Château Hosanna, Pomerol* 🌿 ⚱ ☀

# MERLOT ON THE SIDELINES

"If anyone orders Merlot, I'm leaving," goes the famous Paul Giamatti line from *Sideways*. "I am not drinking any fucking Merlot!" And while the movie may have been great for Pinot Noir and the domestic wine industry as a whole, that one little soundbite was so devastating for the Merlot market in America, they gave it a name: "the *Sideways* effect." The truth is that some of the greatest wines in the world, including the 1961 Cheval Blanc Giamatti sheds tears over at the end of the film, are either largely or entirely made of Merlot grapes. Here are some of the greatest:

1. CHÂTEAU PETRUS, Pomerol in *Bordeaux, France*

2. CHÂTEAU LE PIN, Pomerol in *Bordeaux, France*

3. CHÂTEAU BÉLAIR-MONANGE, St. Émilion in *Bordeaux, France*

4. CHÂTEAU PAVIE, St. Émilion in *Bordeaux, France*

5. MASSETO by Ornellaia, *Tuscany, Italy*

6. REDIGAFFI by Tua Rita, *Tuscany, Italy*

7. MESSORIO by Le Macchiole, *Tuscany, Italy*

8. GALATRONA by Fattoria Petrolo, *Tuscany, Italy*

9. THREE PALMS by Duckhorn, *Napa Valley, California*

10. PROPRIETARY RED BLEND by Amuse Bouche, *Napa Valley, California*

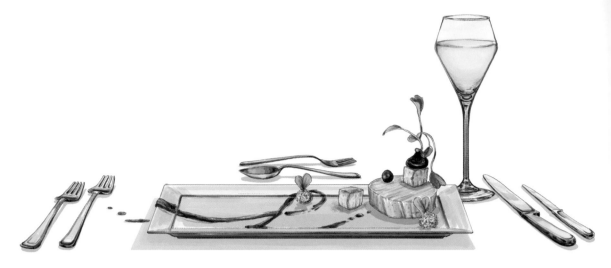

## Foie Gras
### & BARSAC

The French sweet wine Sauternes is the traditional choice for everyone's favorite gout-inducing, force-fed duck liver, but its little brother Barsac is equally suited to the task, and he doesn't get nearly enough attention in the back seat. This is a dish so depraved it needs a wine that's just as comfortable with hedonism. Barsac is geographically encapsulated within Sauternes, so they're from the same family, and producers have the option to put either name on their labels. But while Sauternes has much more name recognition and commands higher prices, Barsac's proud producers choose to use Barsac on their labels because they believe their wines are that much more unique and special.

They're made from Semillon and Sauvignon Blanc grapes, and like Sauternes, they get their intense sweetness from what's called noble rot. That is, the grapes actually rot while they are still on the vine but in a way that raisinates them without introducing any bad flavors. In a process fit for Caligula, when the grapes are harvested they are gently pressed to remove the highly concentrated sugar juice. As weird as it sounds, it is actually devastating to producers in the area if the rot never forms, because they can't produce their debased delights without it.

When these wines are young, they're a deep golden color, and as they age, they turn a deeper, darker amber. I've tried old bottles closer to dark brown and black that approached divinity. The younger ones taste like butterscotch, honeysuckle, mango, and ginger, and the older they get, the more they taste like those things—while also taking on the character of caramel, honey, nuts, and dark reductions of citrus. And yes, all of those flavors sound like they'd be downright tantric with foie gras, which is something the sybaritic Gauls figured out a long time ago. Barsac and Sauternes are both intensely sweet no matter their age, but because foie usually comes early in a meal, Barsac's slightly lighter and drier profile gives it the edge, mostly so your buds don't get blown out before the next course.

Barsacs are a great deal compared with most Sauternes, and they're usually sold in half bottles, so you don't have to make a full commitment to give one a go.

*$$ Château Coutet Barsac* ☀
*$$$ Château Climens Barsac* ❈☀

## Oysters
### & MUSCADET

"If it smells like nothing and tastes like nothing," a wine teacher once told me, "it must be Muscadet." While I find that statement to be woefully inaccurate, I understand the sentiment. Muscadet is an appellation on the western coast of the Loire Valley, and the grape that it comes from is called Melon de Bourgogne. Together they produce a style that's light and easy, but cheaply made Muscadet can and will taste like weakly flavored water. The best ones, however, taste like biting down on a candy gusher with a citrus core and sea-salty finish. They are low in alcohol, so they're your handsome lifeguard on a bright summer day, but also just about anywhere and anytime fresh oysters are being shucked. Still, when it comes to the bivalve mollusk of the angels, some will argue that only a chilled Chablis or top-quality northern Italian Pinot Grigio will do. What can I say, I like the underdog.

Look for Muscadets labeled *sur lie*, which is French for "on the dead yeast." During production, after the yeast eats all the sugar and dies, it turns into lees, which are spongy glycerol-like orbs to the touch. If a winemaker doesn't immediately "rack them off," which is a process that involves moving wine into different barrels or tanks to clear sediment, and instead allows the lees to continue aging for a while with the wine, some of that silky glycerol texture and complexity gets passed on to the end product. They eventually remove them, but their impact remains. So yes, you want a little dead yeast in your Muscadet.

$ *Domaine de la Pépière Muscadet Sèvre-et-Maine Sur Lie "La Pépie"* ✳ ☀ ☼ ☀

$ *Domaine de l'Ecu Muscadet Sèvre-et-Maine Sur Lie "Granite"* ☼ ☀ ☀

# Grilled Salmon
## & WILLAMETTE VALLEY PINOT NOIR

Pinot is the perennial partner for salmon, a meaty, oily fish that's better served by the texture of a red than a white, but without all the tannins that usually come with dark grapes (it's still fish). The rules that say red is for meat and white is for fish have a simple logic, but they're far from absolute. Pinot Noir is the best example of that farce, and wine people have long known this red is king when it comes to omega-packed salmon. So next time someone tells you not to drink red with fish, just smile and take a bigger sip.

You'll be even happier if you explore Pinot beyond the most obvious region of Burgundy. Willamette Valley in Oregon is one of the few places outside Burgundy where great Pinot is being made. On the Pacific side, the Pinot's body and alcohol are bigger, the Dr. Pepper cherry notes more explosive, and the tannins and earthiness more muted. All of which make this particular Pinot the most delicious thing you can do for a classically prepared grilled salmon fillet.

The valley and its sub-AVAs, which include the Chehalem Mountains, Dundee Hills, Yamhill-Carlton, Ribbon Ridge, and McMinnville, have developed their own cult followings. And while the wines aren't exactly cheap, they're nothing close to what you'll pay for Burgundy and can be at the same level of quality as some of the Burg's Premier Crus. In fact, some Burgundy producers have even decamped to Oregon, hoping to produce wines as tasty as France's at a lower cost.

$ *Montinore Estate Red Cap Pinot Noir Willamette Valley* ☼

$$ *The Eyrie Vineyards Pinot Noir Willamette Valley* ☀☼☀ ☀☼

$$$ *Bergström Vineyard Pinot Noir Dundee Hills* ☼☀ ☀ ☀

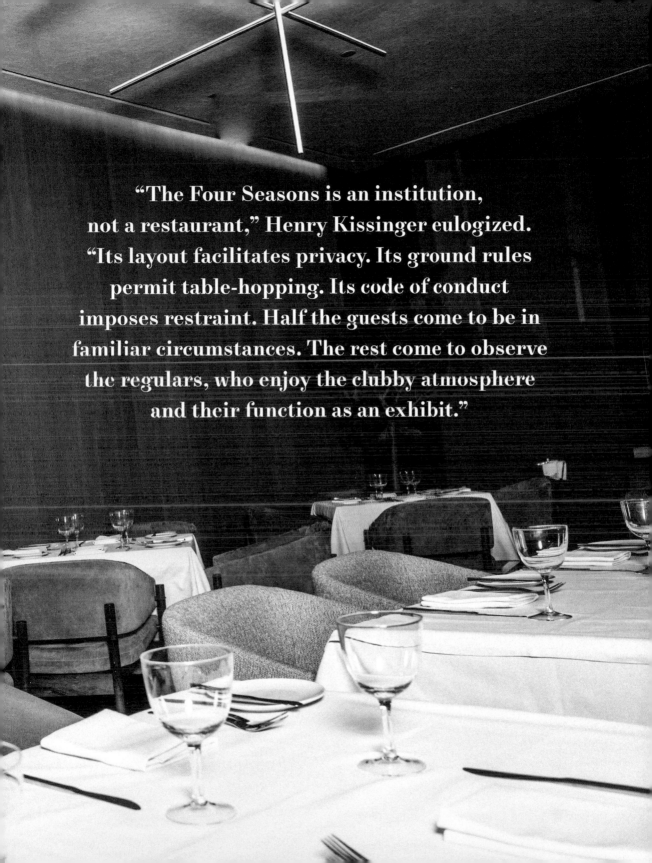

"The Four Seasons is an institution, not a restaurant," Henry Kissinger eulogized. "Its layout facilitates privacy. Its ground rules permit table-hopping. Its code of conduct imposes restraint. Half the guests come to be in familiar circumstances. The rest come to observe the regulars, who enjoy the clubby atmosphere and their function as an exhibit."

# Goat Cheese
## & POUILLY-FUMÉ

The wines of Pouilly-Fumé get their name because they're cultivated in an area of the Loire Valley that makes dry Sauvignon Blanc grown in volcanic ash. Pouilly is the village and *fumé* is the French word for "smoked," which makes sense, given the soil's tendency to impart the wine with a distinctly flinty, smoky character, like the damp alkaline odor that comes off wet stones. It's similar to that, but delicious.

The standard pairing for goat cheese is Sancerre, which is also 100 percent Sauvignon Blanc and grown right next door to Pouilly-Fumé, in the very same region of France that also produces the vast majority of its goat cheese. (As you know by now, it grows so it goes.) And Sancerre's acid and racy citrus are a natural choice for such a tangy, fatty cheese. But unlike Pouilly-Fumé, as Sancerre's popularity has grown over the last eighty years, it has expanded the size of its appellation fourfold to increase production, diluting its very definition in the process. It's a little bit like if Ralph Lauren started selling Polo Sport under the Purple Label to keep up with demand. Or if New York City annexed Connecticut. You can call it Ralph Lauren Purple Label New York City, but we all know it's just Polo Sport New Haven. Expanding the geographical area of an appellation has an impact on its style and overall quality, and that's why little, consistent Pouilly-Fumé, just a hair's breadth from Sancerre with all the same citrus and even more gun-flinty appeal, is the goat-cheese pairing to beat.

Just don't confuse it with Pouilly-Fuisse, which is a Chardonnay grown in southern Burgundy—and very tasty— just very different from what you and your goat cheese are looking for.

$ *Francis Blanchet "Cuvée Silice" Pouilly-Fumé*

$$ *Ladoucette Pouilly-Fumé*

$$$ *Didier Dagueneau "Silex" Blanc Fumé de Pouilly*

# White Truffle Pasta
## & BARBARESCO

Barolo, the Tony Soprano of Italian wine, always gets the nod for white truffles and fresh pasta because it actually embodies the aromas of truffles in a glass. Like Barolo, Barbaresco is made from 100 percent Nebbiolo, which is a grape revered for its aggressive tannin, and both wines are lauded for their long-term ability to age. The "King and Queen of Italian Wine" are actually made ten miles from each other in the same region of Piedmont in the north. But while Barolos have more power, Barbarescos have more finesse. And when it comes to pungent white truffles, it's that soft-shoe Barbaresco panache that makes those decadent little fungi dance like no one's watching. The Nebbiolo works with the truffle to animate the most ravishing qualities of both—that deep-earth, floral, gamey, nutty, mushroomy musk that could bring down empires.

With so much refined tannin, Barbaresco is rigid bordering on harsh as a youth and remains leathery and firm even with age. If your bottle is young, which for these wines means less than twenty years old, open it at breakfast and serve it with dinner. If it's from a truly great vintage, you might even want to open it the night before. In theory, the older it is, the less time it needs to breathe, but these are finicky wines that never follow the rules.

$$ *Pio Cesare Barbaresco*
$$$ *GAJA Barbaresco*

# Dark Chocolate Soufflé
## & BAROLO CHINATO

The soft-baked egg poof requires time and skill, and it's a high-stakes game of culinary Operation from the moment it rises to the instant it collapses under your fork. That lopsided balloon shape is what gave it its name, from the French verb "to inflate." And though the world has many soufflés, both savory and sweet, in the latter category the self-respecting gastronome goes for dark chocolate every time.

For all its enduring appeal, finding something to drink with this Grande Dame of dessert isn't so obvious, beyond the traditional fallbacks like Port. As you know by now, chocolate is the wine pairer's enemy, and the darker it is, the harder it is to pair. Because of all the tannic bitterness, sugar, and fat, most wines end up tasting too bitter, too sweet, or too sharp in the merger, leaving one or more of the cocoa's components out in the cold. While most foodies immediately reach for Vintage Port, a fortified ruby red dessert wine, there's a little-known sleeper of a sweet red called Barolo Chinato from northern Italy that was born for this Mission: Impossible. What starts out as a Barolo made from Nebbiolo grapes becomes something entirely different in Chinato with the addition of a neutral grape spirit that's then infused with herbs and spices like orange peel, clove, cardamom, rhubarb root, cinnamon, coriander, mint, and vanilla. Also present is an essential ingredient called china (*kee-na*), which is made from the quinine bark of the South American *Cinchona officinalis* tree, and most recognizable as the key flavor component in tonic water. What you get is a sweet and bitter wine that's just a little bit medicinal—in the most enticing way—like a vermouth but stranger and more complex. It's one of the few wines with the right amount of body, acid, tannin, sweetness, and baking spice to agreeably French kiss a bittersweet chocolate soufflé.

*$$ Giulio Cocchi Barolo Chinato*
*$$$ Pio Cesare Barolo Chinato* ⁂ ✳

# *Pretty Delicious*
# INSTAGRAM-
# READY
# PAIRINGS

When I personally succumbed to Instagram, it didn't take long to realize that the wine professionals I followed all had the same boring feeds. Mostly bottle shots of coveted producers the average person has never heard of, posted for bragging rights. So I asked my childhood friend Michelle, photographer extraordinaire, whose beautiful work is on display in these pages, if she'd lend me her talents. We were going to shoot wine and make it interesting.

"So we're just going to shoot and drink wine?" she asked. "Just tell me when."

We didn't know then how far that idea would take us, but we've since held multiple gallery showings, started a creative agency, and had opportunities to travel around the world on wine adventures.

One thing we learned: When you take precious time out of your life to wait in some stupid line to purchase the picture-perfect, Instagrammable foodstuff of the moment, you'd better be sure the wine you choose to go with it lives up to the investment. In terms of pure palate pleasure and color coordination, these combos are what I like to call "pretty delicious."

## Dominique Ansel Cronuts
### & ANDERSON VALLEY SPARKLER

First, good luck. Since the moment the cronut was introduced in 2013, there have been lines out the door of SoHo's Dominique Ansel Bakery all day, every day, even after they instituted a preorder system that has more lead time and complex rules than a housing lottery—at least before the Rona. The cronut is basically a French croissant that was jealous of how happy American donuts make people, with their cute little holes and frosting and pretty toppings. So it married a donut and had a baby, which came out shaped like a donut, fried and filled with cream, with its father's crunchy, flaky, layered dough.

There's no other way to celebrate eating one than with bubbles. This is as close to a congruent pairing as it gets, and you won't know where the flaked layers begin and the autolytic flavors of the wine end. The Northern California climate of the Anderson Valley produces some of the best bubbles you can find in the New World, and they smell a little bit like skipping through an apple orchard in the fall with some butter and jam toast. There are sparklers made here that often get confused for Champagne in blind tastings because they're that good. All that fruit in the wine will agree with whatever the cronut cream-of-the-month flavor is—if you don't polish off the bottle before you're finished waiting in line.

*$$ Roederer Estate Brut MV* ☀✳

## The Bagel Store Rainbow Bagel
### & VOUVRAY

**VERSUS**

## Supermoon Rainbow Croissant
### & SAVENNIÈRES

In the world of breakfast pastries, there is a bagel camp and a croissant camp. The friendly divide is a bit more extreme in the world of Chenin Blanc, where some winos are Vouvray fo' life and others are give me Savennières or death. Whether you lean bagel or croissant, we can all agree that rainbows make things pretty. And Loire Valley Chenin Blanc can handle the full color spectrum. Chenin Blanc is the only grape that can rival Riesling for its ability to produce profoundly incredible wines that range from dry to sweet, and all are capable of aging. Both appellations are from the Middle Loire sub-region of the Valley, which runs straight east to west, and both styles give you ginger, sweet saffron, orange marmalade, and enough acidity to decompose a body. While you could easily interchange the two, Vouvray is your choice for festive bagels because it's light and easier going, with a giddy resilience that plays across the mouth and a cutlass of Chenin acid. It's Savennières for the croissant, which, like the pastry, is a little bit haughty and fussy, with a density, layered complexity and *je ne sais quoi* that's deeply satisfying.

*$$ Nicolas Joly Savennières "Les Vieux Clos"* ☀✳
*$$ Domaine Huet Vouvray "Clos du Bourg" Sec* ☀✳

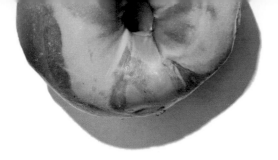

## Milk Bar
## Cornflake-Marshmallow-
## Chocolate-Chip Cookie
## & FALANGHINA
## BENEVENTANO

The bakery and dessert shop Milk Bar rather deviously decided to open a location a few blocks from my apartment, which puts me in a moral tailspin every time I walk by. Do I scoop up a cornflake-marshmallow-chocolate-chip cookie or do I push past the line and avert my gaze, bumper-carring innocent pedestrians until I make it to a safe zone? Who knew that a cookie made with breakfast cereal could make for such an existentially desirable dessert? When I do indulge, the only thing that can build upon that little bite of perfection is Falanghina Beneventano, a white wine from Campania in southern Italy, which also gave us beautiful things like the Amalfi Coast and Sophia Loren (with some points deducted for Capri pants). Imagine a vase of flowers in your living room suddenly turned into perfumed liquid, except someone also added almonds. When you drink it with that Milk Bar cookie it turns into a salty-sweet tidal wave of guilty pleasure. The best versions of these wines are dry with a spiny acidity that's softened just enough by their floral umbrella— and the candied apricot that hides underneath (and does beautiful things to chocolate)—with some gentle minerality that plays right into the cornflake crunch.

*$ Donnachiara Beneventano Falanghina* 🌿✴ 🌱

## Black Tap
## Cotton Candy Shake
## & WHITE SUPER TUSCAN

One of the first times anyone let me and Michelle play with our food in public was at the Black Tap in SoHo. Their specialty is unfathomably large (and beautiful) milkshake concoctions that require skillfully fast eating before they become sticky rainbow puddles on the counter.

White Super Tuscans are just like the red versions in that they use native Italian and non-native grapes blended together. The French grapes are usually fermented and aged in oak, and the Italian grapes in stainless steel. When the two of them are combined, it tastes like someone salted your vanilla cream donut and topped it with lemon verbena and basil. The creaminess of the shake merges with the wine, and the citrus works against the sugar.

*$ Bibi Graetz "Casamatta" Bianco Toscana* 🌞🌿✴ 🌱

# CHAPTER 14

# Frightful Delights

### SOME LIKE IT HAUTE,
### *in* DELICIOUSLY HIDEOUS PACKAGES

y four front teeth are fake. Almost no one knows this. I knocked them out in an eighth-grade sledding accident that started with a plastic toboggan front-loaded with bricks for speed and ended in an open-mouth meeting with a deck post.

They managed to put most of my teeth back in, but the fix had an expiration date. As an adult, I began the long and expensive process of replacing each dead soldier with a permanent implant, one at a time, whenever I could afford to. They charge you $5,000 to remove your tooth, drill a hole in your skull, and insert a titanium rod, and while you're waiting six months for that rod to heal, they give you a temporary "flipper" tooth that snaps into place.

They don't explicitly tell you not to eat blue cheese with Spanish counts during that time, but it's implied.

When you work as a wine importer, lavish "market lunches" are one wonderful perk of the job. They're a way to showcase your vineyard's wines to important clients and journalists over very expensive meals that you also get to eat. Collectors, somms, and powerful buyers come to drink your wines and hear stories about how they were made directly from the people who made them. In this case, the winery was Rioja's storied Marqués de Murrieta, one of my principal

**We were going to be tasting a century's worth of Marqués de Murrieta's most famous Rioja, Castillo Ygay, and it was the talk of the table. I was halfway through my salad discussing it when my front tooth fell out of my mouth.**

accounts, and the market lunch, at one of the city's classic seafood restaurants, was particularly lavish.

Sitting across from me was Vicente Dalmau Cebrián-Sagarriga, the owner of Marqués de Murrieta, who is an actual count of Spain and a luminary in the wine world. He had flown in directly for the meal and the very special event we were hosting later that evening, called a vertical tasting. These are rarefied occasions—my absolute favorite fringe benefit of the wine business—where a winery shows off its very best vintages from multiple decades, and you get to see how the same wines age and evolve over time. We were going to be tasting a century's worth of Marqués de Murrieta's most famous Rioja, Castillo Ygay, and it was the talk of the table. I was halfway through my salad discussing it when my front tooth fell out of my mouth.

Or I should say into my mouth—I could feel it in there, because I was in the middle of chewing a large bite of food. I stopped chomping long enough to review the situation with steadily depleting levels of calm. I couldn't spit it out, because—did I mention the count? But I also couldn't swallow, because now my tooth was lost somewhere in that bite. And I couldn't speak to excuse a sudden departure from the table with a half-chewed chunk of blue cheese falling out of my toothless mouth, mostly because of the count, but also just baseline human decency—the shock of discovering that someone has a black hole where their tooth just was is right up there with a burglar outside your window. So I just sat there in

paralysis with my mouth firmly sealed, nodding along to the conversation. Eventually, I turned to Marqués's export director, João, to my left, and mumble-whispered "emergemthy." Then I quietly disappeared from the table and prayed I didn't swallow my tooth on the way to the bathroom.

I called my dentist from the stall, then texted João to explain. And by the end of the day, they were both my heroes. The emergency dental procedure had me AWOL for the rest of the afternoon, but João covered for me, and when I made it back—just in time for the vertical tasting—the Count of Creixell was never the wiser. Of course, my mouth was still a ticking time bomb, which meant no eating or drinking (or smiling or talking) for the rest of the night—dentist's orders. I never did get to try that 1917 Castillo Ygay.

But I'm thrilled to report that the full set of Cadillacs I've now got drilled into my head will be there well after I'm gone. And having the freedom to eat and drink like a New Yorker again, without fear, made all the market lunches and dinners that much sweeter. One of the great satisfactions of this business has been the portal it opened for me onto a vast culinary universe, often full of strange and hideous fine-dining dishes I otherwise may not have discovered I love.

These are cuisine classics that appeal to even the most rudimentary of palates, once you get past the provincial reflex to recoil in terror. And you can't call yourself a citizen of the food world until you've walked a mile with every last one of these ugly-delicious ducklings.

# Escargot
## & PULIGNY-MONTRACHET

Don't say "eww" until you've tried the good kind, because they're just so good. Baked in a garlic-parsley butter sauce, they aren't even snaily—or fishy or gamey or insecty—or whatever other reason you've always given yourself to avoid them. They are the right amount of warm and chewy, like your favorite doughy bread, drenched in a sauce fit for kings in powdered wigs and face makeup.

This is where white Burgundy affixes its beauty mark and takes a deep, theatrical bow. At the "village" level and above, white Burgundies are the gold standard of Chardonnay, the region that every other region in the world looks to for the top examples of what the grape can do. And of all the villages in Burgundy doing miraculous things with our favorite white grape, one of the very best of them is Puligny-Montrachet—the quintessential Chardonnay. This is where I first learned to love escargot with a special group of humans, Nick, Tony, and Diane, while drinking

the prestigious and mind-boggling local wine at every little bistro in town—over snails bobbing in homemade butter. Limestone soil covers most of Burgundy, yet the wines that come from this particular 514-acre (208-hectare) community are so charged with mineral energy, you'll think you got lost at a Reiki convention. Over the years, a lot of people have spent a lot of money attempting to figure out exactly why that is, and the answer always seems to be the same: it's the terroir, stupid.

That terroir not only accounts for this Chardonnay's gravel, but also its firm core, which creates a lightning field in your mouth, and a dumbfounding display of aromatic diversity. The wines are salty and buttery rich, just like your snail sauce, but they also vibrate with vigor. And the hint of oak used to make them gives them a pleasantly bitter disposition. It's a pairing that's centuries old, and long may it reign.

*$$ Domaine Jacques Carillon Puligny-Montrachet* ☼✳❖

*$$$ Olivier Leflaive Puligny-Montrachet* ✳

*$$$ Domaine de la Romanée-Conti Montrachet Grand Cru* ☼ ⚕ ✳

205

## Steak Tartare
### & CHÂTEAUNEUF-DU-PAPE BLANC

Steak tartare done properly is both savory and sour, with a consistency close to churned butter and a look that screams "brain splatter." But the raw beef really just gives texture to the mix—the palpable flavors come from true extra-virgin olive oil, fresh mustard, cracked pepper, and creamy egg yolks (plus the occasional pickled-vegetable palate cleanser). And though your eyes might see steak and be immediately inclined toward red, that tannin and body will almost always be too much for such an understated dish. What clicks for steak tartare is powerful white.

The Châteauneuf-du-Pape appellation in the Southern Rhône Valley is renowned for its reds, but it also produces world-class whites with big body, lower acidity, and the same kind of arresting herbal and savory aromatic profile you find in steak tartare. The most common grapes used are Grenache Blanc, which share the same DNA as the reds with a white mutation, along with Roussanne, Clairette Blanche, and Bourboulenc. And less than 10% of the yield is blancified, so the wines have developed a much deserved cult following.

High in alcohol with fresh citrus, raw almonds, exotic star fruit, fennel, anise, and quince aromas, Châteauneuf-du-Pape Blancs are some of the most full-bodied and luxurious whites in France. They're also among the few low-acid whites still capable of aging, and while their styles can vary greatly from weightier oaked versions to those that invoke crisp stainless steel, they all share a measured opulence and expansiveness worthy of tartare. Their lip-smacking oily texture is a luge for the raw meat; their saline minerality tucks right into the yolk, mustard, and black pepper;

and their viscous body sweeps all the remaining components down your throat. The only mistake people make is serving both too cold: You'll enjoy them that much more with just a slight chill.

Look for Côtes-du-Rhône Whites for an everyday drinking alternative.

$ *Famille Perrin Réserve Côtes du Rhône Blanc*

$$ *Château de Vaudieu Châteauneuf-du-Pape Blanc*

$$$ *Château de Beaucastel Châteauneuf-du-Pape Blanc Roussanne Vieilles Vignes*

## Sea Urchin
### & CASSIS BLANC

Don't let the spiny globules of orange alien slime put you off. From the port towns of the Mediterranean to the fishing villages of Japan, many ancient seafaring cultures have known for centuries how rarefied and exquisite a single bite of sea urchin can be. Americans are still catching up. A fleeting morsel is often all you are served, and you'll pay handsomely for it, but it will taste like someone turned the ocean into a curious little coral-colored marshmallow cloud of briny bliss.

Just outside of Marseille, Provence is one of those older gastronomic cultures where sea urchin is known as oursin, and the wine they make in this region of southern France is a metaphysical extension of the ocean creature it complements.

It's also the land of pink, with almost 90 percent of its total production having some sort of salmon or rose-flecked hue. But Cassis has made a name for itself in Provence as a white wine producer of high regard—so high that Hemingway wrote about it in *A Moveable Feast*, one of the first books to teach me about the everyday pleasures (and importance) of eating and drinking well. Its Marsanne and Clairette grapes act like a succubus on the soft urchin flesh, with a whisper of sea salt and waves of peach, honey, and dried herbs that will seduce even the most skeptical of palates.

*$$ Clos Sainte Magdeleine Cassis Blanc*

## **Oysters Rockefeller**
## & DRY FURMINT

Created in New Orleans in the late 1800s, the richest dish in America was named for the richest man in America, John D. Rockefeller. And amusingly enough, it was invented because of escargot shortages (that's how good French snails are; see page 205). Molluscs the oil-baron way are oysters on the half shell that have been baked with a top coat of butter, parsley, spinach, Pernod, shallots, Parmesan, and breadcrumbs, with a crucial squeeze of lemon after the fact. Yet the pasty little mucous creature lurking underneath all that upper crust strikes fear in the hearts of many.

And that brings us to Hungary, where I first discovered a wine called Furmint on a trip with my younger brother, Forrest. At a bar in Budapest, we were confronted with a chalkboard full of wines neither of us had ever heard of, so we chose the grape that seemed to be listed over and over again. And we were so fascinated with what we tasted, we spent the rest of the night trying every Furmint on the menu. There were more than I care to mention, mostly to protect my grandmother's delicate disposition.

Furmint is a Hungarian white grape that has traditionally been used in a famous style of dessert wine called Tokaji (toe-kai), and wines named for the grape range from lightly sweet to straight-up diabetes. But there are now a growing number of producers making Furmint in a dry version, and these are the ones you want with your Gilded Era shellfish. They have a nose like someone took a Meyer lemon rind and smoked the citrus in a pipe, and their spice notes range from cumin to pepperoncini. In some, the texture is so minerally, you could be licking basalt volcanic rock, and their long, dry finish with just a little bit of funk is fiercely captivating.

Tokaj is the name of the famous dessert wine and also the place it comes from, the main region known for producing both dry and sweet Furmint. But the lesser-known standout region to look for is Somló. Wherever it comes from, the label almost always indicates "Dry Furmint" to let you know what you're signing up for.

Back in America, I confirmed my hypothesis that this Hungarian revelation would murder with oysters Rockefeller. That two-shot of lemon, the top-baked breadcrumbs gathered up by the acid and carried home by the smoke, the salty kick of both? Hungary like the wolf.

*$ Királyudvar Tokaji Furmint Sec, Tokaj*

*$$ Oremus "Mandolas" Tokaji Dry Tokaj-Hegyalja*

*$$ Peter Wetzer Furmint, Somlo*

## Frog Legs
### & BOUZERON ALIGOTÉ

Close your eyes and imagine you're eating the tiniest, puniest chicken wings. Accented with garlic and parsley, the French croakers taste superior to any drumstick you've ever had. The tender white flesh of the frog turns princely with the light-bodied, dry white made from the Aligoté grape in the AOC of Bouzeron in southern Burgundy. The appellation is dedicated solely to the production of this one white grape, and the leg's buttery sauce and pungent herbs find a life partner in the spicy, smoky tensions just beneath its surface.

*$ Cave des Vignerons de Buxy Bourgogne Aligoté*

*$$ Domaine Ramonet Bouzeron* ✳

*$$$ Coche-Dury Bourgogne Aligoté* ⁝⁝ ⚥ ✳

## Barnacles
### & RÍAS BAIXAS ALBARIÑO

Barnacles look like the gangrened claw of a swamp monster that's come back from the dead to hunt you in your nightmares. Yet people risk their lives to harvest these repulsive creatures from the rocks of Galicia in Spain. The first time I tried one I had to practice meditational breathing. But then I immediately tried ten more. Texturally, they're like the best jumbo crab you've ever had, with the brininess of gourmet salt and vinegar potato chips. Such is the beauty of these little beasts that you forget about their looks entirely. Albariño, a light-bodied white from the cold and rainy valleys of Rías Baixas in northern Spain, is the liquid version of this potato chip of the deep—garnished with lemon.

*$ Bodega Sucesores de Benito Santos Igrexario de Saiar Albariño* ⁝⁝ ✳ ⚘

*$$ Pazo Barrantes "La Comtesse" Albariño* ⁝⁝ ✳

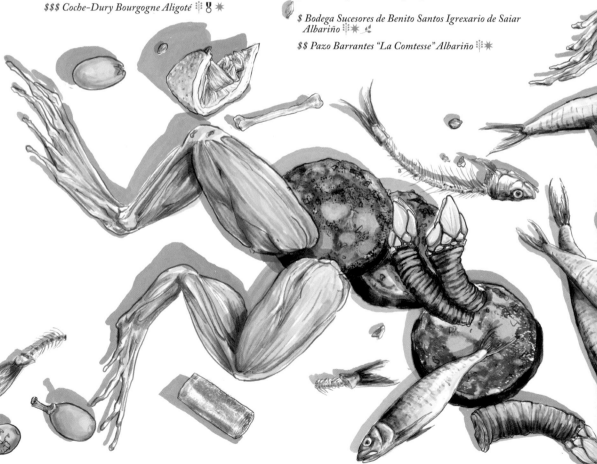

## Sardines
### & SPANISH TXAKOLI

I was in my thirties when I first learned that sardines aren't just gross slugs in a can that smell like fish vomit. The good kind are grilled fresh, like in Basque Country, or yes, even preserved in olive oil, like the Spanish, Portuguese, and Italians do. Txakoli is a northern Spanish wine also from Basque Country that tastes like someone poured fizzy water over some fresh lemon juice and dropped a pack of Sweet Tarts in to dissolve. It has a slight sparkle and tangy shine that turns creamy sprats into pearls.

$ *Ameztoi Txakolina* ⦙❋ ⦂

$$ *Astobiza "Malkoa" Txakoli de Alava* ☀ ⦂

## Blood Pudding
### & HAWKE'S BAY SYRAH

The English and Irish have been enjoying this sausage made from pigs' blood for centuries, but New Zealand's version of boudin noir rivals its Old World ancestor. And the Hawke's Bay Syrah they produce comes with the same elegant threads of olive tapenade, black pepper, and fennel you find in their sausage. But their Syrah is also best known for being sanguine, which is a genteel way of saying bloody. The Kiwi plasma pairing is weirdly primal and pleasing, like sucking the blood from a paper cut.

$$ *Te Mata Estate "Bullnose" Syrah* ⦙❋

$$$ *Craggy Range "Le Sol" Gimblett Gravels Vineyard* ⦙ ⦂❋

CHAPTER 15

# Expense-Account
# Prep Course

*For* LADIES *who* POWER LUNCH

The first time I ate at a truly great restaurant, it was Le Bernardin. (For those who come from flyover country like me, that's Berna-daahn—you have to French it up.) I was in my early twenties, and I was so green, I didn't know what three-star Michelin meant. I was being treated to a very nice meal by a family friend, Stan, who was in from out of town, and I remember being amused that there was a person to take my fork away and a totally different person to bring me my spoon for the next course. There was also a person who brought me my bread and a person who brought me my water, and none of them were the waiter who took our order. They were like a swarm of bees dressed in black, and all the formal pageantry made me a little nervous that I'd do or say something wrong. I did my best to follow my benefactor's lead and didn't order much, because I felt guilty about the prices. I also confess that after we left, I went and got a hot dog because I was still hungry.

Ten years later, I was back at Le Bernardin, but this time under circumstances my twenty-five-year-old self wouldn't have imagined. It was a very special lunch with my two direct bosses, Sergio and Frederic, and the owners of our parent company, Champagne Louis Roederer. We had been assigned the obscene task of taste-testing a long and mind-blowing list of dishes that were going to be paired with seminal vintages of Cristal the following night at a major dinner event. As each dish came out, the head sommelier poured the specific year of Cristal that would be matched with it, and we took our time with every bite, thinking about all of the elements at play, and discussing amongst ourselves. Then we offered our personal opinions to one of the greatest chefs modern cuisine has ever known, Eric Ripert, who as you know if you've ever seen him on TV, is an elegant sweetheart of a man. He took our notes in stride knowing that the wine was what needed to shine.

"Too much richness in the sauce on this one. It's overpowering the wine."

"We need a touch more salt here to go with the minerality of the 2008."

It gave me goosebumps to think back on how much my life had changed since that first meal years earlier. Here I was, sitting at a table with wonderful colleagues and the owners of one of the most famous Champagnes in the world, getting paid to eat one of the best meals of my life and critique it to the three-star Michelin legend who prepared it.

I was caught up in that prideful bit of nostalgia when I felt a gentle nudge from one of my colleagues. "Look at the bar," he said. And there he was. The Raging Corksucker.

The years hadn't been kind, and he sat looking dark and disheveled, with a droop to his shoulders that suggested a heavy weight. He was also half scowling in the direction of my table, and I couldn't help feeling some good old-fashioned schadenfreude. This brief little moment of serendipity, of eras colliding, was all it took for me to realize that the baggage was gone. It wasn't something I needed to shout out loud—it was just for me. I nodded to acknowledge that I had seen him and went right back to my sea urchin and Cristal.

**It gave me goosebumps to think back on how much my life had changed since that first meal years earlier. Here I was, sitting at a table with wonderful colleagues and the owners of one of the most famous Champagnes in the world, getting paid to eat one of the best meals of my life and critique it to the three-star Michelin legend who prepared it.**

People I meet always seem to think that high-level food and wine pairing is just too difficult or complicated, or somehow outside the average pedestrian's ability to comprehend. As you know by now, that's just fear mongering. Fundamentally winning contrasts like fat and acid are an intuition-level thing. And there are a few masterpieces from the contemporary canon that offer a great place to start if you've got fine dining in your future. These are some of my favorite dishes from New York's world of haute cuisine, all of which have transcended their moment and seem destined for culinary immortality— with just the right pairings for the journey.

# Momofuku Ko Egg
## & CENTRAL OTAGO PINOT NOIR

Momofuku Ko is the tiny omakase-themed jewel in chef David Chang's dynasty, where reservations remain near-impossible to get. There, one of his signature dishes is a soft-cooked hen's egg that's lusciously runny with an unctuously sweet onion soubise, a sharp flash of parsley and vinegar, and a big ooze of caviar, topped with crunchy fingerling potato chips. It tends to bring out the Lord Byron in every food critic who crosses its gooey path.

I'm no wine poet, but I know that Central Otago Pinot Noir tends to bequiver my taste haunches and set my cheeks atremble. It's the complex and moody Juliet to Chang's eggy Romeo. Pinot Noir from Central Otago is considered the great red wine of the New World, and from its seat in a remote part of New Zealand where *Lord of the Rings* was filmed, even a challenger to Burgundy's throne (I can hear the Francophiles protest). The other-worldly land sits way down at the 45th parallel of the Southern Hemisphere, at the same level as the bottom tip of South America, where great Chilean and Argentine wines are made. But to give you a better idea, flip the world over to the corresponding 45th parallel in the Northern Hemisphere and you get Bordeaux and the Rhone Valley in France and Piedmont in Italy. Terroir country.

The Pinot Noir of the Hobbits carries the same notes of thyme and parsley that the egg dish does, and all the acid, ripe plum, earth, and spice to temper the indulgent yoke and caviar.

*$ Mt. Difficulty "Roaring Meg" Pinot Noir*

*$$ Burn Cottage Vineyard Pinot Noir*

*$$$ Felton Road "Block 5" Pinot Noir, Bannockburn*

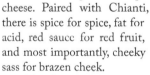

# Carbone
## Spicy Rigatoni Vodka
## & CHIANTI CLASSICO

Chefs Rich Torrisi and Mario Carbone's red-sauce spectacle managed to elevate old-school Italian-American fare to the realm of fine dining. To this day, Carbone's fans are legion, its clientele shinier than ever, and its reservations all but hopeless to book. The space itself, with its narrow corridors, red velvet, and cozy alcoves lit for misbehavior, is straight out of the Rat Pack era (really, Sinatra dined regularly at the restaurant that occupied the space before, and they've never taken down the original sign out of respect for its history). The bow-tied captains have an almost performative, *Goodfellas*-dinner-theater delivery, but where the costumes have been designed by Zac Posen.

I was a sales rep when it first opened, and I was lucky enough to land one of the coveted "by the glass" slots on their wine list with an exceptional Chianti Classico on my roster. Everyone loves Chianti, and Sangiovese was made for pasta. But I didn't realize just how much until I saw the sheer number of Chianti bottles they were moving—and most of it with their Spicy Rigatoni Vodka. Almost mythical, Carbone's version of vodka sauce is less pink than it is Malibu orange, and it practically radiates cheese. Paired with Chianti, there is spice for spice, fat for acid, red sauce for red fruit, and most importantly, cheeky sass for brazen cheek.

There's now so much wine made in the Chianti appellation in central Tuscany that they've had to expand the geographical borders multiple times to keep up with demand. But when the label says "classico," that means it came from the original zone that made these

Sangiovese-based reds, and you don't need to worry about any dilution in quality. Chianti is the wine that first changed my opinion about just how interesting any one wine could be. It was an old bottle so beat up we couldn't read the producer, just the vintage: 1955. And when we drank it, we were awed into silence. That's also pretty much how I reacted when I first tried Carbone's Spicy Rigatoni Vodka. Find yourself a date who looks at you the way I did that Chianti, then make them take you to Carbone.

$ *Monte Bernardi Chianti Classico Riserva* 🌼✳

$$ *Querciabella Chianti Classico* 🌼✳ 🌿

$$$ *Monteraponi Chianti Classico Riserva "il Campitello"* 🌼✳

## Daniel Pressed Duck
## & CORNAS

BIG MACS & BURGUNDY

First things first. It's "Dan-yell," a first name so iconic in the world of cuisine that when you pronounce it the French way you never need the last name. It can only be the one: chef Daniel Boulud, who opened his flagship in 1993. When a friend and his pregnant wife ate there recently, they brought them out a baby onesie at the end of the meal that read "I dined at Daniel." That's how much they've thought of everything at this midtown mainstay, where hospitality has been honed to a pristine gloss, jackets are still required, and expense accounts are strongly recommended.

Daniel's longtime sommelier Raj Vaidya, now a private consultant, is one of those I most look up to in the business. (He's forgotten more than I will ever hope to know about wine, but he'd never let me know it.) Always fair and gracious, even when I was trying to sell him wine I knew he wouldn't buy, he was probably the first bigwig in the industry to show me that success does not have to come at the price of humility. At Daniel, Vaidya presided over one of the most prestigious wine lists in fine dining, and his prowess for pairing is legend.

His favorite duo among the many classics served at Daniel starts with a red from the Northern Rhône called Cornas. "It's the ideal pairing for the 'Bloody Duck,' as we call it in English," says Vaidya, referring to Daniel's timeless and succulent bird, which involves a centuries-old preparation where the blood is vice-pressed out of the meat and then stirred back into the sauce it cooks in. "The savory and iron-rich character of the pure Syrah is key to balance out the meaty, gamey flavors of the dish."

Cornas is an appellation based on Syrah that gets overlooked in the shadow of its more renowned neighbors in the north, Hermitage and Côte-Rôtie. But it's the biggest, baddest, roughest, and toughest of them all. The tannins are teeth-staining and iris hued, and the blackberry, charcoal, and smoked black pepper these wines seem to conjure are nearly as prominent as the olive tapenade and licorice. For now, they're not as expensive as their higher-profile friends, and I hope they stay that way. For a value alternative to Cornas and the swankier appellations of the northern Rhône, look to producers in Côtes-du-Rhône who use more Sryah than Grenache in their blends.

$ *Franck Balthazar Côtes du Rhône* 🌼🦌✳ 🌿

$$ *Domaine Alain Voge Cornas "Les Chailles"* 🌼✳ 🌿

$$$ *Domaine Auguste Clape Cornas* 🦌 🎖 🌿✳

214

# Eleven Madison Park
# Carrot Tartare
## & HERMITAGE BLANC

Known to foodies as EMP, Eleven Madison Park has gone through several chapters at its home in Manhattan's Flatiron District. First opened by the restaurateur Danny Meyer in 1998, it was purchased by his two leads in the front and back of the house, chef Daniel Humm and operator Will Guidara, in 2011. Humm later bought Guidara out and took over. The restaurant now offers a single, outrageously expensive multi-course tasting menu inspired by New York agriculture and French cooking tradition and technique. It's been named the greatest restaurant in the world and has held the maximum three stars from Michelin for years. Though the menu changes often, I was lucky enough to experience an eleven-course retrospective tasting menu a few years ago high-lighting signature dishes from EMP's long run. One of the standouts was a carrot tartare that remains one of the most iconic and innovative dishes in the restaurant's history.

The carrots are put through a meat grinder and presented with a tray full of mix-ins in tiny little bowls. There's pickled ginger, pickled quail egg yolk, smoked bluefish, apple mustard, chives, mustard flowers, grated horseradish, sunflower seeds, pickled apple, sea salt, mustard oil, and a spicy carrot vinaigrette. It's a lot for any wine to confront.

Hermitage Blanc can handle it all. An itty-bitty appellation in the northern Rhône, it's known mostly for its reds, but there's a very small and very precious amount of white wine made here from grapes called Marsanne and Rous-sanne. They have wonky textures that bounce from oily to creamy to salty and are concentrated into a formidable elixir that feels like a karate chop to the mid-palate in a great way. Just as the sweet, fruity taste of the carrots in the tartare play off the bold, bitter, and sometimes harsh flavors of the sides, these full-bodied whites are full of juxtaposition. With components that run the board from quince and beeswax to chamomile and vanilla, they have a retort for almost every taste amalgamation on the platter. And you don't have to shell out for EMP's carrots—put Hermitage Blanc up against the most insane crudités platter you can assemble at home; it's up to the challenge.

If EMP and Hermitage (Blanc or Rouge) are beyond your wallet's reach, look for a Crozes-Hermitage instead. It's the appellation surrounding Hermitage itself and provides an everyday quaffable version of the wines made from the same grapes as the big boys.

*$$ E. Guigal Crozes-Hermitage Blanc* ⁝✳ ⌇

*$$$ Delas Frères Hermitage "Domaine des Tourettes" Blanc* ⁝✳☀

*$$$ Domaine Jean-Louis Chave Hermitage Blanc* ☀ ⵘ ✳

# Le Bernardin Pounded Tuna
## & JURA TROUSSEAU

Le Bernardin is just one of those places. Originally opened in Paris in 1972 and transplanted to New York in 1986, restaurants this fine rarely live so long. With a genius chef who's adored around the world for the way he walks through life and treats people, and a chef-sommelier in Aldo Sohm who's equally kind and talented, at Le Bernardin, service and cuisine of the very highest order converge with genuine care and warmth, resulting in what I believe is an unparalleled experience. And beyond all the accolades and stars and awards, it's got the longevity to prove it.

Seafood has always been the main event, and though the menu is constantly changing, there's one dish that consistently remains—and usually outsells everything else: the pounded tuna. Only a Frenchman could think to put foie gras on a toasted baguette, drape it with thinly pulverized yellowfin, and garnish it with chives. The olive oil it comes with is the finest your tastebuds will ever have the pleasure of knowing.

The deceptively simple combination straddles the thin divide between austerity and opulence, and that's exactly where the light-bodied, electric-cherry red Trousseau is most comfortable. Jura is a region tucked into the hills between Burgundy and Switzerland in eastern France, and it's the affordable, cool-kids version of Burgundy that every budding oenophile should come to know. The area makes Pinot Noir and Chardonnay and also confoundingly good wines from stranger grapes like Savignan and Poulsard. But the indisputable sleeper among them is Trousseau, the pale rider of pounded tuna. Grown on limestone soils, Trousseau wines from Jura are lean and agile, but what they lack in weight they make up for in lively red fruit like raspberry, tannins that reverberate, a spine that tingles, and an easy crush of acid that puts those slivers of tuna and succulent foie in an immaculate little jewel box. Right when you think the fruit and fish have you, the chives and herbaceousness start to shimmer, and when the foie drops in, the acid restores levitation.

*$ Domaine Rolet Père et Fils Arbois Trousseau* ✳☀

*$$ Jean-Francois Ganevat Côtes du Jura "Plein Sud" Trousseau* ☀✳❀

*$$$ Jacques Puffeney Arbois Trousseau* ☀ ⵘ ✳

# Aquavit Arctic Bird's Nest
## & CYPRIOT COMMANDARIA

Aquavit has survived several locations and incarnations since its inception in 1987, but their Bird's Nest is always on offer. It's still one of the craziest and most beautiful desserts you'll ever come across. A confection like this one isn't built overnight, and its form has been perfected over the decades. The current iteration has all the delicious avian layers—plus some—and is as complicated as ever to make:

1. To create the effect of the honey tuile nest, cookie batter is run through a tiling trowel.
2. Tempered chocolate is piped through ice water to resemble loose twigs.
3. Crumbled brownies are scattered around to mimic dirt.
4. Shredded halvah, a sesame-seed based, densely sweet confection, is cotton candied and placed on top to look like bird feathers.
5. Raspberries frozen in liquid nitrogen are shattered for accoutrement.
6. White-chocolate eggs with sea buckthorn yolks get the bird's eye view on top.

Cypriot wines have just as many layers, and even more staying power. They're the oldest and most legendary continually produced commercial wines still in existence. And the sweet Commandaria from this modest little island in the Eastern Mediterranean may be first among them. It got its name in the Middle Ages after Richard the Lionheart conquered the island during the Crusades and sold it to the Knights Templar, though it was likely being made long before that.

Commandaria is produced from two local and ancient grapes, Mavro and Xynisteri, which are black and white respectively. They're grown on the southern slopes of the Troödos Mountains in volcanic soil, where fourteen villages are entitled to make Commandaria. The grapes are picked very ripe, and thus very rich in sugar, and are dried in the sun for a week or two to further increase their sugar content, then fermented for as long as two to three months. After that, winemakers typically fortify the batch with grape spirit and age it in oak barrels for at least four years. The process creates a dark and frosting-sweet red that's high in alcohol (at least 15 percent), with dried citrus fruit and notes of espresso that always make me think of cake—and Aquavit's bird's nest.

*$$ Keo St. John Commandaria* (fortified) ☀

*$$ Tsiakkas Commandaria* (not fortified) ☼🍃☀🌿

# CHAPTER 16

# Surf and Turf

---

## HIGH STEAKS *and* SHORE THINGS

**T**he Montauk Surf Lodge is a beach-town Studio 54 for the Instagram generation where you can high-five 50 Cent before he goes on to perform and live out all your hashtag jetset, hashtag Hamptons fantasies over bottles of rosé. Jayma is the mythical creature who runs it all (and in Montauk requires no last name, like Cher or Prince). So when she reached out a few years ago and asked me if I could write a wine list that would sell, I jumped at the chance, right after making sure she had dialed the right number. Surf Lodge wound up having the best year of high-end wine sales they'd ever had, and Jayma started asking me to guest somm on big holiday weekends.

I toggled between pouring high-end Burgundies for Celine-decked socialites to cracking bottles of Sancerre for Justin Bieber and his crew (they were nice). And before I knew it, I was working on lists for other high-profile spots all over the Hamptons, including the competition, Montauk Beach House, run by the other local one-namer, Yannis. At some point, I knew something had changed when I'd meet new people in town and they'd say, "Hey, you're that wine girl."

Montauk sunk its claws in even deeper two years ago when I became the managing partner on a major new restaurant project conceived as a beach-chic steakhouse that would also host major musical acts in an intimate setting. We found a very special, west-facing plot that looks out over Montauk's Fort Pond, which has the kind of sunsets you don't forget, and my job was to figure out how to bring that vision—and location—to life. So far that has involved moving to the eastern end of Long Island for large parts of the year and learning how to do things like winterize large commercial properties. The ones with fire suppression systems that seize up at midnight in the middle of subzero February freezes, with hardly a soul around, and threaten to flood entire buildings and pretty much put them in the lake before you even get a chance to start renovating.

When you try to start a business in a town known as the "end of the world," there are bound to be a few stumbles, but we still plan on opening what will hopefully be a stunning above-water restaurant called Mavericks sometime in 2022, barring any additional global pandemics. And in the long windup, I've learned more about red meat than I have any business to know. Living in Montauk, I've also had more opportunities to fine tune my seafood game than Jaws at Seaworld.

One of the great pleasures of pairing surf, turf, and wine in a beach town is that you don't need to overcomplicate it. Ocean critters are meant to be eaten simply, and the wine you drink with them should be just as fresh and easy—preferably with some bright summer fruit and a sea breeze of salinity to carry the season through. Pairing turf is just as effortless. All you need to know is that Napa Cab never met a steak it didn't like.

# *Surf* / **Shore Things**

# Lobster Roll
## & BANDOL ROSÉ

If steamers and Vinho Verde (page 222) are simple-on-simple, lobster rolls and Bandol are glitz-on-glam. And there is nothing more titillating on a summer day, or any day really, than someone offering me a glass of pink Bandol with a warm, buttery lobster roll in their hand. Bandol is a separate appellation encapsulated within the larger and more prominent Côtes de Provence because of how distinct (and distinctly expensive) its wines are. What makes them unique from other dry French pinks is that they're primarily based on a grape called Mourvèdre, which makes full-bodied, deeply hued wines with fresh-tilled earthiness and botanical intensities ranging from anise seed to fennel. They are respected for their ability to age where most rosés cannot, and most need a year or two after their release to be completely ready to drink, which is extremely rare in the pink wine category. The region also produces red and white wines called Bandol Rouge and Bandol Blanc, and the best of them are as age-worthy as their westerly Bordeaux neighbors. But when it comes to the crustacean sandwich of heroes, think pink.

As you know, if you get to the end of beach season and haven't had a lobster roll, you've failed summer. But there's plenty of time to redeem the rest of your year. Done right, you want a potato bun that's lightly seared and soft to the touch, with a helping of lobster that's warm and fresh and painted in butter. Bandol Rosés have the strength to take on any briny undercurrents and the delicacy to cradle the mildly supple flesh, but it's their cool spiciness and lean, tropical-fruit spine that give the roll that pink pincher of flavor it needs to walk on water.

*$ Domaine La Suffrene Bandol Rosé* ☀

*$$ Domaines Ott "Château Romassan" Bandol Rosé* ☀✳⁝⁝

# Crispy Soft Shell Crab
## & MOUNT ETNA ROSSO

Sicily's vineyards are planted in the shadow of a not-so-sleepy giant called Mount Etna, one of the world's most active volcanoes, and the ash produced by its constant eruptions lends a signature smokiness to the wines. The island's vintners tempt fate every year, and with global interest in their wines now bordering on obsession, more producers are actually moving farther up the volcano to test planting in the humus-rich black soils left in the wake of the molten lava trails.

The principal grape used to make red wine here is called Nerello Mascalese, and because Etna throws off so many different microclimates, the styles it produces can vary. But what I love most about these wines is their ability to come off as both light and acutely concentrated in the same sip. Their color can be as thin as a translucent Pinot Noir, but as you drink them, their tannin attacks like a stack of dry toast, trailed by smoky electric cherry that's unlike any other red grape. That stout fruit and tannin melt through the crab's fried crust and soft shell like magma, and the ocean-crawler-meets-volcano strangeness of it all brings every beach party to its feet.

*$ Le Vigne di Eli Etna Rosso* ☀✦

*$$ Rovittello Etna Rosso* ⁝⁝ ✳ ✦☀

*$$$ Calderara Sottana "Prephylloxera," Tenuta delle Terre Nere* ☀✳ ✦

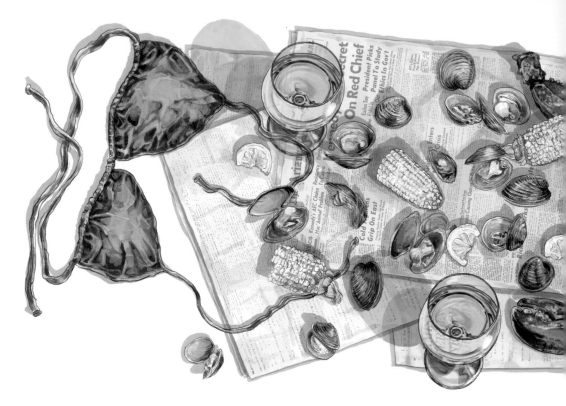

## Clam Bake
## & GEORGIAN RKATSITELI

Rkatsiteli (*caught-suh-tell-ee*) is one of the world's oldest known grape varieties, and it's still cultivated in the country that most likely invented wine. (Earliest records of production in Georgia date back eight thousand years.) And there's a new generation of sommeliers who've made it a mission to make sure we know this grape, mostly in the form of "orange wine." Also known as skin contact (see page 27), the orange stuff is made by leaving white wines to soak or macerate longer with their skins. Since the grapes are white and not red, the color absorbed ranges from gray to neon carrot, which can also be intensified by oxygen exposure.

You get a wine that has grip but isn't bitterly tannic like a red would be, yet with more boldness and a savory quality you wouldn't otherwise get from a white. And that's what's so lovely about pairing skin contact wines like Rkatsiteli with a big steaming pot of shellfish, potatoes,

sweet corn, and butter. Like the silly bib and messy fingers that make clam bakes such a social equalizer, the wildflower tones, moderate acidity, and light-straw hue of Georgian Rkatsiteli take on each element with zero ostentation.

*$ Do-Re-Mi Rkatsiteli/Kakhuri Mtsvane, Kartli Region* 🌿☀️ 🌱

## Steamers
## & VINHO VERDE

Vinho Verde translates to "green wine," in this case meaning young, and it comes from the area around Minho in northern Portugal that makes its wines in much the same way Provence does its rosés. The wines here are vinified and bottled young to be released early the following year, and at around 10 to 11 percent abv, they're an ideal accessory for hot weather. They taste almost like someone made a tart lemonade, then added a little fizz and a dash of sea-spray fruit flavoring (all natural, of course)—a refreshing and simple wine for a light and easy meal by the shore.

this day, Spaniards aren't comfortable with the homage. They even sued in 2011 to get them to change it, but ultimately lost in court. So it would appear Argentine Rioja is here to stay, and it should inarguably be at the top of your beach packing list. La Rioja's low latitude is offset by its high altitude, which moderates what would otherwise be very hot temperatures with cooling winds and chilly nights. The quality white produced by that climate is fleshy and generous with enough saline tension to keep it from toppling over into sensory overload.

Torrontés is so heady you'll wonder if the aromatics alone could get you buzzed. It leaps up into your nostrils like a spicy and pungent rosé that's spent a lot of time with ripe melons and juicy lemon citrus. Torrontés is extremely dry, and what it lacks in acidity it makes up for with an oily texture that's particularly well suited for freshly grilled fish. When you drink this La Rioja, it wraps your fish taco in its own vinous shell and carries each bite happily below deck to your belly.

$ *Pircas Negras Torrontés Famatina* ※

## Fish-n-Chips
### & ENGLISH SPARKLING WINE

From Port to Bordeaux, the English have long brought the wines of other countries into fashion, but they've never exactly been known to produce quality wines of their own. Now the Brits are coming fast and hot onto the scene, thanks in large part to climate change, which is making areas like Sussex in the south more ideal for wine production. Though it's still several parallels north of the 50th, which

Serve your steamers in the broth you cooked them in, with a side of melted butter for dipping. Aided by its soft effervescence and salt, Vinho Verde lights the fuse that gets the clam's flavors to detonate in your mouth. They're practically breezy in body and not overly complex, so the fireworks don't linger too long after you swallow.

$ *Casal Garcia Branco Vinho Verde*

$$ *João Portugal Ramos Alvarinho Vinho Verde* ⁂✳

## Fish Tacos
### & LA RIOJA ARGENTINA TORRONTÉS

Not to be confused with the original in northern Spain, La Rioja is an appellation in Argentina north of Mendoza that's closer to the equator than most wine regions. It dates back all the way to the 1500s, when Spanish immigrants to Argentina named it for their homeland, but to was long considered to be the cutoff point for viticulture, the region's warming temperatures have changed the equation for good. Just as importantly, southern England shares a tectonic plate with France from back when the bulk of the Earth's land mass was still part of the supercontinent Pangea. So as luck would have it, the same distinct chalk soils we prize so much in Champagne also exist in Sussex. Its wines are also made in the Traditional Method and come from the three main grapes used in Champagne—Pinot Noir, Pinot Meunier, and Chardonnay. And though the jury is still out on how long these sparklers can age—the country's wine culture is still very young, and the Champagne houses who have planted here have yet to release commercially—the initial bottlings are showing very real potential in both quality and taste. Soon the Brits might just be known for bubbles, without the squeak.

One iconic export that will always be synonymous with the Commonwealth is fish and chips. The golden fried staple has long since colonized every pub, tavern, and seaside shack the world over. And it should come as no surprise that the crispy batter of their national dish makes for a royal wedding with autolytic British bubbles. The saline notes coming out of Sussex suds are as pronounced as their beaming acidity, and for fried-on-fried cod and potatoes, those are precisely the elements you need in force. They're also bloody brilliant with tartar sauce, ketchup, and vinegar.

*$$ Wiston Estate Blanc de Blancs MV, Sussex* ✻

*$$$ Nyetimber "Tillington" Single Vineyard, Sussex* ✻

# S'mores
## & RECIOTO DELLA VALPOLICELLA

"Campfire" isn't a note you find too often in wine, but as luck would have it, there's a niche style that sets your once-a-summer date with charred s'mores ablaze in more appetizing ways. Valpolicella is an appellation in the Venetian region of northern Italy known for its big red wines, but the sweet, red dessert styles, like Recioto della Valpolicella, are what make the DOC particularly special. Red and sweet is relatively rare because of just how difficult it is to make strong acidity, bitter tannins, high alcohol, and dense sweetness play equally prominent roles in the same wine without turning it into grape-flavored Smirnoff Ice. Normally, balance and restraint make for great wine, but in this case the all-in approach is exactly what drives the appeal.

The main grape used here is Corvina, with Rondinella added to the blend for fruitiness and Molinara a minor player to boost acidity. To make a Recioto, the grapes are left to shrivel and raisin on mats in hot, dry conditions (for more on *appassimento*, see page 87), imparting Recioto della Valpolicella with the flavor of a dry red and the sweetness of a dessert wine—so they're sturdy yet somehow never cloying. The sweet baking spices connect with the s'mores graham cracker, the tannin modulates the chocolate's sugar and bitterness, and the threads of black cherry and tobacco slide through the crispy blackened marshmallow like the perfect stick.

*$$ Serego Alighieri "Casal dei Ronchi" Recioto della Valpolicella Classico* ✻

*$$$ Giuseppe Quintarelli Recioto della Valpolicella Classico* ✻

# CLOSET CASES

I always wondered what it might be like to have a personal stylist, and thanks to my incredible roommate Kelsey Lyle, I didn't have to get my own E! show to find out. Kelsey is not only a close friend and confidant, she's also the Fashion Director for Saks Fifth Avenue, and she lets me raid her bottomless wardrobe on the regular. She also taught me that there are a few key staples everyone should have in their closet—and the same applies for the wines in your rack.

### The Perfect White T-Shirt

We all own a white t-shirt, but rarely one that ticks all the boxes; not too baggy, not too cropped, just the right proportions. When you stumble upon your Goldilocks, it's better than owning a dozen tees that don't quite do you justice. And that's the crisp, clear **French Mediterranean Picpoul de Pinet**, a dry, high-acid white you can wear with anything and always fits to a T.

### Outfit-Making Denim

A great pair of go-to jeans is all about the cut and the wash, and when you find your tried-and-true denim that's tight in all the right places, in the perfect blue, you hold on to that prize for years. **Mendoza Malbecs** are the vintage Levi's you've always dreamed of—well-made crowd pleasers equal to any occasion and consistently good even at the value tier.

### The Tailored Blazer

They're every wardrobe's treasure, and they're not just for corporate meetings and cucumber sandwiches. A well-tailored blazer can prop up an evening look or add a hint of effort when you go casual. They're an investment piece, just like a great bottle of **Italian Barolo**, the foundation for any good adult wine rack.

### The Classic Trench

A timeless icon like the Burberry trench is your portfolio's most steadfast asset. It's Jackie O' and Audrey Hepburn, or Meryl Streep in *Kramer vs. Kramer*, a must-have classic—much like the perfect **Rosé Champagne**. They can roll with any situation and add plenty of flair without being loud about it.

### A Piece of Prized Leather

Leather weather is all year round nowadays. Whether you go pants, jacket, skirt, or shirt, a stylish piece of hide always adds texture to your basics. And like a **vintage Port**, it only gets better with age. The more distressed, the more evolved the flavor, and the bottles can last for months even after you've popped them.

*Turf /* **High Steaks**

# MEAT CUTE

## Napa Cabs Love Red Meat

Whenever a restaurant is focused on steak—which, believe it or not, is still the most successful restaurant model in America—wine will always be an outsized part of its success. And there's a reason most steakhouses have Bible-sized wine lists disproportionately filled with Napa Cabernet Sauvignon.

Together, red meat and Napa Cab can move nations. Few wines deliver the kind of high-alcohol and tannic body blow required to tangle with such a full-flavored protein. That tag team creates tension with the beef and helps the experience linger after the bite is gone, like a vinous A.1. sauce. The buttery-black sear on a good steak also mirrors the toast of the oak barrels Napa Cabs are aged in, allowing the char and the tannin to merge while the wine's considerable fruits dart through. And because nothing is more American than a steakhouse, big, bold, USA-sized wines are almost always a natural fit.

Napa Valley is surprisingly vast and the Cabernets are often significantly different, depending on where they're grown within the American Viticulture Area, which is the stateside version of an appellation. There are now sixteen sub-AVAs in Napa alone, all with their own distinct flavor profiles, which can taste as uniquely different as a Barolo from Piedmont does to a Brunello from Tuscany. Napa's roster is so deep and varied that we can be as specific with Napa Cab sub-AVAs as we are with cuts of beef.

On a basic level, Napa wines fall into two general categories: Valley Floor and Hillside. The Valley Floor is the region's OG, and the vineyards here are what Napa's reputation was built on. (For more on the great story behind that, see "The Judgment of Paris" on page 143.) This is where the cornerstone was firmly laid back in the 1970s, and

wines that come from Valley Floor vines are the most lush, bold, and opulent versions of Napa Cab. They're usually dominated by plush fruit, and have a violet-licorice backbone. For anyone pursuing a Napa wine collection with a depth of vintages, five years of age is usually a good starting point, while ten to fifteen years is the sweet spot.

Hillside vineyards have very low yields because vine growth is limited by infertile and shallow soil, which give you small berries with thick skins. The modest output means the wines here tend to carry girthy price tags—in some cases almost twice those of the Valley Floor. But if you've got money to burn, by all means burn it on the Hillside. These wines are audacious and fascinating and fiercely structured, with Tesla-coil acidity and gum-clenching tannins. They're known for their burly black fruit, but their smoky minerality steals the spotlight. The youngest you want to go is ten years, which is just enough time for the tannin to come to heel and the acid to amalgamate, letting the mid-palate expression bloom. These wines really start to shine at the twenty-year mark.

When it comes to red meat, the general rule to apply is congruent over complementary. The more tender the cut, the more plush the tannin (that is, extra smooth with the tiniest hint of sweetness). The tougher the cut, the more acid and abrasive tannins are required for balance. Choose Valley Floor for the softer cuts and Hillside for the chewier ones. Pairing by sub-AVA involves more than a little nuance, but the fact that these fine distinctions are even possible on such a granular level is part of what makes these wines so exquisite—and worth knowing inside out.

### Tenderloin
# Filet Mignon
## & YOUNTVILLE CABERNET SAUVIGNON
*Valley Floor*

Taken from the smaller end of the tenderloin, the most velvety-lean part of the cow has less connective tissue and fat, yet with all the lusciously rich, melt-in-your-mouth texture. A delicate flower when it comes to flavor, this precious cut calls for a wine with soft tannins that won't run roughshod over your flamed carbon. For this we turn to Yountville, an enviable location in the heart of Napa Valley. The most coveted of cabs for the most coveted of cuts, the wines from Yountville are like satin teddy bears, with tannins that roll through your mouth just as tenderly as the loin. The textures are similar, and the luxurious fruit, warm cassis, and minty inflections of Yountville Cab bring forth just about all the flavor you can throttle from one of the butcher's quietest top-flight delights.

*$$$ Dominus Estate*

### The Ultimate Rib Eye
# The Tomahawk
## & DIAMOND MOUNTAIN CABERNET SAUVIGNON
*Hillside*

One of my partners at Maverick's loves this rarefied cut so much, we nicknamed him "the Tomahawk." It's the very best version of a rib eye, with at least five inches of bone that can also serve as a handle if you decide to go Flintstones on it. Tomahawks are insatiably rich and juicy, teeming as they are with little white ribbons of fat. Diamond Mountain offers the kind of mouthwatering potency you want to go with it. These wines are so rugged and burly, they almost seem chewy themselves, with a wet-dark earthiness that feels like drinking a glass of Leonardo DiCaprio in *The Revenant*. If you aren't careful, they might be just brawny enough to make you grab that tomahawk by the bone.

*$$$ Diamond Creek "Volcanic Hill" Cabernet Sauvignon*

# BROAD STRIPES

*Unlike Napa, which has clearly defined sub-AVAS, many American Viticulture Areas are too big and loosely regulated to tell you much at all.*

In the Old World, geographically delineated wine regions are called appellations, which you know as places like Sancerre, Chianti, and Rioja. In the United States, they're known as American Viticulture Areas, or AVAs. The big difference between the two is that in the United States, AVAs are defined purely by geography, and never by grape. The Alcohol and Tobacco Tax and Trade Bureau, or TTB, sets those geographical lines. And just why it is that the same people who collect the taxes on our firearms and ammo have been entrusted to regulate America's winegrowing is a question only the United States Congress can answer. But because of it, we have none of the rigorous quality controls and oversight that exist in Europe, where there are many more safeguards on everything from crop yields to approved grape varieties and aging requirements, and even more when you get down to the specific appellation quality levels. The French, Spanish, and Italians have strict rules. They take their wine very seriously, and because of it, so does the rest of the world. It's hardwired into their culture—and bureaucracy—which in this case is a good thing.

In many parts of the country, our AVAs are so broad as to be almost useless. Wines from my home state of Kentucky, for example, get lumped in under the Ohio River Valley AVA, which spans four states and sixteen million acres (6.5 million ha). It's hard to imagine that wines from such geographically distinct areas aren't marked by stylistic differences—because they so obviously are. And in the United States, classifications like reserve, which in the Old World indicate higher quality wines, are considered by the TTB to fall under brand names, meaning any garbage juice in a bottle can put the word "reserve" on its label—and often does. This is what happens when you make the tax people the wine people.

Much more work needs to be done, but fortunately, in a handful of American wine regions that have more history and production, like Napa, the AVAs are pretty specific—only because the wine communities have taken it upon themselves to self-regulate. Napa Valley itself is its own AVA, but inside it, they've created sixteen sub-AVAs, all with their own distinct styles.

229

### Short Loin
# New York Strip
## & ST. HELENA CABERNET SAUVIGNON
*Valley Floor*

The steak so nice they named it twice, then about eight more times—this supple slice of the short loin is known by many handles, most notably the Ambassador, the boneless club, the Hotel-Style, the Kansas City, the Delmonico, the top loin, the veiny steak, and the French contre-filet. But most will recognize the New York strip at the Broadway-sized crosswalk of texture, flavor, and fat that made it so famous. It's one of the most versatile cuts for pairing with different styles of Napa Cab, but one sub-AVA announces itself as the strip's most natural counterpart. St. Helena is a powerful expression of Jolly Rancher fruits like cranberry and raspberry, with a savory jamminess and violet-laced cedar core that drops a big red Times Square ball of flavor on any New York strip.

*$$$ Nickel & Nickel "Hayne Vineyard" Cabernet Sauvignon* ❖✳❀

### Plate
# Skirt Steak (with Chimichurri Sauce!)
## & MOUNT VEEDER CABERNET SAUVIGNON
*Hillside*

Long and thin and cut from the undercarriage, the lowly skirt steak is a lean little utility player. But add some chimichurri sauce and all the sudden it's a star. Because of its tough and fibrous texture—and so little fat to soften the chew—you'll want to uncork something with about as much acidity and tannin as a glass of wine can pack. I know I've talked a lot about cutting fat with acid, but when you have a high amount of lean protein, the tannin and acid structure have to be just as firm. Mount Veeder is a taut and herbaceous wine with the metallic gleam of a freshly chromed bumper and acid like a lemon curd kneed you in the salivary glands. Combined with a sauce that's shaped by red-wine vinegar, parsley, and garlic, it can split any skirt steak wide open.

*$$ Hess Collection Cabernet Sauvignon, Estate Grown, Mount Veeder* ❖✳

### Chuck
# Flat Iron Steak
## & COOMBSVILLE CABERNET SAUVIGNON
*Valley Floor*

A shoulder cut of increasing popularity, the flat iron is a relative newcomer to steakhouse menus. Sliced thinly enough, the deep marbling of the top-blade chuck makes it nearly as tender as tenderloin at a fraction of the cost. It has a blood brother in the up-and-comer of Coombsville, an AVA that was, until recently, also something of an afterthought. The grapes from this area were once considered only good enough to be blended with other wines from farther up the valley for acidity, but the combination of spirited producers and climate change have quickly turned Coombsville into a somm-approved darling. The wines here have a vivid expression, with blue and black fruits, lean energy, stern acid, and graphite-level minerality that are as tasty and deserving as any of their fellow Valley Floor neighbors.

*$$$ Stags' Leap Winery Coombsville Cabernet Sauvignon* ❖✳

### Tenderloin and Short Loin
# Porterhouse
## & HOWELL MOUNTAIN CABERNET SAUVIGNON
*Hillside*

The most gluttonous answer to the question of which steak to eat is: "All of the good ones at once." And that's where the Liberace of meat raises its big, bejeweled hoof. Half filet mignon, half juicy strip, the XXL T-bone is required to have a filet thicker than 1¼ inches to even be classified as a porterhouse. The mohunke nest piece of meat there is can be tricky to pair because of its two different personalities, so you'll need a Hillside Cab with the same dichotomies in acid, tannin, fruit, and flavor, giving you the Hulk of a pairing you're after, as opposed to the Bruce Banner you're not. (The Hulk is also the Liberace of Marvel meat metaphors.)

The porterhouse finds its Colossus in the wines of Howell Mountain, which flaunt gargantuan tannins, rugged texture, and a menthol-mocha esprit. They're a personal favorite. Dominated by volcanic soils and steeply planted vineyards, the area produces compact grapes, and thus wines that are as dense as they come. Their power is amplified by mesmerizing dark bramble fruit and a tar-like tannic clutch.

*$$$ La Jota Vineyard Co. Cabernet Sauvignon* 〰※

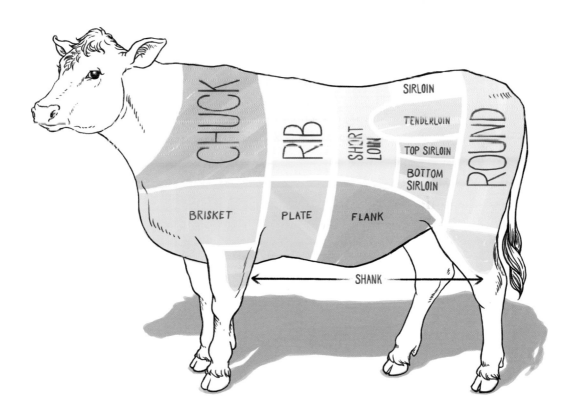

# VANESSA'S RECOMMENDATIONS

## Favorite Glasses

Riedel. They have a thoughtful line for every budget range. I'm a personal fan of the Riedel Veritas series.

## Favorite Wine Key (also called a corkscrew!)

Forget the fancy and newfangled; something that gives you control and is easy to carry is all you need. A reliable double-lever wine key from a trusted supplier like Pulltap is the best way to go. You can even custom make your own for less than the cost of the fancier versions.

## Favorite Ah-So (the thing that helps you open older bottles with fragile corks)

While there are swankier versions, they can be heavy and cumbersome. Inexpensive and easy to find, Monopol Westmark makes a great one.

## Favorite Wine Fridge

For top-of-the-line, hashtag goals: Eurocave

For a starter fridge while you figure out how much space you'll actually need: Check *Wine Enthusiast* for a number of options at whatever budget you're living in.

## Favorite Wine Books

For beautiful gift-giving on my favorite subject: Champagne: *The Essential Guide to the Wines, Producers, and Terroirs of the Iconic Region* by Peter Liem

For becoming a blind-tasting expert: *Beyond Flavour* by Nick Jackson

For an all-around wine study reference: *The Oxford Companion to Wine* by Jancis Robinson

For an everything-you-need-to-know quick reference guide: *The New Wine Rules* by Jon Bonné

For an interesting history lesson: *Wine and War: The French, the Nazis, and the Battle for France's Greatest Treasure* by Don and Petie Kladstrup

## Favorite Online Resources

For a focus on wines under $25: Reverse Wine Snob

For a wine newbie trying to get a lay of the land: Wine Folly

For a wine geek looking to dive in deeper: Vine Pair

For a factual in-depth look at classic wines and wineries around the world: The Wine Cellar Insider

For a smart look at the intersection of wine, business, and politics: Dr. Vino

For the largest online community and informational resources on natural wine: Raw Wine

## Favorite Online Shops

For deals on older wines and a look at the auction market on a budget: Winebid.com

For the largest online selection and convenient local store pickup: Wine.com

For some of the most coveted small-production bottles in the wine geek world: Chambers Street Wines (chamberstwines.com)

For options on customizable or engraved gifts: Reservebar.com

## Favorite Periodicals

For up-to-the-minute wine reviews: *Wine Spectator*

For a geekier look at up-to-the-minute wine industry news: *Decanter*

For a helpful guide to vintage ratings: *Wine Enthusiast*

For the most visually stunning and creative disruptor in the food and wine space: *Noble Rot* magazine

For monthly wine classes and a thoughtful look at producers and regions: Eric Asimov, the *New York Times*

For a contemporary outlook into the natural wine world: Marissa Ross, *Bon Appétit*

## Favorite Wine Subscriptions

For the best pop culture wine info: Winc

For sampling small amounts of different wines and cute gift sizes: Vinebox

# ACKNOWLEDGMENTS

## Vanessa Price

There are more people that made this book possible than there are actual pages in this binding. The first person to support my dream of writing a book one day was my sister Breanna Mackenzie Price. Though she may be gone now, her light in the world and her belief in me are imprinted on these pages and in my heart forever. Thank you to my brothers, Forrest and Garrett, for putting up with their overbearing older sister. Thank you to my parents, Gene and Renae, for raising me to have the courage to follow my dreams. Thank you to my step-family, Diane, Walt, Cherie, Evan, Philip, and Jordan for adopting me as your own. Thank you to my grandparents, Granzie, Hootie, and Memom, for fighting for a world where a girl like me can do a thing like this. Thank you to my Aunt Carlene, Uncle John, and cousins Erin, Megan, Addison, Willie, Hank, Bart, and Barrett for being a family to me and my siblings that could never be replaced. Thank you to Michelle, my heart, photographer, and co-creative; we really did it. Thank you to The Ellaphant in the Room, who could have known back then where our "pairing" would take us. Thank you to Colin, my best friend since second grade, for not only putting up with me for the last three decades but for continually inspiring, loving, and holding me up along the way. Thank you to Yannis, a scoundrel after my own heart, for always protecting and supporting me, even when you wanted to kill me. Thank you to Alan, my editor at *New York* magazine, you saw a diamond in the rough and took the time to polish it. Thank you to Barbara, we went to hell and back together, and survived. Thank you to Susan, you helped me find myself when I was lost. Thank you to David, Frank, Frederic, and Sergio, for showing me what a good boss (and leader) looks like. Thank you to Dave, you changed my life, more than you may ever know. Thank you to Lisa and David, you are the definition of chosen family. Thank you to Mariel, for always being my biggest cheerleader. Thank you to Lana and Youad, you have lovingly picked me up every time I have fallen. Thank you to Barret and Adam for showing me what generosity of spirit and kindness can do in this world. Thank you to King, for making me and my sister always feel like princesses. Thank you to Maya and Dean, your faith in me changed everything. Thank you to Mike, for indulging every whimsical notion I ever expressed. Thank you to Tom, that year in New York will eternally mean the world. Thank you to Walt, you pushed me because you believed in me. Thank you to Nathan, you showed me how to fight for myself. Thank you to Phil; you gave me solace and shelter when I needed it. Thank you to Kellee, you showed me what a big dream and a bigger work ethic could accomplish. Thank you to Nick, no one challenges and pushes me more. Thank you to Raegan, you've been my partner in mischief for nearly three decades. Thank you to Pooks, the best big brother a lost kid could ever hope to find. Thank you to Jean-Remi. Your selflessness and support carried me when I couldn't carry myself. Thank you to Kelsey, Kurt, Peter, Merri, Massimo, Roberto, Dan, Barbara, Megan, Dehan, Maeve, Bradley, Sarah, Mandy, Kelsey, Allison, Allie, Heidi, Erica, Claire, Angela, Cherayne, Michelle, Liz, Gina, Rachel, Carlos, Matthew, Gabriella, Violet, Michael, and Cyprien for your eyes, time, contribution, and support on this labor of love. It seems it takes a village. Thank you to every winery that ever hosted me or considered me worthy of representing your wines, I was proud to have the honor. Thank you to Kari, my amazing agent, for believing in this project from the beginning. Thank you to Laura, the best editor one could hope for. Above all, thank you to my co-writer, Adam, for taking almost every 3 A.M. call, for the endless conspiring and creating, and most importantly, for helping this grasshopper to grow. I truly could not have done this without you.

## Adam Laukhuf

Adam would like to thank Vanessa Price for turning what he thought was some innocent advice for a neighbor into a years-long odyssey he's still trying to wrap his head around. For being a force of nature who drew him in slowly with an offer of wine in exchange for help with her first few bylines, which turned into a wine column, which turned into a book proposal. For not murdering him even once despite all the editorial torture, and for never using the words *fruity* or *intense* in a sentence ever again. For all the late-night phone calls, texts, and emails that were always very urgent at the time. For teaching him more about wine than he has any business knowing, and for a season of Sag Harbor sunsets he won't soon forget. He wouldn't change a thing, except for maybe a few lines here and there.

Above all, Adam would like to thank his mother, Lynne Laukhuf, the most wonderful human being he knows, for her unwavering love and support, her endless reserves of patience, kindness, and positivity, and for a lifetime of teaching him how to be a better person by her example. Thank you to his amazing sister, Shannon, for forcing him to learn all the Indigo Girls harmonies in middle school, and for loving life and family as purely as she does the animals she protects; her huge-hearted partner, Debbie, and the rest of the Forever FFD, Tracey and Joe, Kathy and Ric, Debbie, Max, Casey, Liam, Jocy, Jay, and Brooke (he loves you all and is sorry you just got this book for Christmas). He'd also like to thank his life-wife, Sloane Crosley, for getting nearly all of his jokes, and sister wives Jebediah Reed and Chris Tennant, keepers of the eternal text chain, for getting the rest of them; Fiona Thomas and Ann Whitman, who've put up with him since college, and Charlotte Kidd, for what probably seems like longer; the other fam, Zoe Turnbull, Kimrah Blackwelder, Joie Jalleo, Marshall Heyman, Brina Milikowsky, Dave Goldweitz, and Sarah Christmasballs; the original Strangers, Brendan Taylor and Mike Aaron, who along with Cate Ellison, Janine Carendi MacMurray, and John Gauld have been dealing with him since before the internet; the incomparable ClamzRica, Claire Mazur and Erica Cerulo, the incorrigible Chris Wilson, the angel creature Marie-Therese Hohenberger, who never once complained despite all the late nights, and the absolute greatest, Hamid Awan, who always took care of him, even in a pandemic. And thank you to the friends, colleagues, mentors, and former bosses who've made it all seem worth it over the years or offered a helping hand, including Jeff Bercovici, Maer Roshan, Paige Ferrari, Ruthie Baron, Kayleen Schaefer, Ross Schneiderman, Sean Alfano, Krista Freibaum, Ben Robinson, Casey Kelbaugh, Ian Mohr, Wilmot and Ana Kidd, Noel Parmentel, Jr., OJ Burns, Joe Keohane, Chris George, Dave Katz, Greg Williams, John Banta, Willa Paskin, Steve Garbarino, Sarah Hoffman, George Gurley, Mike Sacks, Callie Wright, Justin Torkelson, Courtney Colavita, Chris Cechin, Nicole Vecchiarelli, John Cook, Aaron Gell, Jamie Johnson, Bob Morris, Eric Spitznagel, Clara Sedlak, Andrew Bradfield, Carol Lacoss, Bryan Ricchetti, Tod Thiele, Shane Dixon Kavanaugh, Linda Hall, who'd absolutely hate this book, and the late, great Ross Drake.

Editor: Laura Dozier
Designer: Heesang Lee
Production Manager: Larry Pekarek

Library of Congress Control Number: 2020931084

ISBN: 978-1-4197-4491-4
eISBN: 978-1-6833-5925-8

Printed and bound in the United States
10 9 8 7 6 5

Abrams Image books are available at special discounts
when purchased in quantity for premiums and
promotions as well as fundraising or educational use.
Special editions can also be created to specification.
For details, contact specialsales@abramsbooks.com
or the address below.

Abrams Image® is a registered trademark of Harry N. Abrams, Inc.

**ABRAMS** The Art of Books
195 Broadway, New York, NY 10007
abramsbooks.com